STUDIES IN THE HISTORY OF
WORSHIP IN SCOTLAND

STUDIES IN THE HISTORY OF WORSHIP IN SCOTLAND

Edited by

DUNCAN B. FORRESTER

and

DOUGLAS M. MURRAY

SECOND EDITION

T&T CLARK
EDINBURGH

T&T CLARK LTD
59 GEORGE STREET
EDINBURGH EH2 2LQ
SCOTLAND

First published 1984
Second edition 1996

ISBN 0 567 08504 X

British Library Cataloguing-in-Publication Data
A catalogue record for this book is available from the British Library

Typeset by Waverley Typesetters, Galashiels
Printed and bound in Great Britain by Bell & Bain Ltd, Glasgow

CONTENTS

INTRODUCTION

W. D. Maxwell's *A History of Worship in the Church of Scotland* (London, Oxford University Press, 1955) has been out of print for some considerable time. This book is not a revision of Maxwell; its focus is broader, as we have endeavoured to give attention to at least the major strands of Christian worship which have been found in Scotland; and our contributors represent no unified theological position or historical stance but come at the subject from very diverse angles. Accordingly we are aware that we have not said the last word, but we hope this book will stimulate interest in a field of study which has been sadly neglected in recent years. Our hope is that it will be stimulating rather than definitive, and will provoke discussion, research and writing, as well as being useful to students who wish a reliable guide to lead them into this fascinating but inadequately mapped terrain. We believe that the history of worship is a matter not only of interest to the Churches, but of far wider significance. Certainly it is a field littered with the debris of battles of long ago. There can hardly be another aspect of Scottish history which has been so dominated by prejudices, sectarian bias, parochialism, and carefully nurtured myths as this. The time is ripe for a fresh look at the history of worship in Scotland in a broader and more ecumenical context than was possible in the past, re-examining received opinions and scrutinizing interpretations which are still sometimes defended passionately by a particular denomination or party. This scholarly process cannot but involve an element of demythologizing.

The Scots have been prolific producers of handy and influential historical myths. They claimed for long to be an ancient people who had come in the fourth century BC from Egypt by way of Ireland, to found in Scotland a dynasty of kings of unbroken succession and venerable antiquity. By the time Jacob de Wett came to paint the portraits of this royal line in the Palace of Holyroodhouse in the 1680s, there were reckoned to be one hundred and ten kings in the lineage – and most of them shared an extraordinary family resemblance in de Wett's paintings! In the seventeenth century it was commonly held that the Scots had been converted to Christianity as early as the second century, and had enjoyed the blessings of Presbyterian government until the imposition of bishops in the fifth century brought lasting discord to the Church. The monks of St. Andrews ingeniously devised the tale that St. Regulus had brought relics of St. Andrew to Kilrymont, later called St. Andrews, at a date so early that claims of Canterbury or York to primacy over Scotland could conveniently be rebutted. Later Presbyterians discovered an affinity for the shadowy Culdees, and declared them their spiritual ancestors, thus inventing the 'Celtic Church' as the true ancestor of the Reformed Church of Scotland before the unfortunate medieval episode of Romanism – a myth carefully demolished in this volume.

The worship of medieval Scotland could be, and was, ignored or deplored by Presbyterians, and lauded by nineteenth-century Roman Catholics, while the high church Episcopalians preferred to avoid the issue by looking to the East for their liturgical inspiration. It was for long assumed by most Presbyterians that the forms of worship of the Reformation period had been continued without significant alteration (apart from a few periods of Episcopal deviation) right up to modern times. But nineteenth-century high church Presbyterians argued that the purity of reformed worship had been subverted by English sectarian influences flowing in during the Cromwellian period, so that *Knox's Liturgy* was quite forgotten. And then there was the romantic saga of the Covenanters, with their lonely hillside conventicles, and all their sufferings at the hands of the dragoons, agents of a prelatic government. Saints or fanatics? Myth or reality? Sir Walter Scott's *Old Mortality* aroused a storm of controversy because it challenged the exalted view of the Covenanters and their worship which was particularly dear to most Presbyterians who saw in the Covenanters their spiritual ancestors. 'The religion of the Covenanters', wrote Thomas McCrie in reviewing *Old Mortality*, 'has now obtained the sanction of the national laws and is the established religion of this country . . . everything for which the Covenanters contended . . . is contained in the standards of the national Church . . . If, therefore, there is any justice or force in his ridicule, the weight of it must fall upon the established religion of Scotland.'* Nobody likes myths that are dear to them being challenged or disturbed, and myths that have to do with worship seem to arouse peculiarly strong passions. Myths and history, memory and worship all have to do with our sense of identity, personal and collective. That is why they are such important, as well as emotive, matters in which narrowness or distortion is positively dangerous.

Segregated Churches worshipping in isolation from one another produce their own mythologies and interpretations of history to explain and justify their separation and their sense of identity. In the history of worship, as in all history, we must come to terms with our fragmented

* Cited in Marinell Ash, *The Strange Death of Scottish History* (Edinburgh, 1980), p. 126.

past and seek to possess a fuller and more accurate understanding of our historical roots. Our contributors do not present a uniform view, nor were they asked to do so. On some issues they differ quite sharply from one another. And that is as it should be. All have tried to keep in mind the economic, social and political context, to note the interaction between differing forms of Christian worship in Scotland, and to give attention as appropriate to the theology as well as the practice of worship.

We hope that in putting these essays together, reflecting as they do a diversity of religious commitment but a common conviction of the importance of worship and the significance of its history, we have made some contribution to the encouragement of further study of the history of worship on a broad, ecumenical and scholarly basis.

Duncan B. Forrester
Douglas M. Murray
Autumn, 1983

INTRODUCTION TO THE SECOND EDITION

It is gratifying that there has been a demand for a second edition of this volume. We are grateful to those contributors who have revised their chapters where appropriate, taking account of developments since the book was first published, and bringing the bibliographies up to date. It is hoped that this edition will be of interest to those engaged in the study of worship in Scotland, and will stimulate more research and writing in this field. It is also hoped that this book will continue to be of encouragement to all who are engaged, in whatever capacity, in the activity which is at the centre of the Church's life and service.

Duncan B. Forrester
Douglas M. Murray
Autumn, 1995

Acknowledgement

Acknowledgement is due to the Trustees of the Church Hymnary Trust for the extract from *Church Hymnary* (No. 568) on p. 192.

CONTRIBUTORS

The Right Rev. Dr. Mark Dilworth, O.S.B., is a member of the Benedictine community of Fort Augustus, Inverness-shire, where he was ordained priest in 1947. He has worked as a parish priest and acted as Headmaster of the Abbey School. His Edinburgh doctoral thesis was awarded the Hume Brown Senior Prize and published as *The Scots in Franconia* (1947). His other publications are on Scottish monasticism and the Roman Catholic Church in Scotland. He was a Post-doctoral Research Fellow in Edinburgh University's Institute for Advanced Study in the Humanities in 1972–73, and was Keeper of the Scottish Catholic Archives, Edinburgh, 1979–91. In 1991 he was elected Abbot of Fort Augustus.

Professor Emeritus Gordon Donaldson, C.B.E., M.A., Ph.D., D.Litt., Hon.D.Litt., Hon.D.Univ., F.B.A., F.R.S.E. (1913–93), was Professor of Scottish History and Palaeography in the University of Edinburgh from 1963 to 1979. Previously he had been lecturer and then reader in the Department, and was Assistant Keeper of Scottish Records, 1938–47. He was appointed Her Majesty's Historiographer in Scotland in 1979 and was awarded the St. Olaf Medal by the King of Norway in 1991. He was President of the Scottish Church History Society, and among his many publications are *The Making of the Scottish Prayer Book of 1637* (1954), *The Scottish Reformation* (1960) and *The Faith of the Scots* (1990).

The Rev. Professor Duncan B. Forrester has been Professor of Christian Ethics and Practical Theology, New College, University of Edinburgh, since 1978, and Principal of New College since 1986. Previously he was Chaplain and Lecturer at the University of Sussex, and for eight years an educational missionary, teaching at Madras Christian College, Tambaram, South India. He is a member of the Faith and Order Commission of the World Council of Churches. In addition to publications on political and social ethics and Christianity in India he has published articles and reviews on liturgical topics and is joint author (with Ian McDonald and Gian Tellini) of *Encounter with God: An Introduction to Worship and Christian Practice* (2nd edn., 1996).

James D. Galbraith, M.A., M.Litt., Dip.Med.Stud., was formerly Curator of Historical Records (Deputy Keeper of the Records) at the Scottish Record Office. He is a graduate of the University of Aberdeen where he did research on the sources of the Aberdeen Breviary, and has since published papers on various aspects of the medieval Scottish liturgy for the Friends of St. Machar's Cathedral, Aberdeen, and others.

The Very Rev. Allan Maclean, M.A., has been Provost of St. John's Cathedral, Oban, Argyll, since 1986, and is also Examining Chaplain to the Bishop of Argyll and The Isles. He was awarded the James Elliott Prize in Scottish History in 1971 for work on Episcopalian History, and was Tutor in the Scottish History Department of Edinburgh University, 1977–80. He was also Chaplain at St. Mary's Cathedral, Edinburgh, where he was ordained in 1976.

The Rev. Ian A. Muirhead, M.A., B.D. (1913–83), was educated at the University of Glasgow and was Minister of St. James', Forfar, and of Brandon Church in Motherwell before becoming Lecturer in Ecclesiastical History at Glasgow University in 1963, and Senior Lecturer in 1972. On his retirement from the University he was Minister of Monymusk, 1979–82. He was President of the Scottish Church History Society, and contributed numerous articles to learned journals, including the *Records of the Scottish Church History Society*, *The Innes Review* and the *Scottish Journal of Theology*.

The Rev. Douglas M. Murray, M.A., B.D., Ph.D., is a graduate of the Universities of Edinburgh and Cambridge, and was ordained at St. Bride's Church, Callander, in 1976. He later served as Minister at Polwarth in Edinburgh before being appointed Lecturer in Ecclesiastical History at the University of Glasgow in 1989. He was Editor of *Liturgical Review*, and served as Convener of the Panel on Doctrine of the General Assembly of the Church of Scotland, 1986–90. He gave the Chalmers Lectures at the Universities of Edinburgh and St. Andrews in 1991 which were subsequently published as *Freedom to Reform: The 'Articles Declaratory' 1921* (1993).

The Rev. Dr. David H. C. Read has been minister of Madison Avenue Presbyterian Church, New York, since 1956. He was educated in Edinburgh, Montpelier, Strasbourg, Paris and Marburg. He was a Chaplain during the war, held two Scottish charges and was Chaplain to the University of Edinburgh as well as being appointed a Chaplain to the Queen before he moved to the United States. He holds ten honorary doctorates and has published extensively, particularly on preaching and worship, including *Preaching about the Needs of Real People* (1988).

The Rev. Henry R. Sefton, M.A., B.D., S.T.M., Ph.D., was ordained in 1957 as Assistant Minister at Glasgow Cathedral and served subsequently at St. Margaret's, Knightswood, St. Mark's in Wishaw, and Hope Waddell Training Institution, Calabar, Nigeria, before induction as Minister of Newbattle, Midlothian, in 1962. For six years he was Assistant Secretary in the Church of Scotland Department of Education and thereafter taught Church History in the University of Aberdeen for twenty years. He was Master of Christ's College, Aberdeen, 1982–92. A study of *John Knox* was published in 1993, and he has contributed numerous articles to learned journals and dictionaries, including the *Dictionary of Scottish Church History and Theology*.

The Very Rev. Professor James A. Whyte, M.A., LL.D., D.D., D.Univ., was ordained in 1945, and served as Chaplain to the Forces, and as Minister of Dunollie Road Church, Oban, and Mayfield Church, Edinburgh, before being appointed, in 1958, to the Chair of Practical Theology and Christian Ethics in the University of St. Andrews. He retired in 1987, and in 1988 was Moderator of the General Assembly of the Church of Scotland. He has been Guest Lecturer at the Institute for the Study of Worship and Religious Architecture in Birmingham, Kerr Lecturer in Glasgow, Croall Lecturer in Edinburgh, and Margaret Harris Lecturer in Dundee. He was joint-editor of *Worship Now*, Vol. 1 (1972) and Vol. 2 (1989), is the author of *Laughter and Tears* (1993), and has contributed to many composite volumes, including *Towards a Church Architecture* (1962), and *A New Dictionary of Liturgy and Worship* (1986).

Chapter One

THE BEGINNINGS

Ian Muirhead

In the first age of Christianity in the British Isles, Scotland is no more than a geographical name for that area of mainland and islands which lies to the north of Hadrian's Wall. Distant, inhospitable and inaccessible as most of this territory was, it was the homeland of many tribes, and it was inevitable that the Christian Church would eventually make its appearance in it, either by percolation up eastern or western land routes from the Christianity of Roman Britain, or from more distant places by means of the western seaways. Christianity must be present before any discussion of its ways of worship can arise, and so this chapter must first consider how the Christian faith came to be in Scotland, and what forms it took in the six or seven hundred years before Queen Margaret and her sons established the medieval Church there. The remainder of this chapter will then consider what can be ascertained about the ways in which the Christian faith maintained its worship and celebrated its rites during this period.

At the commencement of the eighth century, the English church historian Bede wrote, 'At the present time there are in Britain, in harmony with the five books of the divine law, five languages and four nations – English, British, Scots and Picts. Each of these have their own language, but all are united in their study of God's word by the fifth – Latin – which has become a common medium through the study of the scriptures.'[1] Though the speech of Bede's four nations was incomprehensible to each other without interpreters, three of them did share an ancestor in the *Common Celtic* branch of the Indo-European stem. According as it retains the original Q-sound, or replaces this with a P-sound, Common Celtic is divided into Q-Celtic and P-Celtic. The Britons spoke P-Celtic, and this had originally prevailed between Hadrian's Wall and the Forth–Clyde isthmus.[2] The expansionism of the Anglo-Saxon kings of Northumbria, sometimes more, sometimes less successful, had gradually restricted the British speech to Strathclyde, and introduced English as far north as the Forth. East of the mountains of central Scotland, the *dorsum Britanniae*, or 'spine of Britain', the Picts spoke a form of Q-Celtic, perhaps intermingled with an older, and totally different linguistic tradition.[3] Northern and southern Picts were

1

divided by the Mounth, the mountainous border on the south of Aberdeenshire, but Pictish influence may at times have been wider, since Columba is said to have obtained Iona from them, and a few carved stones,[4] typical of the Pictish kingdoms, are to be found in the north and west. In the west, since the beginning of the fourth century, the significant factor was the growing enclave of Scotti from Ireland. These Scots of Dalriada also spoke a form of Q-Celtic, but it was sufficiently different from that of the Picts, for example, for Columba to need an interpreter.[5]

Bede's fifth language was only just represented. The political decision taken within Roman Britain to make people, rather than defensive works, the protectors of the northern frontier was significant.[6] Among these *foederati* (allies) north of Hadrian's Wall, there is no Romanization comparable to that in the south, but there are some traceable results. The genealogies of local chiefs include native versions of Roman names (Quintilius, Clemens, Tacitus, Paternus, Aeternus).[7] There is a handful of Latin inscriptions and one or two graffiti.[8] It would have been surprising if the cultivation of Roman style amongst the *foederati* had not also included some signs of Christianity as one of the invisible imports. By the fourth and fifth centuries there is widespread evidence of the presence of Christianity in Roman Britain, one of its focal points being in the Carlisle area.[9] Tertullian, claiming that 'places in Britain, inaccessible to the Romans' were yielding to Christ,[10] may himself have been yielding to rhetorical flourish, but the Christianity of the Provinces must have crossed the borders and when Ninian came, it was as bishop of an already-existing Christian community in the south-west, dependent perhaps upon Carlisle. Such Christianity as existed reflected the patterns of Roman Britain – inscriptions speak of bishops, priests and deacons.[11] Charles Thomas has argued that other proto-bishoprics may have existed in addition to that of Ninian of Whithorn, suggesting Glasgow or Govan, somewhere in the Edinburgh area (perhaps Abercorn), and somewhere (Old Melrose? Peebles? Stobo?) in the valley of the River Tweed as possible sites,[12] but these possibilities await more evidence.

This is not the place to discuss the tangle of problems associated with the name and achievements of Ninian. Our main source is Bede, who may have had his information from Whithorn, or even from Pictland,[13] but there is also a seventh-century laudatory poem, and an almost useless medieval life. Almost everything claimed for Ninian has also been denied to him – including his alleged contacts with Martin of Tours, his own monastery, even his association with Whithorn except as an imported patron.[14] It is not, however, easy to dismiss Bede's evidence completely, and there is a little confirmatory evidence in a letter of St. Patrick to Coroticus (Ceretic Gwedig). Patrick was dead by 461, so the letter must be placed in the first half of the century, perhaps between 425 and 450.[15] It was occasioned by a raid on Ireland in which Coroticus had abducted some newly baptized communicants, and Patrick's protest assumes the possibility that there was some Christian public opinion, even among the 'apostate Picts', which might be rallied to moral indignation at the outrage. It seems reasonable to see in this some traces of Ninian's work, but how far this mission, either as the work of Ninian himself, of his contemporaries, or of immediate successors, extended beyond the Forth–Clyde isthmus remains in debate.[16]

What is clear is that the next important thrust of Christianity into geographical Scotland came by way of the western seaways, and from the Christianity already established in Ireland.[17] The sea routes from France and Spain, the lands on either side of the Irish Sea, the Isle of Man and the scattered landfalls up the west coast and among the western isles of Scotland formed an area in which trade-goods and travellers had moved up and down and to and fro since prehistoric times. Here were the routes by which Christianity had reached Ireland and by which contacts between the Irish Christians and those of the Continent were maintained, and though the importance of the sea routes had for a time diminished, now, as the invaders from the European northlands spread over what had once been Roman Britain, the western seaways resumed their significance as a means of maintaining the contacts of what had become the Christian fringes of Britain, with Ireland, Gaul, Spain and the Mediterranean.[18] The early Christian monuments which now appear are predominantly littoral, on the coastlines of Cornwall, Wales and south-west Scotland, and the affinities between their *formulae* and those of the Continent, and even of North Africa, have been noted.[19] Winejars and other pottery (some with incised crosses), found on western and Scottish sites, can also be linked with Gaul and with the Mediterranean,[20] and, most important of all, the ideas and practices of the Christian Church no longer required to enter through the south-east coast of England and spread slowly, if at all, west and north. They had ready access to both sides of the Irish Sea, where they were accepted, developed and at times re-exported along the common sea routes.

Bede tells us that Ninian's own episcopal see was 'named after St. Martin'[21] and although expansions of this statement which make Ninian a pupil of Martin, or profess to date the building of Candida Casa by the latter's death, are suspect, the Ninian–Martin association cannot be denied in our earliest source.[22] The importance of St. Martin was two-fold, representing the arrival from the east of new concepts of monasticism, and introducing new standards of episcopal concern. 'An ex-soldier of insignificant appearance, ill-dressed, unkempt and excitable', he set up a semi-eremitical community on a bed of the River Loire about two miles from Tours, one of the first monasteries in the west. Here there lived about eighty monks, dressed in clothing of camel's hair, and dwelling in wooden cells or in caves. It was Europe's introduction to the extreme forms of monasticism which characterized the desert fathers of the east.[23] Martin's intellectual endowments may have been meagre, but the intellectual foundations of the movement were secured when Cassian wrote his *Commentaries*[24] for the monks of a new foundation, Apt near Marseilles. A third important community was set up on the island of Lerins, which in time gained a reputation as 'a nursery of bishops'. When Martin was himself raised to the bishopric his zeal set new standards of episcopal care. Hitherto a weakness of the Continental Church had been its 'neglect of the country folk outside the immediate ambit of the urban churches'.[25] The type of bishop exemplified by Martin was committed to the deliberate evangelization of the countryside. If Ninian knew of this, and applied it in his own situation, one could see how his traditional image as bishop and apostle arose, though the area in which he exercised his mission to the Picts remains a matter for debate.

The new monasticism spread swiftly and widely, and was especially welcome to the Irish situation. Outside the urban patterns of Empire, the emphasis was on tribe and community, rather than on a geographical area, or a given place, and the new patterns were congenial to the shape of society in which the early bishops were of a 'tuath' or tribe, rather than of a regional diocese. Reaching Gaul by the end of the fourth century, the new monasticism was in south-west Britain and Wales by the fifth century and firmly established in Ireland by the beginning of the following century in a widespread movement the influence of which was to persist for a long time, absorbing the bishops into the monasteries, where, subordinate to the abbot, the episcopal functions might be performed by a relatively minor monastic official.[26] Illtud, a Breton, had a community on Ynys Pyr (Caldey) in the Bristol Channel, from which were said to come such famous leaders as Samson of Dol (Brittany), Cadoc, Gildas and David, national apostle of Wales. David's own monastery, Ty Dewi, was visited by a number of Irish saints, Finnian of Clonard, Finharr of Cork, and Brendan of Clonfert among them.[27] A manuscript called the *Catalogue of Irish Saints* (the exact date of which is debated) distinguished three 'orders' of Irish churchmen, of which the second was said to have received 'a *missa* from David, and from Gildas and from Docus', *missa* having the sense of a particular liturgy of the Mass. They were, in fact, borrowers on a considerable scale from the early Church in Wales.[28]

While recent scholarship has tended to deny to Ninian himself a monastic community, by the sixth century Candida Casa was a centre of monastic life, drawing from across the sea such men as Enda of Aran, Tigernach of Clones, Finnian of Moville and others.[29] In return there came from Ireland the man who provided the first strong impulse of the Christian faith in Dalriada, and, it is also claimed but with less certainty, in Pictland, Columba or Colum Cille, the one whose familiar name has perhaps appropriated to itself and to its community the credit for the missions of many workers.

Colum Cille, descended maternally from Niall of the Nine Hostages, and from Loarn, ruler of Dalriada, was of the line of some of the most famous kings of Leinster, and ten cousins in his lifetime were said to have been rulers in Ireland. Trained in Finnian's monastery of Clonard, Colum Cille founded his own first monastic community at Derry, to be followed by Durrow and many others. In 563, wishing to be 'an exile for Christ', he left with twelve companions for Scotland. Though the last thirty years of his life were spent on Iona, he was one of the greatest of the Irish monastic leaders, with a large *paruchia Columbae*, a linked family of monastic houses in Ireland founded in his lifetime and added to by his followers,[30] a *paruchia* to which Iona was largely peripheral.[31]

Whether in the hands of Colum Cille or of others, the monastic pattern in Scotland as in Ireland had certain clear advantages. It is to a high degree unlikely that the tumult and congestion of a tribal king's dun or rath would offer congenial surroundings for the lives of churchmen. Monasteries offered a practical answer, the creation of a separated community, of which the *vallum*, the enclosure, was a significant element. It was a boundary either drawn *ad hoc* or received ready-made by the gift to the monks of a deserted fort. Within this, a church or churches, a graveyard, accommodation for the indwellers, and whatever else the needs of the community suggested were erected[32] and the patterns of the Christian life could be firmly maintained in a base from which mission could go out on occasion to the surrounding country. That such missions were undertaken is clear, but the balance between mission and the even tenor of the monastic life is obscure[33] and the results of mission appeared in the creation of daughter monastic communities, rather than of anything adumbrating secular parish communities.

Iona's most successful enterprise came, not through self-initiated mission, but through a royal invitation.[34] With the arrival of St. Augustine of Canterbury in 597 a slow ascent from heathendom had been begun amongst the English peoples, marked by times of advance and of retreat. During one of the later revivals of paganism, some of the northern princes took refuge in Iona. Converted to Christianity and baptized there, one of them, Oswald, on his successful return to Northumbria, sought help from Iona for the rechristianization of his land. Under Aidan and his successor Finan, Northumbria came under the Iona tradition. By now, however, there was an extended period of controversy over the celebration of Easter and other points of discipline, the lines being drawn between the 'Romani' and the supporters of the local traditions, and the climax for Northumbria being reached at the Synod of Whitby (664).[35] Though the debate has often been represented as one between the Roman and the Celtic Church, the contestants would hardly have recognized themselves under such descriptions, since neither then nor at any other time was there a 'Celtic Church'. Nor indeed was it ultimately a debate about ways and times of worship, however much these were superficially in question. In Northumbria the debate did take place at a point at which Anglo-Saxon and Scots traditions were meeting and conflicting, but this is only partly relevant, for the debate was as intense in Ireland. The ultimate conflict was between two understandings of church structure, one monastic, the other episcopal. Was the church to continue to be based on monastic *paruchiae*, with the bishop subordinate to the abbot, or was it to return to the older system of bishops and dioceses? It may be significant that the immediate consequence of Whitby is the appearance of a number of new bishoprics.[36] For political reasons some of these had short lives. Anglican expansion under Ecfrith was halted by his defeat and death at Nechtansmere, and the flight of Bishop Trumwine from the new bishopric of Abercorn followed. The dominance of monasticism was to endure for a long time, but throughout the late seventh and early eighth centuries, the choices made at Whitby were repeated elsewhere and by others. Even Columba's biographer Adomnan, on a visit to Northumbria, was convinced and accepted the Roman usage. He failed to convert his own monks in Iona, but was much more successful in Ireland, and perhaps elsewhere.[37]

Bede reports that, about 710, Nechtan, king of the Picts, sought advice on Easter from Ceolfrid, abbot of the monastery of St. Peter and St. Paul. He had decided to adopt Roman usage, but this decision must have had a considerable gestation period in which rather more than 'an assiduous study of Church writings' affected his views.[38] He would certainly not have had any encouragement from the 'family of Iona', except in the person of Adomnan. The latter was dead by the time Nechtan wrote, but there are evidences for his work in Pictland. There are churches bearing his name at Dull (in Atholl), and Forglen, near Turriff, and originally connected with Adomnan's church at Forglen is the Monymusk reliquary, a box which once contained a relic of Columba set in a small metal casket of Pictish work.[39] It is to the example of Adomnan, 'the renowned priest and abbot of the Columbans', that Coelfrid directs the attention of Nechtan in his reply, and there seems at least a case for speculation about his influence. Pictland was placed 'under the direction of Peter', and a number of churches now appear bearing Peter's name. The uncooperative members of the family of Iona were finally expelled across the *dorsum Britanniae* about 717.[40]

By the ninth century a new situation had been created by the appearance of the Vikings among the islands, along the coastlines and in the estuaries. In the years of destruction the abandonment of Iona became necessary; the relics of Columba were divided between Kells and the Columban monastery at Dunkeld, a 'physical recognition of the separation between Ireland and Scotland at this date'.[41] Hence, when in mid-century Picts and Scots were united under Kenneth mac Alpin, it is not likely that this involved any strong reassertion of Columban/Irish influence in the former Pictish kingdoms. There was certainly some renewed presence, demonstrated by the round towers of Abernethy and of Brechin, in placenames involving the term 'annat', and perhaps in some of the St. Bride dedications. But communications with Ireland must have been much less secure, and the establishment of peace over the Easter issue may have involved other changes of outlook so that the slow changes and developments in Scotland were not hindered. The monastic-centred life of the Church was waning, and we hear of 'three elections of bishops in Abernethy, when there was but one bishop in Pictland', and of the death of Tuathal son of Artgus (865) the *primepscop* of Fortriu (though older ways still lingered, and he was also abbot of Dunkeld).[42] The Keledei (Culdees), who appear from now onwards, bear only a faint relationship to their Irish namesakes.[43] The latter were a reforming élite, associated with Maelruain (died 792), founder of Tallaght. They followed the Rule of St. Carthage, and were ascetics who regarded woman as 'man's guardian devil', and, at Tallaght at least, banned all fermented liquor. They were 'enclosed', i.e. restricted to their own monastery, and were a minority among the other monks. In Scotland the name became widespread and the great number of 'Culdee sites' – St. Serf's, Lochleven; St. Andrews; Dunblane; Monymusk; Abernethy, etc. suggests not a small élite, but rather a generic name for clergy, sometimes married, but sometimes living in some kind of community or 'minster' of secular clerks. There is an implication that they were the representatives of the 'old' and not very strict Church. Where they did not *de facto* become the canons of a bishop's church, they were most often tidied up by later ages into the more strictly medieval pattern of Augustinian priories. The changes summarized here may be studied in detail in I. B. Cowan's article, in which he concluded that the Church in Scotland was 'consistently moving onwards towards a diocesan system from the eighth century onwards' and that when it clearly takes its place in the medieval Church this is 'not a violent break with the past but the natural consummation of an extended evolutionary process'.[44]

What this slow transformation meant in terms of the Church's worship remains very largely opaque. Innate resistance to change in established ways of worship probably kept ancient forms and customs alive, and when a European princess appeared as Queen, Margaret certainly found things to displease her, even though it is hard to decipher to what she is taking exception.

During the six hundred years or so in which Christianity was establishing itself throughout the geographical area of Scotland, whatever else was happening, the Church was baptizing, confirming, celebrating the Eucharist, tending the souls of the sick and endeavouring by monasticism and in other ways to maintain the spirituality of the people and clergy, but direct historical evidence of what went on is scarce, and its interpretation often speculative.

There is an initial generalization of fundamental importance; although one will meet the phrase constantly in the older literature (and in not so old literature) there was never a 'Celtic Church'. Christianity operated in lands linguistically Celtic, as in others, and its material objects – manuscripts, monuments, ecclesiastical furnishings – might show the imprint of Celtic art forms. There is no evidence that it used any language other than Latin for its services, or in its scriptures (though sermons might be in the vernacular). As Jocelyn Toynbee wrote many years ago, 'the so-called Celtic Church, surviving continuously in the west and north, was thoroughly Roman in Creed and origins; Roman too, initially in its organisation and practice'.[45]

Local variations and idiosyncracies came to exist, as they did in Gaul, in Spain and in other areas of the Christian world. The manuscript called the *Catalogue of Saints*, to which reference has already been made, says of the second and third periods of Irish churchmanship, 'They celebrated different masses, and had different rules' but there was no schismatic thought or intention. They wished, as Colman told the Council at Whitby, to remain faithful to their own particular past; 'all our forefathers, men beloved of God, are known to have observed these customs'.[46] Monasteries were particularly liable to take a pride in keeping their own Rule which might include varieties of liturgical custom, and perhaps this intensified the situation where monasticism was the most prominent part of the structure of Christian society. But the intention was always, whether in Gaul, or Spain, in Ireland, Pictland or Dalriada, to believe and live in the way of the Church. The missionary priest who celebrated Eucharist in the wilds of Midmar, Aberdeenshire, believed himself (though no doubt with some *naïveté*) to be doing exactly what the Holy Father in Rome did. Whatever differences, or conflicts, might at times be seen were 'the results of peripheral survival, not the outcome of a separatist heresy'.[47] It was left to the Scottish historians of the eighteenth century, and their followers, to invent a separatist Celtic Church to serve their own polemical interests. It goes with this that in a sense there was also no 'Celtic' way of worship. The universality of the rites of the Christian Church was taken for granted. Admission to it was through Baptism, and life in it was centred upon the Mass. There could be, and there were, 'different masses', but this was never understood as contradicting a unity which did not of necessity demand uniformity.

When we pass from generalization to detail, we discover how meagre our materials for knowing this worship are. Of the existing lives of Scottish churchmen, only Adomnan's life of Columba can help, and that not without qualification. Written about a hundred years after the time of Columba, one can never exclude the possibility that its author has in fact told his stories within the matrix of the religious life of his own time. Strictly, Adomnan's life is as much evidence for his own age as for the age of Columba. Again we must note that what it describes is the life of an enclosed monastic community, and it gives little help as to what might be the worship of a missionary band, until they had set up a daughter monastery.

Monasteries, or families of monasteries, had their own family pattern of life, the Rule. Irish sources claim eight chief Rules followed in the Irish monasteries,[48] and named the fifth and eighth as the Rules of Columba and of Adomnan. No authentic Rule of the former has survived, though Colum Cille's 'rules and customs' were referred to in the Whitby debate,[49] and an Irish manuscript claims to quote from the Rule the prescription of a double allowance of food for both *Sabbatum* (Saturday) and the *dies dominica* (Sunday).[50] The community's worship, the Divine Office (*cursus, synaxis, horae, celebratio*), consisted of daily services based essentially on the recitation of the Psalms at the 'canonical hours', each service probably announced by the bell-stroke of the *clocca*. Adomnan provides us with names for some of these services; *hymni matutinales, prima diei hora, hora diei tertia, hora sexta* (= midday), *hora nona; vespertinales Dei laudes* could be regarded as beginning the celebration of the following day, after which the monks slept until the *clocca* called them to *media nocte*.[51] Columba was supposed by some to have been in the habit of celebrating ten canonical hours.[52]

Mass was only said on Sundays (usually at *sext, hora sexta*), and on such *sollemnes dies* during the week as were marked by church feasts (Christmas, Epiphany, Maundy Thursday, Ascension, etc.) or by the *dies natales*, the commemorations of the deaths of the brethren.[53] The service, called in Irish *Oiffrenn*,[54] was called *Sacorfaicc*[55] in the Book of Deer. The fragment of a service for the administration of Communion to the sick which this manuscript contains is the solitary witness from Scotland, and to obtain some idea of what happened we have to draw on Irish sources. These are scanty enough. Another service for the sick is in the Book of Mulling (before 697).[56] Fragments of a palimpsest from Reichenau contain, under a later manuscript of a glossary, traces of a much-erased sacramentary.[57] The Stowe Missal (ninth century, with earlier material) is the most complete collection of services.[58] Two collections of hymns, the Bangor Antiphonary (end of seventh century), and the *Liber Hymnorum* (eleventh-century manuscript including much earlier materials), with a few scattered leaves of manuscripts from Continental libraries, complete the available material.[59]

The worship of the Lord's Day (and of feast days) was a pattern of prayers and responses, lessons from Scripture or at times from lives of saints, hymns, the Lord's Prayer, and, at the centre of all worship, the consecration, and distribution of bread and wine. In the manuscripts the substance of prayers was accompanied by rubrics (directions) in Latin, or occasionally in the vernacular. Thus, the Book of Deer has at the distribution, *Hisund dubar sacorfaaicc dau*, Here give the sacrifice to him.[60] The form and content of prayers, and their inclusion or exclusion from a particular service, was determined by the Christian Year, and the Stowe Missal shows alterations for Christmas, Epiphany, Circumcision, Maundy Thursday (*natalis calix*), Low Sunday, Ascension and Pentecost.

Phraseology and content, exclusion or inclusion of specific items, and the order in which these appear mark off different 'families' of liturgy, and give clues by which individual manuscripts can be assigned to this or that family or tradition. Choice of the saints who are to be commemorated, particularly if they have local or regional significance, are also identification marks. Origins of particular families of liturgies were the subject of much mythology. Colman, at Whitby,[61] claimed the authority of St. John for the way in which he and his people worshipped, and so we sometimes hear of what is called an Ephesian rite. An Irish author claimed an Alexandrian rite as the source of the Irish liturgies, but, while there may be traces of more distant customs, it seems that their sources were largely Gaul and Spain. Bede tells that Augustine of Canterbury asked the Pope, 'Why does the method of saying Mass differ in the Holy Roman Church and in the Church of Gaul?' He was advised in the reply that whatever customs, Roman, Gallican or other, were found to be most helpful should be used.[62] This was a process going on all the time. In Gaul itself many influences came together, Mediterranean influences coming up from southern France and eastern influence brought by the inflowing tide of monasticism. The process went on amongst the Britons and the Irish, as materials were compared, combined, mutated and permutated. It was only later in our period that Rome began to put a value on uniformity and to attempt to promote the Roman rite to the exclusion of all others, an attempt never completely successful.

In the only Scottish fragment, the Book of Deer, the prayers show signs of Gallican influences, but also may contain elements from Spain (Mozarabic) and from Mediterranean sources. The Stowe Missal shows a stage in the attempt to promote the Roman Rite. As well as a number of services, it contains a Treatise on the Mass which is earlier than the services and has 'a wholly different set of rubrics' showing strong eastern influence.[63] But by the eighth or ninth century to which the Missal belongs there are signs of the Roman pattern; 'the Stowe canon and the Roman canon are practically identical'.

To those accustomed to the Roman forms there was much to offend in other masses,[64] the number of strange collects at the commencement of the service, the unfamiliar introduction to the Lord's Prayer, the equally strange *embolismus*,[65] and the custom in Iona at least, that in the absence of a bishop, two presbyters broke the bread.[66] The number and order of the lessons was another point of difference, the Gallican liturgy beginning with the Gospel, and having a *lectio prophetica* as well as a Pauline lesson. Even the giving of the benediction might vary, Columba blessing the monastery with both hands upraised, and Diormat blessing the brethren with his holy right hand.[67]

Prayers for (but not to) the departed had a recognized place – the benefit of the souls of the departed was claimed to be one of the three chief objects of the eucharistic offering.[68] The deacon brought the diptych to the celebrant who read the names out to the congregation during the offertory, after the first oblation of the unconsecrated elements and before the Canon. Columba, celebrating immediately after news had reached him of the death of his friend Colman, bade the congregation add his name to their prayers.[69] No formula for the consecration prayer (the Canon) has survived in our scanty materials. It was, however, said in an audible voice, an anthem, *Sancti venite*,[70] was sung while the clergy communicated, and other anthems followed during the communion of the people. The wine was mixed with water, and surviving evidence suggests that communicants received both bread and wine.[71] The breaking of the bread was accompanied by an elaborate ceremony of separating and rejoining the two halves, and then the construction of a pattern of small fragments set out in the form of a cross on the paten, different numbers of pieces being associated with different feast-days.[72]

In this, as in other things, we are probably in contact with very distant original sources, perhaps the monasteries of the desert fathers of the middle east.

Outside the monastery, groups of travelling monks kept the pattern of the monastic hours as best they could, as when Columba with a few brothers sang the *vespertinales Dei laudes*, on their visit to King Brude.[73] This was primarily a political mission and a relatively large group. For what happened on missionary travels, one finds some evidence in Bede. Two brothers Hewal, Englishmen, had long lived in exile in Ireland, before devoting themselves to missionary journeys on the Continent. These missionaries 'devoted themselves to psalms and prayers, and daily offered the sacrifice of the saving Victim to God, having with them sacred vessels and a consecrated table for use as an altar'.[74] What they did on the Continent, or what Bede describes Aidan doing in Northumbria, could well describe the ways of the missionaries in, for example, Pictland.[75]

We get glimpses of them in the lively sculpturings of the Pictish stone-carvers. Groups of clergy appear on several stones. Three figures on a stone from Kirriemuir, Angus, all wear primitive, full, circular-shaped chasubles.[76] Two carry square or rectangular objects, while the third wears a triangular shape which has been identified as a *rationale*, a vestment of varied shape, often in gold, or silver, studded with precious stones, supposed to have been derived from the Aaronic breastplate. On a stone from Invergowrie, three clergy carrying rectangular objects, and perhaps showing the Roman tonsure, are shown. Two wear large shoulder brooches.[77] Clergy from St. Vigeans, Arbroath, are apparently provided with *flabella*, liturgical fans to keep insects from the chalice.[78]

The rectangles often carried by these missionaries have been variously identified as altar slabs, relic boxes, book-satchels, or, most likely, actual books. The book, primarily a gospel or gospels, was essential to the missionary. No one left the community of Finian of Clonard 'without a backall (book-satchel), or without a gospel, or without some well-known sign, so that round these they built their churches and their cathedrals afterwards'.[79] Again the Book of Deer gives the only surviving Scottish example, containing the Gospel of St. John, with parts of Matthew, Mark and Luke. Others are known to tradition; St. Ternan had four Gospel books, one of which, St. Matthew, was still on show in his church at Banchory in the sixteenth century. In the mid-fourteenth century, a Gospel book in a silver case, attributed to the early Bishop Fothad, was preserved at St. Andrews.[80] Legend said that Colum Cille had obtained St. Martin's Gospels for his church at Derry, bringing it as a gift from the people of Tours in return for showing them where their saint was buried.[81]

Monks and missionaries could, of course, rely on capacious memories. All would know the 'three fifties' of the Psalter by heart,[82] and a similar knowledge of the Gospels was, according to some Rules, a condition of being allowed to remain in the monastery. But possession of a Gospel and the copying of such books had great virtue. For taking notes, and perhaps for practice, leaves of wood covered with wax were used. An early copy of some of the Psalms on such *caudices* was uncovered in an Irish peat bog,[83] and we know that Adomnan used such aids on Iona.[84]

Wandering or settled in a place of his choice, the missionary preached, if necessary, like Columba, through interpreters, but ultimately, like Aidan in Northumbria, learning the language. He would exhort to belief and to Baptism. He would exorcise springs and wells devoted to pagan rites, and consecrate them to Christian rites. Hence comes the significance in placenames of wells bearing the names of early preachers. St. Patrick writes of his newly baptized converts seized by Coroticus. Columba baptizes converts and their families.[85] The Stowe Missal contains a late order for the rite which probably for the most part follows the sixth-century forms. The cross on the forehead, laying on of hands with prayer, and use of saliva are not mentioned, but the acts of exorcism, the blessing of salt laid on the catechumen's lips, a double renunciation of the devil, his works and pomps, and a three-fold confession of faith are included. After the Baptism the new convert put on a white dress, the sign of the cross was made on one hand, and the feet ceremonially washed, and finally adult or child received both the bread and wine of communion.[86] This might be done by intinction, that is, the bread soaked with wine would be given in a spoon. Silver spoons with Christian symbols or inscriptions have survived from a variety of contexts, and a spoon together with a knife-like object from the St. Ninian's Isle treasure were explained by Monsignor McRoberts as a spoon for giving communion, and a knife for the elaborate *fractio panis*, the dividing and arranging of pieces of the host on the paten.[87] While his arguments for regarding all twenty-eight objects in the hoard as being strictly ecclesiastical in use are not equally convincing, it seems reasonable to see here the treasures of some early monastery buried, as the monks of Iona buried their goods in 825, in times of stress.

Other ecclesiastical objects have been handed down, such as the 'bachalmore of St. Moloch',[88] or have resulted from archaeological finds. Such are the silver spoons with Chi-Rho and fish symbols, and other pieces from Traprain Law, and several typical early bells. These were probably not primarily for calling to worship, but were, with the mass book and *cruisce*, part of the altar furnishings for Mass.[89] There is undoubtedly a certain oddness in the glimpses we get of worship in the early Christian centuries, and one can understand how clerics like Wilfrid, fresh and enthusiastic for Roman ways, or Queen Margaret's chaplain Turgot, unaware of any principles of historical development, meeting 'peripheral survivals' mistook them for 'separatist heresies'. Turgot spoke of the Queen's subjects celebrating Mass in 'I know not what barbarous rite'.[90] Oddities and survivals must not blind the student to the fact that the differences are superficial and the underlying patterns are those which develop into the medieval forms of worship of the next period.

NOTES

The most important books and articles are asterisked. Many of them have bibliographies which can be used to guide further reading.

1. Bede, *A History of the English Church and People*, trans. Leo Sherley-Price (Penguin Classics, 1955), p. 35.
2. According to K. H. Jackson, 'British was spoken all the way from Penzance to Edinburgh'. Quoted by Charles Thomas, *Christianity in Roman Britain to A.D. 500* (1981), p. 61 (hereafter referred to as *CRB*).
3. Discussion by K. H. Jackson in F. T. Wainwright, ed., *The Problem of the Picts* (1955), chapter vi and appendix.
4. Bede, *op. cit.*, p. 143. Carved stones at Fiscavaig, Skye, and in Caithness, Orkney and Shetland.
5. A. O. and M. O. Anderson, *Adomnan's Life of Columba* (1961), p. 397.
6. I. A. Richmond, *Roman and Native in North Britain* (1958), pp. 112–158.
7. Kathleen Hughes, *The Church in Early Irish Society* (1966), pp. 25–26 and note. H. M. Chadwick, *Early Scotland* (1949), pp. 149–150.

8. Latin scribblings from objects found on Traprain Law, East Lothian.
9. Charles Thomas, *Early Christian Archaeology of North Britain* (1971), pp. 11ff. (hereafter referred to as *ECANB*).
10. Tertullian, *adv. Iudaeos*, iii 4, quoted in H. Williams, *Christianity in Early Britain* (1912), p. 75.
11. Thomas, *ECANB*, p. 102.
12. Thomas, *idem*, pp. 17–18. Later discussion in Thomas, *CRB*, p. 291.
13. Bede, *op. cit.*, p. 143. The poem is discussed by W. Levison, 'An Eighth-century Poem on St. Ninian', *Antiquity* 14 (1940), 280–291. Ailred's *Life* is in *Historians of Scotland*, V. Some of the literature on Ninian is summarized in J. T. McNeill, *The Celtic Churches* (Chicago, 1974), p. 235.
14. It has been suggested that Ninian's association with Whithorn only belongs to the period of the poem (eighth century) but K. Hughes has written 'It was far more likely a revival and fostered an old cult and tradition'.
15. Modern translation by L. Bieler, *Works of St. Patrick* (1953).
16. C. A. R. Radford, *'The Early Church in Strathclyde and Galloway', Medieval Archaeology* 11 (1967), 105–126. C. Thomas writes, 'Christianity in southern Scotland so far as its derivation can be made out, sprang from that early fifth-century see at Whithorn; and the Whithorn bishopric, unless some totally eccentric phenomenon is represented, came out of late Roman Britain.' *CRB*, p. 347.
17. L. Alcock, *Arthur's Britain* (1973). 'The concept of the isolation of the Celtic west is a myth', p. 206.
18. C. A. R. Radford, 'The Archaeological Background on the Continent' in M. W. Barley and R. P. C. Hanson, eds., *Christianity in Britain 300–700*, p. 32. 'A reactivation of the Atlantic sea-routes opened the way to close contacts between the *foederati* states and the unconquered lands of the north and west.' A good study of the importance of the sea routes is E. G. Bowen, *Saints, Seaways and Settlements* (1969).
19. Thomas, *ECANB*, chapter iv.
20. *Ibid.*, pp. 23ff.
21. Bede, *op. cit.*, p. 143.
22. W. H. C. Frend finds it 'difficult to disbelieve entirely' that Ninian was a disciple of Martin, and decides that the 'tradition of missionary activity was not ill-founded'. Barley and Hanson, *op. cit.*, p. 43.
23. See Hughes, *op. cit.*, p. 17 and notes 1 and 2. Martin was widely esteemed in Ireland, Bowen, *op. cit.*, pp. 129–130. For Adomnan's use of the Life of Martin, in his life of Columba, see Anderson, *op. cit.*, p. 86.
24. Hughes, *op. cit.*, p. 18.

25. J. N. L. Myers, in Barley and Hanson, *op. cit.*, pp. 4–5.
26. P. J. Corish, *The Christian Mission* (History of Irish Catholicism, I, 3, 1971), pp. 11–12, 34ff. W. F. Skene, *Celtic Scotland* (1877), II, p. 44.
27. John Ryan, *The Monastic Institute* (History of Irish Catholicism, I, 2, 1971), p. 5. McNeill, *op. cit.*, pp. 35–37.
28. Ryan, *op. cit.*, p. 6; McNeill, *op. cit.*, p. 72. F. E. Warren, **Liturgy and Ritual of the Celtic Church* (1881), p. 81.
29. Ryan, *op. cit.*, p. 5; McNeill, *op. cit.*, p. 71.
30. The best edition of the Life is Anderson and Anderson, *op. cit.* (cp. n. 5 *supra*); Ryan, *op. cit.*, pp. 3–4; McNeill, *op. cit.*, chapter vi and bibliography.
31. Skene writes, 'For Columba as for Adomnan the real centre of church life was in Ireland.'
32. Thomas, *ECANB*, chapter ii.
33. Adomnan, for example, seems only to refer to one journey of Columba into Pictland, the visit to Brude, a political rather than a missionary occasion.
34. Bede, *op. cit.*, book iii, chapter 3.
35. *Idem*, book iii, chapters 25–26.
36. Ian B. Cowan, **'The Post-Columban Church'*, *Records of the Scottish Church History Society* 18 (1974), 247.
37. Bede, *op. cit.*, book v, chapter 15. Some evidence might suggest that Adomnan, on his return to Iona, sought to increase the status of the bishop by providing a *cathedra*, 'the chair of Iona', Anderson and Anderson, *op. cit.*, pp. 25, 102.
38. Anderson and Anderson, *op. cit.*, pp. 94–95; Skene, op. cit., II, pp. 174–175.
39. D. M. Wilson, *Reflections on the St. Ninian's Isle Treasure* (Jarrow Lecture, 1969), p. 8.
40. Bede, *op. cit.*, book v, chapters 21–22. Skene, *op. cit.*, II, p. 178.
41. Cowan, *op. cit.*, p. 252.
42. Cowan, *loc. cit.*
43. Ryan, *op. cit.*, pp. 47–49; Cowan, *op. cit.*, 253; Hughes, *op. cit.*, pp. 173–181.
44. Cowan, *op. cit.*, pp. 259–260.
45. J. C. M. Toynbee, quoted in Barley and Hanson, *op. cit.*, p. 24; cp. Thomas, *ECANB*, p. 5.
46. Bede, *op. cit.*, p. 184.
47. Thomas, *ECANB*, p. 5.
48. Ryan, *op. cit.*, pp. 32ff.
49. Bede, *op. cit.*, p. 187.
50. Anderson and Anderson, *op. cit.*, p. 120.
51. Anderson and Anderson, *op. cit.*, pp. 121–123.
52. Louis Gougaud, *Christianity in Celtic Lands* (1932), p. 330.

53. Anderson and Anderson, *op. cit.*, p. 123; Ryan, *op. cit.*, pp. 58–59.
54. Gougaud, *op. cit.*, p. 323.
55. John Stuart, *The Book of Deer* (1869, Spalding Club), p. 90.
56. Existing MSS. are described by Warren, *op. cit.*
57. Ryan, *op. cit.*, pp. 59–60.
58. G. F. Warner, *The Stowe Missal*, 2 vols. (1906, 1915), Henry Bradshaw Society. Cp. Warren, *op. cit.*, pp. 198ff. 'It may have had a direct connection with the liturgy of Iona', Anderson and Anderson, *op. cit.*, p. 69. They do not, however, elaborate.
59. Warren, *op. cit.*, chapter iii.
60. Stuart, *op. cit.*, p. 90.
61. Bede, *op. cit.*, p. 185.
62. Bede, *idem*, pp. 72–73.
63. Ryan, *op. cit.*, p. 59.
64. Warren has gathered a number of points, *op. cit.*, pp. 96–100.
65. *Embolismus*, a prayer 'inserted' between the Lord's Prayer and the breaking of bread.
66. Anderson and Anderson, *op. cit.*, p. 305. Warren, *op. cit.*, pp. 128–129.
67. Anderson and Anderson, *op. cit.*, pp. 525, 529.
68. Warren, *op. cit.*, pp. 102–105.
69. Anderson and Anderson, *op. cit.*, pp. 489, 491.
70. Warren, *op. cit.*, p. 110.
71. Warren, *idem*, pp. 133–134 (mixed chalice); pp. 134–136 (communion in both kinds).
72. This, and other customs such as the 'half-uncovering' of the chalice, will be found in the Stowe Missal, vol. ii, pp. 40–42.
73. Anderson and Anderson, *op. cit.*, p. 289.
74. Bede, *op. cit.*, pp. 280–281.
75. Bede, *idem*, p. 145. Compare also the description of St. Cuthbert in Bede's Life, *Lives of the Saints*, J. F. Webb, translator (Penguin Classics), pp. 83–84.
76. J. Romilly Allen and J. Anderson, *Early Christian Monuments of Scotland* (1903). Warren, *op. cit.*, p. 113.
77. W. D. Simpson, *The Celtic Church in Scotland*, frontispiece and p. 111 n. 1. D. McRoberts, *'The Ecclesiastical Character of the St. Ninian's Isle Treasure' in Small, ed., *The Fourth Viking Congress*, p. 234.
78. McRoberts, *idem*, p. 241.
79. P. McGurk, 'The Irish Pocket Gospel Book', *Sacris Eruderi*, VIII (1956), p. 249.
80. Stuart, *op. cit.*, p. xxii.
81. Skene, *Celtic Scotland*, II, p. 483.
82. Hughes, *op. cit.*, p. 175.
83. The Springmount Tables, containing Pss. xxx–xxxii in a sixth-century hand, see C. Thomas, *CRB*, pp. 84–85 and notes.

84. Adomnan noted on his tablets the travel-talk of Bishop Arculf, storm-stayed for a winter on Iona, and turned his notes into a book on 'the Holy Places'. Bede, *op. cit.*, p. 294; Anderson and Anderson, *op. cit.*, p. 94.
85. Anderson and Anderson, *op. cit.*, p. 397.
86. Warren, *op. cit.*, pp. 64–67.
87. McRoberts, *op. cit.*, pp. 237–238.
88. On pastoral staves in general, see Warren, *op. cit.*, pp. 115–116. That of St. Moluag was in the keeping of the Dukes of Argyle; St. Kentigern's staff, which he had received from St. Columba, was displayed at Ripon in the fifteenth century, but its authenticity must be doubted.
89. McRoberts, *op. cit.*, p. 230.
90. Skene (*op. cit.*, II, p. 349) thought the 'most probable explanation' was that the service was in Gaelic, but there is no evidence for Scotland or for Ireland for services in the vernacular, though preaching might be. 'The official language of the church in the Celtic-speaking parts of the British Isles was Latin, as elsewhere', C. Thomas, *ECANB*, p. 5. Warren had long ago realized this (*op. cit.*, p. 155) 'no trace of a vernacular liturgy'. See also M. V. Hay, *Scottish Gaelic Studies*, II, pp. 30ff.

Chapter Two

THE MIDDLE AGES

James Galbraith

Many fifteenth-century Scotsmen evidently believed that the form of public worship followed in their secular cathedrals and parish churches had been imposed on the country as a deliberate political act by Edward I of England, when his forces overran Scotland in 1296. The poet Blind Harry says of Edward:

> The Roman bukis at than was in Scotland
> He gart be brocht to scham quhar thai thaim fand
> And but radem thai brynt thaim thar Ilkan
> Salysbery oys our clerkis than has tan.[1]

The surviving liturgical books of medieval Scotland, comparatively few in number, provide the bulk of the evidence available for a study of Scottish worship between the thirteenth and sixteenth centuries. These books are of the types which were used generally in the Western Church during that period, of which the most important were the missal, containing both the variable and fixed material for the daily service of the Mass throughout the year, and the breviary, which provided the texts of the divine office – that is, those psalms, scriptures and other matter which were to be read by the clergy on each day of the year and during each part of the day, as divided into the seven 'canonical hours' of matins, lauds, prime, sext, none, vespers and compline. The order to be followed in Baptisms, marriages and such 'occasional' services was the province of a further book, the manual or ritual. Like their counterparts used elsewhere in Europe, these Scottish books of the later Middle Ages do not deviate in dogma, or in any essential point, from the universal rite of the Western Church. That rite had been fixed at the start of the ninth century, from a fusion of the original Roman and other early rites; however, individual churches in the West remained free to develop their own ceremonial practices and to create texts appropriate, or 'proper', to the feasts which they observed, so that by the thirteenth century, there were in Europe a considerable number of local 'uses' or variants of the basic rite. Most of the extant Scottish books are based on the 'Salysbery oys', one such local variant, itself derived from the Continent in the eleventh century, which had developed in the diocese of Salisbury (or

19

Sarum) and eventually became the predominant 'use' in England, Wales and Ireland. Yet there is enough evidence to suggest that by the sixteenth century, if not earlier, the Scottish Church had, at least in the opinion of its clergy, developed a 'use' which was as distinct from that of Salisbury as those of Cologne, Hereford or Rouen.

There appears to be no direct evidence to support Blind Harry's assertion that 'Roman bukis' were used in Scotland before the introduction of the Sarum use, but in fact this is not unlikely. Following the Synod of Whitby in 664 the practices of the Roman Church were established in Northumbria, and the long withdrawal of the Celtic Church began. It is not unreasonable to suppose, in view of the existing contacts between Northumbria and the adjacent parts of Lowland Scotland, that in time the original Roman rite, or the ninth-century synthesis made by Alcuin of York which was to become recognized as the Roman rite, should have percolated to the church in Lothian, the embryonic Church in Scotland. If there was indeed such an early link between the Anglo-Saxon Church and that in Lothian, we may have a convenient explanation for the otherwise puzzling fact that many Scottish churches observed the feasts of certain saints native to the north of England before these feasts were regularly incorporated in the use of Salisbury.

Doubtless, Blind Harry had none of this in mind. He may simply have echoed a tradition that Queen Margaret and her son David I had introduced Roman practices to Scotland. More probably, his belief in the use of 'Roman bukis' derived from some awareness of the unique position which the Scottish Church held in Christendom. Possibly by 1192, but certainly by 1219, the Scottish bishops had obtained a papal privilege which removed their dioceses from the control of the archbishopric of York and placed each in direct subjection to the papacy, so that the Church in Scotland became the 'special daughter' of the Roman Church. Thus, the bishops of Scotland were left in a position of virtual independence, but with respect to the form of worship used in their churches, they already enjoyed the same freedom as other diocesans, so that the '*filia specialis*' privilege did not of itself encourage the growth of separate 'uses' in their bishoprics, or the piecemeal introduction of the 'Salysbery oys'. For Harry was certainly in error when he tells us that Sarum practices were forced on this country.

In the late twelfth and early thirteenth centuries, the emerging Scottish cathedrals turned naturally to their English counterparts as models whereon to base their constitutions (though none of them seems to have considered York as eligible, despite its proximity). Moray, perhaps prompted by the enduring influence of its first effective bishop, Richard of Lincoln (1187–1203), went to that diocese for its constitutions in 1212. However, Glasgow had already turned to Salisbury for that purpose, and in the years between 1250 and 1255 Dunkeld and Fortrose followed suit. In 1242 Moray confirmed its Lincoln constitutions, with the proviso that the usages of Salisbury should be followed in worship. Thus it was apparently by voluntary adoption, and in the train of the Sarum constitutions, that the use of Salisbury came to this country.

That use was never consistently practised by all the clergy in Scotland. The highly centralized orders of regular clergy, such as the Franciscan and Dominican friars and the Cistercian monks, must have followed their own 'uses', at least by the fourteenth century, though it cannot be said whether the same was true of other orders which were more liberal in this respect, for example, the Augustinian canons who composed the chapter of St. Andrews. Among the secular clergy, there were evidently individuals who preferred to read, or to continue to read, their office according to the use of Rome. Neither the diocese of Galloway, nor that of Orkney, had been included in the 'special daughter' privilege, and these may have followed some version of the uses of York and of Trondheim to which they were subject, in name at any rate, until 1472, while in the Celtic west of Scotland, some distinctive practices presumably existed. At the lower end of the scale, we find indications that some parish churches possessed books of the uses of York, Chichester and Lincoln; some of these anomalies may have come to Scotland in the same way as the set of vestments held by Aberdeen Cathedral which had formed part of the 'spoils of the battle of Bannockburn'.[2]

The Wars of Independence did rather more to shape the worship of the Scottish Church than to provide a medium for the exchange of books and furnishings. The use of Sarum did not enter Scotland during these wars, but the Anglophobia which prompted Blind Harry's comments on it certainly did. The severance between Scottish churchmen and their English counterparts which these wars encouraged was reinforced by the Great Schism of the Western Church (1378–1418) in which the two countries took opposite sides. Instead, the outlook of the Scottish Church and people was turned more fully to the Continent, and particularly to the Low Countries. One result was the growth of major deviations from Sarum practices in worship.

The library of Aberdeen Cathedral contained a copy of the 'Statutes of the churches of Cologne and Liège' sometime before 1429, when the dean who had lost the volume was expelled.[3] It is probably a coincidence that this same cathedral had elements in its constitution which cannot be attributed to either Lincoln or Salisbury,[4] but there is abundant evidence that, in the context of worship and the ceremonial associated with it, Continental elements were adopted until the 'purchasing and in-bringing of novelties and innovations in the kirk' had become a matter of national concern in that it contributed, in the view of the Parliament of 1496, to the 'uter heirschip and destituting of the realme of all money'.[5] Such 'innovations' in clerical dress, church furnishings and the like were relatively minor and must usually have been confined to individual churches. This cannot be said of the developments in ceremonial associated with the sacrament, nor of the new devotions which the Scottish Church adopted during the fifteenth century.

Since the laity of the Western Church were virtually excluded from the act of corporate worship expressed in the Mass which was celebrated in what was to them an alien tongue, it is easy to understand why the high point of the service, the consecration of the host, should have come to be signalled by some dramatic gesture which all could see and understand. It is likely that the practices of raising the host at the moment of consecration, and of censing while it was so elevated, had come to Scotland directly from the Continent, for Scottish records contain some of the earliest evidence for the general introduction of these customs. It is, however, certain that many Scottish churches of the later Middle Ages were 'Continental' in their treatment of, and attitude to, the consecrated host. Part of the sacrament was reserved for the communion of the sick or dying. In English churches, this was kept in an ornate box or 'pyx' placed on, or suspended over the altar. Scottish churches used the same method of reservation, but by the late fifteenth century, many had changed to that practised in the Low Countries, where the consecrated sacrament (which was, of course, believed to be the real Body of Our Lord) was displayed in an elaborate monstrance or 'eucharist', 'for the sake of the adoration of the Body of Christ by the people'.[6] These ornaments were carried in processions and, in church, were set where the Body could be seen and venerated, either on top of the rood screen which separated clergy and congregation in larger churches or, in smaller buildings, within a decorated wall-cupboard or 'sacrament house'.

Sacramental veneration was accompanied on the Continent by the growth of particular devotions centred on the Divine Humanity and Passion of Christ. Certain of these, most notably of the Holy Blood, the Five Wounds and the Most Holy Name of Jesus, had reached Scotland by the late fifteenth century, as had other 'new feasts' of the period such as the Presentation of the Virgin (21 November), St. Mary of the Snows (5 August), the Visitation of the Virgin (2 July), St. Barbara (4 December), and the Cologne feast of the 11,000 Virgins (21 October). Much of the available evidence points to the rather unsurprising conclusion that a number of these late medieval devotions were known in Scotland before they were regularly incorporated in the use of Salisbury; certainly the proper material used for their observance in Scotland very often varied from that provided in later Sarum books. The most striking example is the feast of St. Joseph (19 March) which never became part of the Salisbury use, and in fact appeared in few calendars, even on the Continent, before 1510. Known exceptions are calendars of Freising, Antwerp and Utrecht of the years between 1482 and 1497, and that of a missal completed in 1491 by James Sibbald, vicar of Arbuthnott

Church in the Mearns, in which Joseph is already the venerable 'foster-father of the Lord' who figures in later Scottish books.[7]

It would be difficult to claim with confidence that the devotional life of fifteenth-century Scotland was influenced by one place more than by any other; it can, however, be argued that if such a place existed it is unlikely to have been Salisbury – though it may just possibly have been Bruges. Bruges was the site of the Scottish staple through which much of the country's trade with the Continent passed, and through which also passed those (far too numerous, in the parliament's view) members of the Scottish clergy on their way to Rome. The community of Bruges treasured a relic of the Precious Blood; at least one Scottish bishop, James Kennedy of St. Andrews, is known to have participated in the regular Holy Blood processions there,[8] and these religious processions provided a model for those of Edinburgh, which were to be mustered in the manner 'lyk as thai haf in the towne of Bruges or siclyk gud townes'.[9] At any rate, it is clear that the Scottish clergy were very much alive to the development of new expressions of devotion in the Church as a whole. This does not necessarily mean that they simply copied wholesale from Continental models, or that the traffic was entirely one-way. For example, the missal which James Sibbald wrote for his church at Arbuthnott contains a Mass for one of the 'new feasts', that of St. Salvator (commemorating the miraculous bleeding of a crucifix pierced by Jews), including a rather fine rhyming sequence which may be peculiar to Scotland; since it was to St. Salvator (9 November) that Bishop Kennedy had dedicated his college at St. Andrews, there is at least a possibility that Sibbald's mass was composed in that diocese.[10] It is less easy to explain why the book of hours which was produced in Ghent or Bruges for Nicolas von Firmian, an Austrian courtier, sometime before 1510, should contain a memorial in honour, apparently, of David I, King of Scotland.[11] The Church in Scotland was evidently not immune from the general urge to create liturgical material, and, as was the case elsewhere, most of its compositions were designed to grace the feasts of local saints.

One of the most obvious characteristics of the fifteenth-century Scottish clergy is their nationalism. This was, for the most part, a positive and constructive nationalism; it led, among other things, to the foundation of the collegiate churches and of Scotland's first three universities, and it also led to a great revival in the cultus of the national saints. Apparently, these saints had rarely been venerated beyond the particular churches traditionally associated with them, but in the fifteenth century certain hitherto 'local' shrines, like that of St. Duthac at Tain, began to draw pilgrims from many parts of Scotland. The relics of some saints had passed into secular hands, and these were sought out and re-instated; for although such relics fulfilled a secular function, in oath-taking for example, they were increasingly regarded in popular belief as the repositories of miraculous power, particularly against plague. Also in this century the masses and offices composed in honour of the Scottish saints came to occupy a significant place in the worship of the national Church.

The growth in popularity of the national feasts is reflected in three liturgical books dating from the period between 1450 and 1510. The earliest of these is probably a breviary usually associated with the collegiate church of Fowlis Easter. This contains rather scanty material for four Scottish feasts in the body of the text, and for a further three at the end of the book; thus the volume was evidently supplemented as new 'propers' were composed or copied from elsewhere.[12] The second book, Sibbald's 'Arbuthnott Missal' of 1491, provides more extensive material for six national feasts, and the fly-leaves have been used for the addition of masses of the Holy Blood and the other 'new' devotions. It should be pointed out that the calendar in each of these books contains more Scottish feasts than are actually provided for in the text; but in our last example, a Sarum Missal printed at Rouen in 1506 which was adapted for the use of St. Nicholas' Church, Aberdeen, the calendar has been overrun by the Scottish and other feasts which were inserted in manuscript.[13]

The end-papers of the St. Nicholas Missal contain 'propers' for only one Scottish feast, that of St. Ninian. It is unlikely, however, that the users of this book would have been prepared to endure the tedium of observing all these additional feasts without appropriate material, despite the evident nationalist sentiments of the Scottish clergy. Probably by this stage the Scottish and Continental accretions to the use of Sarum were too extensive for fly-leaves or margins to contain them. Thus the proper texts for these additional Masses or offices may usually have existed in the form of separate manuscript supplements to the missal or breviary, similar to the 'quires' used by other churches in Europe or in England which aspired to a distinct and developing 'use'.[14] There are several indications (though little positive evidence) that a considerable quantity of Scottish liturgical material was in circulation by 1510, and even that some of it – the proper prayers for the feasts of St. Ninian and St. Mungo, for example – had become virtually standard throughout the country.

At the start of the sixteenth century therefore, the liturgical practices of Scotland were quite noticeably distinct from those of Salisbury. The clerics of St. Nicholas' added some ninety feasts to the calendar of their Sarum Missal, and not all of these were Scottish in origin. Moreover, it appears that Scottish books frequently differed from their Sarum counterparts in the contents of several offices which both churches had in common. For example, the Fowlis Easter breviary provides non-Sarum offices for the feasts of St. Edmund of Canterbury, the Immaculate Conception (8 December) and the Visitation of the Blessed Virgin (2 July). Further deviations from Sarum practice can be found elsewhere in this book and in the Arbuthnott Missal, particularly in the texts of those 'new feasts' which were incorporated in the English use from the fourteenth century onwards. However, all these variants were comparatively minor. The Sarum basis of the liturgy used by Scottish clerics was practically untouched. Thus, it would be an overstatement to claim that the Fowlis Easter breviary, the Arbuthnott Missal, or the St. Nicholas Missal were more than local adaptations of the use of Salisbury. This view, however, was evidently not shared by the clergy who used them.

Both the breviary and Sibbald's Missal make casual references to the 'use of Sarum' as if that were something quite different from the practices of Fowlis Easter or Arbuthnott, while an even more explicit distinction between the 'use of Glasgow' and the 'use of Sarum' can be found as early as the thirteenth century.[15] By the end of the fifteenth, the Scottish amalgam of national, Continental, Sarum and other material had evidently been dignified in the eyes of its practitioners as the 'use of Scotland'. This supposed 'use', then almost at the high point of its development, may already have been under threat of extinction because of its sheer impracticality.

Sarum books were printed from the 1470s onwards. They effectively swamped all but two of the uses of other English cathedrals and, as they were among the items imported by Scots from the Continent, may also have endangered the distinctive practices of the Scottish Church. Printed books were not only comparatively cheap; they were also comparatively standard in content, so that the guides variously called the 'ordinal', 'pye' or 'directory', which were designed to steer the reader through the complexities of the use, could also be produced in bulk. These directories were essential because of the large number of saints' feasts which were observed in the use of Sarum; for these feasts, each of which was allotted a specific day in the calendar, had to be reconciled with the feasts 'of the season' some of which (like Christmas) were also fixed, but most of which (like Easter) varied in date from year to year. It was not really sufficient to know from a calendar that the feast of All Saints, for example, should always be observed on 1 November if it happened to be a year when 1 November fell on a Sunday, a day of particular importance with its own observances. To find what should be said or sung in this case and in any other possible combination of feasts, the celebrant would have had to turn to the directory. Now, the clergy of St. Nicholas' Church in Aberdeen had at least one of these printed guides to the conduct of the Sarum use, a copy of the short tract called *Crede Michi*.[16] One wonders what they did with it, for the calendar of their printed Sarum Missal contained, as we saw, a mass of additional feasts, and there is no evidence that any serious attempt was made to fit these into the already complex Sarum structure. If the St. Nicholas' calendar was typical, the 'Scottish use' of the early sixteenth century must have been a burdensome and virtually unworkable clutter in which several feasts were frequently celebrated on the same date. Presumably not averse to using the cheap Sarum books, but unable to take full advantage of the printed Sarum directories, the Scottish clergy seem to have been left with a number of unattractive options, one of which was to adopt the Roman, or even the Sarum use, without local modifications. Probably the best available solution was that conceived by William Elphinstone, Bishop of Aberdeen (1483–1514). This was a project to compile and print books of a standard, revised 'Scottish use' which would have its own directories.

By 1507 Elphinstone and his associates had apparently collected material for a comprehensive series of Scottish liturgical books. On 15 September in that year James IV granted a patent to Walter Chapman and Andrew Millar, burgesses of Edinburgh, who had undertaken to establish Scotland's first press. The patent gave them the exclusive rights of printing missals, manuals and breviaries 'eftir our awin Scottis Use', which were to include the propers 'gaderit and ekit' (added) by Elphinstone and others for the feasts of Scottish saints. These books were to be used throughout the country, and the importation of 'sik bukis of Salisbury use' was to cease, on pain of confiscation.[17] The only survivors of this ambitious scheme are four copies, more or less incomplete, and a few loose sheets, of the 'Breviary of Aberdeen' completed in 1510.

The compilers of the Aberdeen Breviary relieved the extreme congestion of the Scottish–Sarum use by simply removing almost all the English material from it. Those few English saints whose feasts remained – and not always with the standard Sarum texts – were mostly associated with the Celtic mission in Northumbria (St. Cuthbert of Durham, for example), and were therefore presumably regarded as 'adopted' Scots. Yet the Breviary was rather more than a de-Anglicized Sarum book (if such a thing could still be described as a 'Sarum' book). It incorporated offices for most of the major new devotions which were fashionable in Europe at the time of its production, and in these there can be found material, particularly hymns, of undoubted Continental origin. The most obvious example is the office of St. Mary *ad Nives* (5 August) which was to be partly observed 'according to the use of Rome', but the use of Continental material was not purely restricted to such new feasts.[18]

The chief interest of Elphinstone's work, however, lies in the legends and other proper texts which had been 'gaderit and ekit' for the feasts of most of the eighty-one Scottish saints named in the calendar, since few examples of such material can be found in earlier books or fragments. Nevertheless, enough of these earlier propers have survived to show that compilers of the Breviary drew on the existing practices of churches throughout the country for their national material. Thus, the book appears to have been a straightforward combination of the various ingredients which made up the 'Scottis Use' at the start of the sixteenth century, but there is insufficient evidence to indicate how far it was really innovatory. We may never know, for example, whether the Scottish Church as a whole had already abandoned the Sarum custom of holding a weekly commemorative service in honour of St. Thomas of Canterbury, in favour of a commemoration of St. Andrew.[19] However, the main characteristics of the Aberdeen Breviary can be discussed with a little more confidence.

This rendering of the 'use and custom of the very famous Scottish church'[20] was, in fact, just that. It was a distinct variant of the rite of the Western Church, and it was moreover a viable one, since it incorporated a 'pye' which made the whole, still rather complex compilation more or less workable in practice. Also, despite its name and certain peculiarities which may have derived from the 'use of Aberdeen', Elphinstone's breviary seems to have been a sincere attempt to provide an acceptable standard use for the whole of the Church in Scotland. It provided offices for local feasts from all parts of the country, including the western Highlands and Orkney. Moreover, its calendar may be unique in comparison with those of other medieval uses, for it gave no indication of local provenance; it was not an Aberdonian calendar (in which the feasts of St. Machar or St. Nicholas, the patrons of the town, would have been of greater rank than those of other local saints), nor did it obviously pertain to any other diocese or church since the offices of Machar, St. Kentigern of Glasgow, St. Moluag of Lismore, St. Magnus of Orkney and the patrons of all the other Scottish cathedrals were given equal precedence. All one can say of this calendar is that it was Scottish. In addition, the legends of the Breviary constitute a remarkable work of nationalist propaganda.

A cleric reading the Breviary in the course of his private devotions would have learned from the office of St. Palladius (6 July) that the Scots had been almost the first to receive the Gospel and from the legend of St. Regulus (17 October) that this early Church had been subsequently strengthened and confirmed by the special favour of St. Andrew himself (who was, significantly, the first of the disciples to be called, besides being the brother of St. Peter). Thus Palladius came to Scotland from Rome in 410, not as a missionary but to all intents as a papal legate whose task was to bring the flourishing 'primitive church' in Scotland into line with Roman usages.[21] The existence of an ancient and intimate connection between the churches of Rome and Scotland is repeatedly emphasized in these legends, suggesting that the fifteenth-century Scottish clergy could see no difference in the doctrine or practices of the Roman and Celtic Churches. Saints of such diverse backgrounds as Machar (a disciple of St. Columba and therefore supposedly Celtic) and St. Ternan, patron of Arbuthnott (baptized by Palladius and thus presumably Roman), cooperated in their missions, and were consecrated in Rome, usually by no less a pope than St. Gregory. According to one legend, St. Columba himself had visited Pope Gregory in Rome.[22] Neither the historical differences between

Rome and Iona, nor the very real – and in 1510 very present – divisions between Highland and Lowland Scotland existed, so far as the authors of these legends were concerned. Taken together, they present 'this poor little Scotland beyond which there is no dwelling-place at all' as a united and independent country which had a unique and very privileged place in Christendom.[23] The ends of the earth had been committed to Christ, and Scotland was one of them.

The nationalist outlook and devotional interests of Elphinstone and his fellows are obvious, but any attempt to assess how far these were reflected by the laity must be largely based on speculation. There are, however, certain pointers. During the late fifteenth and early sixteenth centuries, donations by laymen to collegiate churches and cathedrals were usually made in honour of the Name of Jesus, the Holy Blood, the Five Wounds and the national saints, which may show that the clerical enthusiasm for these devotions had spread. Also, the belief that the local saints of Scotland had power against the plague seems to have outlasted the Reformation, as did the association of their names with local fairs, which suggests that the veneration of these saints was deep-rooted. The poems of the early sixteenth-century Scottish 'makars' indicate the probable existence of a popular vernacular piety, associated among other things with the devotion of the rosary, which like so much else had apparently reached Scotland from the Low Countries.[24]

None of this evidence, however, can be construed to prove that the devotional life of Scotland was exceptional in comparison with that of the rest of Europe. It must be assumed, for example, that although the laity were excited by the display of the consecrated sacrament and despite efforts to encourage regular communion, most of them – perhaps the bulk of the adult population – only communicated at Easter. Yet attendance at Mass may have been regular enough in most places.

In any case, the participation of the layman in the formal act of worship was small. He might go on pilgrimage, take part (whether motivated by piety or the offer of indulgences) in religious processions, or exemplify his devotion in other ways; but his place in church, whatever his social status, was basically to see and to hear. The first part of this role must have had its attractions, at least in the larger churches. Surviving inventories of church furnishings testify to a wealth of splendid vestments and ornaments. Moreover, the interiors of such churches were brightly – and often magnificently – decorated, though presumably not all these decorations were as didactic as the heraldic ceiling of St. Machar's Cathedral in Aberdeen, which demonstrates the place of Scotland, and of Aberdeen itself, in Christendom as a whole. What the Scottish layman heard in a large church at the start of the sixteenth century might also have been magnificent, though puzzling. Elphinstone and his contemporaries clearly regarded the improvement of church music as an integral part of any programme of reform in worship, and set out to achieve a high standard. Surviving evidence shows that Scottish liturgical music of this period was, like the liturgy itself, an ornate and complex compound, made up of newer native and Continental compositions and of the older plainsong presumably inherited from Salisbury.[25] One wonders what the laity thought of it. A High Mass for one of the major feasts would probably have taken some two hours to sing, and it seems that for some people then – as now – a taste for polyphony was something which had to be acquired. Moreover, such elaborate music may have been regarded by some laymen as a distraction from their own vernacular devotions, repeated privately while the liturgy went on around them, which were presumably common in Scotland as they were elsewhere.[26] One thing which the pious layman may particularly have wished to 'hear' in church was a sermon. It appears that he usually did.

It was not until the thirteenth century that the Western Church as a whole came to recognize the necessity of regular preaching as a means to confirm and maintain orthodox belief. Until then, only the bishops had been required to preach on Sundays, but this arrangement was obviously inadequate to satisfy the general enthusiasm for preaching evinced by the laity at the start of that century. This enthusiasm was presumably shared in Scotland, though there is virtually no evidence on the subject of preaching until the start of the sixteenth century. What little there is does, however, suggest that the bishops of Scotland had gone some way towards implementing the canons of the Fourth Lateran Council of 1215, which recognized that bishops were unable for a variety of reasons to preach to all the people in their care, and urged them to promote the increase of preaching in their dioceses by licensing men suitable for the task. Apparently some bishops and secular clergy continued to preach, for the surviving inventories of Scottish cathedral libraries show that these churches, at least, possessed materials which could be used in the construction of sermons. Aberdeen, for example, had two copies of the *Manipulus Florum*, a collection of quotations from doctors of the Church and other authorities which was compiled for this purpose at the start of the fourteenth century.[27] Also, Hector Boece in his *Lives of the Bishops of Aberdeen* (1522) names several of them as active preachers. All this probably means, though, is that Boece considered a concern for preaching to be one of the characteristics of a 'good' bishop, for he does not refer to any personal preaching by his hero Elphinstone; he does state, however, that Bishop William took pains to gather round him men who were trained in theology and skilled in preaching.[28] Probably other bishops did the same; it is hard to believe that men such as Robert Blackadder of Glasgow (1483–1508) or George Brown of Dunkeld (1483–1515) would have neglected a part of the Church's function in society which had long been considered of vital importance.

Even in the later years of the sixteenth century, when the medieval Church was supposedly in decline, there seems to have been no lack of preaching. Sir David Lindsay in the person of his Squire Meldrum was apparently well accustomed to hearing a sermon after the offertory of the Mass; though he states in his most celebrated work, *Ane Satyre of the Thrie Estaitis* (1554) that such preaching was rarely, if ever, undertaken by the parish clergy or bishops. As Spirituality the bishop put it:

'I have ane freir to preiche into my place'.[29]

The Dominicans or preaching friars received official sanction in 1216, and by the middle of that century at least one member of the order was preaching in Scotland, whence he had come by way of France and England.[30] The other main order of friars, the Franciscans or Friars Minor, also quickly became preachers. The friars virtually monopolized theological studies and preaching until the Reformation. Since the feasts of St. Francis and St. Dominic appeared in Scottish liturgical books before they were regularly incorporated in those of the Sarum use, it is possible that these orders were even more influential in Scotland than in England, but very little can be said about the style, content or impact of their preaching in Scotland, and that mainly by deduction from English and other evidence.

Preaching, like the liturgy, could be used as a vehicle for national propaganda. The 'faus prechours' of 1307 who encouraged the people of Scotland to support Robert Bruce's rebellion by means of 'lor faus prechement' may well have been friars.[31] In less exceptional times the preaching of the friars was essentially moralistic. It was based to a large extent on '*exempla*' – short, moralizing stories drawn from saints' lives, personal experience and other sources which were used to illustrate particular themes, such as the power of prayer and confession.[32] Another standard characteristic of their preaching was apparently its appeal to the emotions; by dwelling at length on the Passion they aimed to encourage the virtuous and soften the hard-hearted. It seems, however, that the element of actual religious instruction in their sermons was small.[33]

In Scottish, as well as English contemporary literature, the friars are associated with 'feigning', 'flattery', and 'fleiching'. Thus, there must have been some cases in which the preacher's aim was to persuade his audience to make donations to his order. Much of the Dominican preaching in the sixteenth century was evidently very different. John Adamson, provincial of the Dominicans (and one of Elphinstone's associates) had revived the art of preaching in his province, and there are other indications that the quality of preaching was improving. Yet the preaching of all the orders of friars in Scotland, whether good or bad, may frequently have had one common feature. The fact that the friars were dependent on a bishop's licence to preach did not – at any rate in England – prevent them from attacking the corruption of the secular clergy. It may never be possible to assess how far the friars accustomed the Scottish laity to open criticism of the Church hierarchy. Lindsay, for one, thought that there was not enough of this type of preaching, but to judge by the action taken against several friars during the sixteenth century, there was certainly some.[34]

Setting aside the real or supposed defects of the clergy, there was ample matter for criticism in the worship of the Scottish Church during the years before the Reformation, without seeking further. Scottish churchmen were evidently well aware of this. To begin with, unorthodox opinions were being introduced to a people who were largely ignorant of the rudiments of their faith; a fact recognized by the issue of a catechism in 1552 under the auspices of Archbishop Hamilton of St. Andrews. Possibly, more than forty years earlier, Elphinstone had planned to meet such a requirement by the printing of manuals, which – in England, certainly – usually included tracts concerning the religious instruction of the laity.[35] If so, his plans never came to fruition.

The revised 'Scottish use' did not apparently become popular, far less general, and the liturgical printing project seems to have died with the closure of Chapman and Millar's press shortly after the publication of the Aberdeen Breviary. There are occasional references to the 'use of Aberdeen' later in the sixteenth century, but it must by then have been confined to that diocese. Why the project failed (and why Chapman turned instead to brewing) is by no means clear. The catastrophe of Flodden in 1513 may provide part of the explanation. Another part may be found in Chapman's approach to the Privy Council in 1510, when he complained that his patent had been infringed by the continued importation of Sarum books. This, with other evidence, suggests that the Sarum use, burdened by its own and by the additional Scottish complexities, remained in general use in Scotland until the Reformation.

Even if Elphinstone's 'Scottish use' had been adopted by all the secular clergy in Scotland, the position would have been little better, for though his Breviary can be called revisionary, it can hardly be said to have provided the reforms in worship which were increasingly demanded both by the orthodox and by those less so. Indeed, it is a magnificent illustration of the Scottish clergy's preference for 'superfluities and inessentials' as opposed to the divine office itself.[36] The office had originally been intended to ensure that clerics would read all the psalms and scriptures during the course of any one year; but in the use of Salisbury, and even more so in Elphinstone's, virtually every day had its saint, and each saint his special office. Thus, in 1510, the first year in which the Aberdeen Breviary might have been circulated, its users would not have read the whole book of Ezekiel, or even a substantial part of it, but only as far as chapter 3, verse 10 – provided, of course, that they did not 'skip' passages. Other portions of Scripture were similarly truncated. Perhaps Lindsay makes the point in the *Thrie Estaitis* where the Bishop Spirituality, on being asked to read from the Bible, replies

'I never red that, thairfoir reid it your sel'.[37]

Moreover, the 'superfluities' of Elphinstone's use were not always of an edifying nature, as witnessed by its legend of St. Baldred of the Bass, who had three identical bodies – 'a thing not frequently heard of', as the Breviary rather coyly put it.[38]

In concentrating on an elaborate form of worship coupled with ornate music, Elphinstone and his fellow-clerics of the early sixteenth century came under the condemnation which John Wyclif had pronounced against their English counterparts at a far earlier date, when he claimed that more thought and concern was devoted to 'song and Salisbury use' than to studying and teaching the scriptures. The traditional 'Scottish use' may have been rejected for this very reason by clerics who desired substantial reforms in worship. It appears that such men chose to exercise an option they had always had, by turning from the Scottish or Scottish–Sarum use to the Roman rite, or rather to a revised version of that rite devised by the Spanish cardinal Francis Quignonez, which was published in 1536.

Despite its defects, the 'Scottish use' of the Aberdeen Breviary was a considerable innovation for its time. By 1500 many churchmen were well aware that the worship of the Western Church was desperately in need of reform; what was not clear was the means by which this could best be accomplished. Some would-be reformers evidently thought that the first and most essential step was to produce uniformity in worship within individual provinces of the Church. The first prelate to achieve this, and at a comparatively early date, was Erik Walkendorf, Archbishop of Trondheim (1510–22), who in 1519 issued a standard printed breviary, followed by a missal, 'for the use of the whole of the kingdom of Norway'. However, Walkendorf was not the first bishop to devise such a national use, and this, if anything, is Scotland's small, unsuccessful but unique contribution to the history of worship in the Middle Ages.

NOTES

1. *Hary's Wallace: Vita Nobilissimi Defensoris Scotie Wilelmi Wallace militis,* ed. M. P. McDiarmid (Edinburgh, 1969) II, pp. 71–72.
2. *Registrum Episcopatum Aberdonensis,* ed. C. Innes (Spalding and Maitland Clubs, 1845) II, p. 189.
3. *Ibid.,* p. 133.
4. F. C. Eeles, 'The Relation between the Constitutions and Liturgical Uses of the Cathedrals of Aberdeen and Salisbury', *Transactions of the Scottish Ecclesiological Society* 12 (1936–39), 99–106.
5. *The Acts of the Parliaments of Scotland,* ed. T. Thompson and C. Innes (Edinburgh, 1814–75) II, p. 238.

6. F. C. Eeles, *King's College Chapel, Aberdeen* (Edinburgh, 1956), p. 30; D. McRoberts, 'The Medieval Scottish Liturgy Illustrated by Surviving Documents', *Transactions of the Scottish Ecclesiological Society* 15 (1957), 29.

7. *Analecta Liturgica (Kalendaria)*, ed. W. H. J. Weale (Bruges, 1889), pp. 240, 249, 266; *Liber Ecclesie Beati Terrenani de Arbuthnott*, ed. A. P. Forbes (Burntisland, 1864), p. cv.

8. A. J. Dunlop, *The Life and Time of James Kennedy, Bishop of St. Andrews* (Edinburgh, 1950), pp. 15, 135, 353.

9. *Extracts from the Records of the Burgh of Edinburgh 1403–1528* (Edinburgh, 1869), p. 32.

10. *Liber Ecclesie Beati Terrenani de Arbuthnott*, ed. A. P. Forbes (Burntisland, 1864), p. 392.

11. M. R. James, *A Descriptive Catalogue of Fifty Manuscripts from the Collection of Henry of Yates Thompson* (Cambridge, 1898), pp. 111–112.

12. *Breviarium Bothanum sive Portiforium Secundum Usum Ecclesiae Cujusdam in Scotia* (London, 1900), pp. 487–489, 530, 668–669.

13. F. C. Eeles, 'Notes on a Missal Formerly Used in St. Nicholas, Aberdeen', *Proceedings of the Society of Antiquaries of Scotland* 33 (1899), 444–447.

14. D. McRoberts, 'A Legendary Fragment in the Scottish Record Office', *Innes Review* 19 (1968), 82–85. The only known Scottish example of a 'quire' not associated with a book of worship, but presumably copied in a handy place for the purpose of the writer's personal devotions, is an office (of Continental origin) for the 'new feast' of the Compassion of the Blessed Virgin; noted in *Selkirk Protocol Books, 1511–1547*. eds. T. Maley and W. Elliot (Stair Society and Walter Mason Trust, 1993), p. 41. It is, to date, unique in Britain and, of the four known offices which might have been observed for this feast in British churches, it is the third to appear in a Scottish source.

15. *Lives of St. Ninian and St. Kentigern*, ed. A. P. Forbes (Edinburgh, 1874), p. xciv.

16. *Cartularium Ecclesiae Sancti Nicholai Aberdonensis*, ed. J. Cooper (Aberdeen, 1892) II, p. 245. *Crede Michi* (literally 'trust me') is printed in *The Tracts of Clement Maydeston*, ed. C. Wordsworth (Henry Bradshaw Society, 1894).

17. *Registrum Secreti Sigilli Regum Scotorum*, ed. M. Livingstone and others (Edinburgh, 1908–   ) I, no. 1546.

18. *Breviari Aberdonensis ad . . . ecclesie Scotorum potissimum usum et consuetudinem* (Edinburgh, 1510) *pars estivalis, proprium sanctorum* fo. liii.

19. *Ibid., commune sanctorum* fos. cxxxi–cxxxii.

20. *Ibid.,* title-page.

21. *Ibid., pars estivalis, proprium sanctorum* fo. xxv.
22. *Legends of the Saints in the Scottish Dialect of the Fourteenth Century,* ed. W. M. Metcalfe (Edinburgh, 1891) III, pp. 35–37.
23. The description of Scotland is from the celebrated 'Declaration of Arbroath' of 1320.
24. D. McRoberts, 'The Rosary in Scotland', *Innes Review* 23 (1972), 81–86.
25. A. Oldham, 'Scottish Polyphonic Music', *Innes Review* 13 (1962), 54–61.
26. For example, *The Lay Folks Mass Book,* ed. T. F. Simmons (Early English Text Society, 1968).
27. *Registrum Episcopatum Aberdonensis,* ed. C. Innes (Spalding and Maitland Clubs, 1845) II, p. 128. Though there is much less, even than such scanty evidence, concerning secular clergy outwith cathedrals, it seems that they, too, might possess such materials. The Selkirk notary Ninian Brydin had (or at least planned to acquire) books which could be used for the preparation of sermons as well as guides to hearing confessions and to the cure of souls, and this does not seem to sit well with the sort of 'ignorant, indifferent, one-psalter-between-five' image of the pre-Reformation local Scottish clergy which is sometimes projected. (Walter Mason Trust papers, Protocol Book of Ninian Brydin 1536–1564, no. 432).
28. Hector Boece, *Murthlacensium et Aberdonensium Episcoporum Vitae,* ed. James Moir (Aberdeen, 1894), pp. 18, 21, 24, 92–93.
29. 'The Testament of Squyer Meldrum' in *The Works of Sir David Lindsay of the Mount 1490–1555,* ed. D. Hamer (Edinburgh, 1931) I, p. 193; 'Ane Satyre of the Thrie Estaitis', *ibid.* II, p. 313.
30. J. Th. Welter, *L'Exemplum dans la Littérature Religieuse et Didactique du Moyen Age* (Paris, 1927), p. 245.
31. *Calendar of Documents Relating to Scotland,* ed. J. Bain (Edinburgh, 1884) II, p. 536.
32. For instance, the story of how St. Mungo of Glasgow recovered a ring from the belly of a fish was used in some collections of *exempla* to demonstrate the power of confession as in *Liber Exemplorum ad usum praedicantium . . . secundum codicem Dunelmonsem,* ed. A. G. Little (Aberdeen, 1908), pp. 53–54.
33. This statement should be qualified to avoid an unbalanced picture of medieval preaching as a whole. As a contrast to much of the preaching of the friars, see Fr. Gilbert Hill 'The Sermons of John Watson, Canon of Aberdeen', *Innes Review* 15 (1964), 3–34.
34. Anthony Ross, 'Some Notes on the Religious Orders in Pre-Reformation Scotland' in *Essays on the Scottish Reformation 1513–1625,* ed. D. McRoberts, pp. 202–204.
35. W. A. Pantin, *The English Church in the Fourteenth Century* (Cambridge, 1955), pp. 189–219.

36. This fault was not, of course, confined to the secular clergy or to Scotland; the quotation is from a complaint made to the great reforming council at Basle (1431–49) – Ven. Martin of Senging 'Tuitiones pro observantia Regulae S.P. Benedicti in Concilio Basiliensi' in *Bibliotheca Ascetica antiquo nova,* ed. R. P. Bernard Pez (reproduced, Farnborough, 1967) VIII, p. 545.

37. Lindsay, 'Thrie Estaitis', ed. Hamer, *op. cit.,* II, p. 275.

38. *Breviarium Aberdonense pars hyemalis, proprium sanctorum* fo. lxiiii.

BIBLIOGRAPHY

Breviarium Aberdonense, ed. W. Blew (Bannatyne, Maitland and Spalding Clubs, 1854).

Breviarium Bothanum sive Portiforium secundum usum Ecclesie cujusdam in Scotia (London, 1900). (The Fowlis Easter Breviary.)

Dix, Dom Gregory, *The Shape of the Liturgy* (London, 1978).

Liber Ecclesie Beati Terrenani de Arbuthnott, ed. A. P. Forbes (Burntisland, 1864). (The Arbuthnott Missal.)

McRoberts, David, *Catalogue of Scottish Medieval Liturgical Books and Fragments* (Glasgow, 1953).

McRoberts, David, 'The Medieval Scottish Liturgy Illustrated by Surviving Documents', *Transactions of the Scottish Ecclesiological Society* 15 (1957) 24–40.

McRoberts, David, 'Scottish Sacrament Houses', *Transactions of the Scottish Ecclesiological Society* 15 (1965) 33–56.

McRoberts, David, 'The Scottish Church and Nationalism in the Fifteenth Century', *Innes Review* 19 (1968) 3–14.

Missale ad usum . . . ecclesie Sarum, ed. F. H. Dickinson (Burntisland, 1861–83).

Chapter Three

REFORMATION TO COVENANT

Gordon Donaldson

The revolution in worship which came in the sixteenth century was rooted in theology. Negatively, the Protestant reformers condemned the sacrificial attributes of the Mass as idolatrous, blasphemous and derogatory to the sufficient sacrifice of Calvary, and in particular denounced Masses for the dead. Positively, they emphasized salvation by faith in the redeeming work of Christ through His Passion. The rejection of the Mass and also of the five 'commonly called sacraments' (less politely styled the Pope's 'five bastard sacraments') carried an element of anti-sacerdotalism, and the reformers were anti-clerical in a wider sense. They pressed so strongly for the participation of the laity in the services that it is possible to interpret some of their practices as indicating a concept of a kind of corporate priesthood of believers vested in the congregation or the Christian community, of which the pastor or minister was only the leader and from which, under God, he derived his authority. Worship had therefore to be in the vernacular and the laity had to be fitted for their responsibilities by instruction, education and preaching. The appeal was to be to the intellect through the spoken or written word, rather than to the senses, and this meant that the ceremonies, the symbolism, of the medieval Church, which had been appropriate for an illiterate populace, would be outmoded. All in all, whether for theological or other reasons, a lot of the traditional services became irrelevant almost at a stroke.

Experiments in worship, to some extent reflecting the reformers' ideas, had made headway long before the Roman rite was formally prohibited in 1560. Whatever may have happened even earlier, we do know that in 1543 'preaching of the Word of God' was authorized by a government which was in favour of alignment with Henry VIII's anti-papal England. Although the authorities thereafter set their faces against any concessions to the reformers' specific demands for changes in the services, in 1549 and 1551 'the preaching of the Word of God' was officially acknowledged as an element in public worship, and the phrase suggests an emphasis closer to that of the Reformation than to that of the medieval Church.[1] In 1552 a *Catechism* was issued, giving the people the Commandments, Apostles' Creed and Lord's Prayer in their own tongue and instructing them how to prepare for Communion, and in 1559 came a *Godly Exhortation*, to be addressed to communicants; these were designed to encourage the intelligent and devout participation of the laity, and the emphasis on Communion, rather than on sacrifice, was significant.

Concurrently with such official moves, reformed worship had been emerging at unofficial levels. The years from 1544 to 1547 saw George Wishart preaching widely and administering Communion according to a reformed model, and then the murderers of Cardinal Beaton and their supporters holding Protestant services, including Communion, in St. Andrews Castle. It is hard to believe that there was ever a point thereafter when some kind of reformed worship was not being conducted somewhere in Scotland. By the mid-1550s congregations were organized, sometimes surreptitiously, in a number of places, and these 'privy kirks' had services comprising confession, lections, exposition and prayers of thanksgiving and intercession. Some such groups of worshippers, with no ordained minister, discussed the scriptures among themselves rather than listened to sermons, and it appears that they sometimes celebrated Communion under one of their number who had no authorization or qualification beyond their acceptance of his leadership.[2]

There is no evidence that the idea of conducting worship without written or printed guidance had yet taken root, and in any event the demand was for 'common prayers' in which the people would take part, with books in their hands, instead of being more or less passive while a service was conducted by a priest who alone had a book. The presumption must be that Scottish Protestants obtained suitable material from other countries where the Reformation had been accepted earlier. There were plenty of men among them who could, and did, translate from Latin, German, Danish and French, but south of the Anglo-Scottish border there was an ample reservoir of printed works in a tongue which Scots understood well enough. Long before an English Prayer Book appeared, Primers were readily available.[3] The earliest Primers had been in Latin and contained a Calendar, the Hours of the Virgin, some Psalms and the Litany, but already in the fifteenth century Primers in English had appeared, to serve those who did not know Latin. By the 1530s there were Primers with prayers for morning, noon and night (in place of the traditional Hours), the Commandments, the Creed, the Lord's Prayer, Epistles, Gospels, other scriptural passages and the psalms, and some of them now included material which was condemned by the authorities as heretical. Well over a hundred editions of Primers are known to have been printed before 1558, and between 1534 and 1547 there were twenty-eight wholly in English. In Henry VIII's later years there were Primers authorized by the government, and they paved the way for greater novelties under Edward VI (1547–53). The first of these was the 'Order of the Communion' (1548). This was designed to authorize administration in both kinds and to ensure due preparation on the part of communicants, and it consisted of elements which were to be repeated, with little change, in every Anglican Prayer Book down to the twentieth century – the long Exhortations, the short Invitation 'Ye that do truly . . .', Confession, Absolution, Comfortable Words, Prayer of Humble Access and Words of Administration. These, taken together, formed the portion of the service which directly concerned the Communion and they were intended to be inserted in the Latin Mass, which otherwise remained unaltered. Little over a year after the Order of the Communion came the First Prayer Book of Edward VI (1549), in which the whole service was in English, and in 1552 there followed the much more protestant Second Book. An official Book of Homilies, useful for clergy who were unable to compose sermons, first appeared in 1547. Metrical versions of some psalms and of other items for singing were becoming available even before the Psalter or Sternhold appeared in 1547 and 1549.

As early as 1543 Scotland had been recognized as a likely market for English Primers and Psalters, as well as Bibles,[4] and it would be unreasonable to suppose that the productions of the Edwardine revolution in worship did not also find their way there, as well as being used by Scots who had gone to England. In Scotland the Prayer Book would be especially welcome in the 'privy kirks', where a literate layman could turn to it for ready-made confessions and intercessions. Yet it seems that it was not only half-secret gatherings which used these English compilations, for a vicar who claimed in 1560 that for years he had read 'the common prayers and homilies' to his parishioners is unlikely to have been unique, and the ecclesiastical authorities were finding it necessary to try to suppress novel forms of worship.[5] It is not surprising that once the reformers were able to formulate a programme the adoption of the Prayer Book was in its forefront. At the end of 1557 or the beginning of 1558 they asked that parish priests or suitable laymen should be authorized to read 'common prayers . . . with the lessons of the Old and New Testaments, conform to the order of the Book of Common Prayers'. In 1558 there was talk of a compromise whereby the 'common prayers' and litany, in the vernacular, were to be read alongside the Latin Mass. When the reformers became successful revolutionaries in 1559, it was the 'book set forth by godly King Edward' that was used in at least some churches, and it was reported that the services were 'the very same or differed very little' from those of England.[6] It is unlikely that copies of any service-book other than the English were as yet available in any numbers, and those Scots who did not approve of everything Edward's book contained had complete freedom to pick and choose from its pages. The presumption must be that with the abandonment of the Latin rite, which often preceded its official proscription in August 1560, the services of Edward's second book would be those in most general use in Scotland.

The Book of England already, however, had a rival, in the Book of Geneva, which within a few years was generally to prevail. This rival, the Book of Common Order or 'Knox's Liturgy', was no less English than the Prayer Book was, for it had been the service-book of the congregation of English exiles to whom Knox had ministered in Geneva and who deliberately decided to reject the Prayer Book in favour of a more radical order. The Book of Geneva represented views widely held in England as well as Scotland, for in Elizabeth Tudor's reign the tone of the Church of England and even the episcopal bench was so unfavourable to much that the Prayer Book contained that, if the English had had the freedom the Scots had, the Prayer Book would have been swept aside or drastically purged of conservative elements. It must be remembered that the Prayer Book was then a novelty, to many a disagreeable novelty, and its phraseology had not yet been hallowed by use to become part of the literary heritage of all English-speakers and win the affection which has caused such hostility to recent attempts to displace it.

Although copies of the Book of Geneva cannot have been plentiful, its use was not unknown in Scotland even in 1560. Editions were printed at Geneva in 1558 and 1561, but only with the first Scottish edition, in 1562, can the book have become generally available. At any rate, by 1562 it was practicable for the General Assembly to prescribe its use for the sacraments, and two years later it was prescribed for 'common prayers' as well. A stream of over sixty editions (including one in 1567 which was the first book printed in Gaelic) continued to come out until 1644. For nearly eighty years it was the official Scottish service-book. It was usually bound with metrical versions of the psalms and other items, but when, already in 1561, the Scots called it the 'Psalm Book' they were imitating their cousins in Scandinavia, where a 'Salmebog' contains the liturgy.

The Book of Common Order was not a fixed liturgy like a medieval service-book or the Book of Common Prayer, but it was not a mere directory either. While the instruction sometimes runs, 'The minister prayeth in these words or like in effect', elsewhere no possibility of deviation seems to have been envisaged. There is, besides, ample testimony that 'the *reading* of public prayers' was universally acknowledged as a constituent of worship.[7] The language and thought of the Book owe a certain amount to the Prayer Book, clear echoes of which can be found here and there. The introductory exhortation to the Communion contains substantial passages taken verbatim from the Prayer Book; a good deal of the marriage service is verbally identical in the two books; a pre-Communion prayer in the Book of Common Order contains noticeable borrowing from the Prayer of Humble Access.[8] Elements of traditional worship were not jettisoned: provision was made for the use of the Lord's Prayer (in the Prayer Book version), the Apostles' Creed (at the Sunday morning service and at Baptism) and the

Doxology (at the end of psalms); there were metrical versions of the *Veni Creator*, the Commandments, the Lord's Prayer, the Creed and the canticles familiar in Evensong (the *Nunc Dimittis* and 'the song of Blessed Marie, called *Magnificat*'), each with its tune; lessons were to be read in a regular order. Kneeling was the understood posture for prayer. Although there were no responses there was provision for congregational participation, not least through the psalms. Some metrical psalms had long circulated in Scotland as in England, and a complete Psalter, based largely on English compilations, was issued in 1564. It seems that, despite a prejudice against organs, there was not a total ban on instrumental music and that musical standards were sometimes high, under the guidance of men trained before the Reformation.[9]

The structure of the Sunday morning service was shaped by attitudes to the Lord's Supper. The reformers would have contended that their aim was to restore Holy Communion as the service for every Lord's Day (which Calvin regarded as the ideal), and the Book of Common Order recommended a monthly celebration as a minimum. The people, however, had so long been accustomed to communicate only once a year, at Easter, that they were unwilling to come oftener, and the ministers on their side would not celebrate with few or no communicants. For years after 1560, too, the shortage of ministers would have made weekly or even monthly celebrations impossible in most parishes. Thus infrequent Communion lingered on as a heritage from the medieval Church and made the fulfilment of the reformers' plans impossible. The Book of Discipline (1561) said that a quarterly celebration would suffice in towns and one half-yearly in the country, but nothing like this was attained in practice. Yet, despite such infrequency, the reformers were able to make it clear where their ideals lay. For one thing, actual celebrations, though infrequent, were not to be on traditional holy days but on Sundays selected to avoid coinciding with Christmas or Easter; the implication was that Communion was not just for a special occasion, but for an ordinary Sunday. Secondly, when there was no Communion, worship on Sunday morning included the first part of the Communion service, the equivalent of the Ante-Communion and like it providing for a long intercession after the sermon. This intercession concluded with the Lord's Prayer, after which the Creed, a psalm and the Blessing followed. However, this component of the Sunday morning worship, conducted by the minister, was preceded by the 'reader's service', consisting of confession, psalms and lessons, conducted by the reader from his desk before the minister entered the church to take his part of the service from the pulpit. The reader's service had a content like that of the Prayer Book's Matins, so that in England and Scotland alike the pattern was of Ante-Communion preceded by Matins, for English Protestants had then little more appetite for frequent Communion than had the Scots. In principle the reformers upheld the equal importance of Word and Sacraments, and were emphatic that the Sacraments should always be accompanied by preaching. Therefore, when there was a Communion measures were sometimes taken to ensure that no one should either hear the sermon and not remain to communicate or be admitted to Communion without having heard the sermon; but non-communicants were not always rigidly excluded from the service.[10] In practice, however, despite the theoretical equality of Word and Sacraments, the infrequency of celebrations of the Eucharist meant that preaching was soon apt to be thought of as the core of public worship.

Partly because of the insistence that preaching of the Word was indispensable and partly out of the practical necessity to instruct the people, arrangements had to be made in a situation where for a time only about a quarter of the parishes had ministers. For a few years there were 'exhorters', who were authorized to preach but not to administer the sacraments, as well as readers, who were not qualified even to preach. The latter, besides reading the service and the lections, were authorized to read homilies from 'the buik callit the Omeleyis for reidaris in kirks', evidently the well-known English compilation which had been published in Edward's reign and (in enlarged form) was authorized afresh in 1562. For some years after 1572, it should be added, readers were authorized to administer Baptism and officiate at marriages, probably in an attempt to upgrade their status to something like that of an Anglican deacon.[11]

When Holy Communion was celebrated, the long intercession, concluding with the Lord's Prayer and followed by the Creed, led on to the recital of the words of institution and an exhortation or invitation, after which the minister debarred unrepentant sinners from the Table. Then the minister came down from the pulpit and, sitting with the people round the Table, took the elements. He next knelt to read a 'prayer of thanksgiving' which was in effect the consecration prayer. The Order for the Lord's Supper in the Book of Common Order gives a version of this prayer, preceded by the direction to use 'these words following or like in effect', but it also contains another version, dating from 'the time of persecution by the Frenchmen' (that is, before July 1560). This version runs: 'We . . . beseech Thee . . . that fruitfully we may possess His body and His blood, yea, Jesus Christ Himself, very God and very man, Who is that Heavenly bread which giveth life unto the world. Give us grace so to eat His flesh and drink His blood, that hereafter . . . He may live in us to conduct and guide us to that most blessed life which abideth for ever'. The minister next broke the bread, and the elements were delivered to the people, who passed them round among them-selves, while 'some place of the Scriptures is read which doth lively set forth the death of Christ . . . that our hearts and minds also may be fully fixed in the contemplation of the Lord's death, which is by this holy sacrament represented'. Probably psalms were sung while one group of communicants replaced another at the Table. A post-Communion prayer of thanksgiving was followed by Psalm ciii 'or some other thanksgiving' and a Blessing. Somewhat bald or sparing of words as this order was, it was far more explicit about the 'four-action shape' of the liturgy than was the contemporary Prayer Book, which gave no directions either for 'taking' the elements or for the fraction.

The Communion was clearly a corporate act in which the communicants played an essential part and of course received in both kinds. The gathering of minister and people round a table set lengthwise in the church left no room for the concept of a priest at an altar, and such an arrangement operated at that time in England as well, although there the communicants knelt (or at any rate were supposed to kneel) whereas in Scotland they sat. It seems that in some Scottish churches a Communion Table might have a permanent place in the chancel or in a 'Communion Aisle',[12] but it was also usual to erect tables in the body of the church when they were required. It is clear that from the earliest days the minister was assisted at the distribution by elders, deacons or other members of the congregation, though only as a matter of custom; this again broke down the medieval severance between priest and people.[13]

The stress which the reformers laid on congregational participation is noticeable in other services as well as Communion. As Baptism was 'not ordained of God to be used in private corners, as charms or sorceries, but left to the congregation and necessarily annexed to God's Word', the child was to be brought to the church and baptized after a sermon on a day appointed for common prayer and preaching (not necessarily a Sunday, for weekday services were common). Thus, the emphasis could pass to acceptance of the child by the congregation in its capacity as corporate priest. The Book of Common Order provided for the presence at Baptism of only 'the father and godfather', but evidently 'man embraces woman', and godmothers appear in registers of Baptisms. From the same motive of making the services congregational acts, it was intended that marriages should be celebrated only on Sundays, but when it was seen that the accompanying jollifications were unseemly on the Lord's Day, marriages were allowed on weekdays when a congregation assembled for 'common prayers' and sermon. Private Baptisms and private marriages were apt to be frowned on, like private Communions, but the demand for all three persisted and was sometimes met.[14]

The revolutionary change to a stress on the centrality of the congregation was demonstrated yet again in the arrangements for discipline. The sacrament of penance had been mainly a matter between the individual penitent and his confessor, though public penance and public punishment were not unknown, but now the main emphasis was on public penance in face of the congregation, and excommunication and absolution alike became proceedings in which there was congregational involvement. Excommunication was pronounced by 'the minister in public audience of the people' or 'at the commandment of this Thy present congregation', and when the penitent received absolution 'the elders and deacons with ministers (if any be), in the name of the whole church' were to 'take the reconciled brother by the hand and embrace him, in sign of full reconciliation'. This procedure was related to the wider subject of preparation for Communion. Apart from measures to exclude sinners from the Table, there was much emphasis on reconciliation among members of the congregation who had been at variance. Another aspect of preparation was instruction, provided by Catechisms used not only for children and at special meetings, but as part of public worship, when they were taught by ministers or readers. The duty of examining intending communicants was laid on the elders, who were at first the annually elected representatives of the congregation, and possibly from the very earliest days tickets or tokens were given to those whose fitness to approach the Table was approved. It was a minimum requirement for admission to Communion that one should know the Lord's Prayer, the Creed and the Commandments, and it seems that familiarity with them was ensured, as it was in England, by having them painted on panels displayed in churches.[15]

The Scottish reformers set their faces resolutely against the observance of the Christian Year, on the ground that the Lord's Day alone could claim scriptural authority. In this they met strong resistance from the public, who stood to be deprived not only of their traditional religious observance and secular festivities on holy days, but literally of their holidays. The logic of the 'sabbatarian' position was that men must work six days a week, with no remission, and for generations argument went back and forth about the propriety of 'vacances appointit in time of superstition', which in time of puritanical ascendancy were abolished.[16] But the Book of Common Order itself was not in conformity with the proposed austerity, and instead gave some support to popular demand, for it contained a Calendar. True, there were secular reasons for this: the fairs and markets of many burghs were on saints' days; the legal terms – Candlemas, Whitsunday, Lammas and Martinmas – were all based on the Christian Year and the most important of them, Whitsunday, was a moveable feast; and the terms of the Court of Session continued to be determined by Fastern's Eve or Shrove Tuesday, Palm Sunday, Low Sunday and Whitsunday. The most rigid Presbyterian lawyer of the seventeenth century must have had recourse to the Book of Common Order for its Calendar and its table giving the dates of moveable feasts for a period of years. Whitsunday was not fixed on 15 May by statute until 1693. Not only civil courts, but courts of the Reformed Church, made frequent use of days in the Church's Calendar for dating purposes.[17] But the Calendar contained, besides the dates required by lawyers, a variety of others, including, almost incredibly, 'The Assumption of Mary'.

There is considerable evidence that, despite occasional fulminations from the General Assembly, some ministers did celebrate Holy Communion at or about Easter and had Christmas services as well. The fact that there were regular preaching days throughout the week, of course, meant that services would from time to time be held on Christmas Day, Good Friday and Ascension Day. The continued observance of Lent and of Wednesday, Friday and Saturday as days of abstinence from flesh was a secular rather than a religious matter, enforced by legislation in the interests of the fisheries and the conservation of stocks of cattle, and for more than a century after 1560 licences to eat flesh in Lent had to be obtained from the civil authority. But the traditional religious attitude to seasons of austerity lay behind the general avoidance of marriage in Lent.[18] Why the Reformed Church was against Communion in Lent as well as at Easter is not very clear, but its reiterated condemnation of celebrations at those times had the paradoxical effect of reminding people of the Christian Calendar. There was no doubt about a continued belief in the spiritual value of abstinence in diet, which lay behind the practice of going fasting to Communion (often celebrated at a very early hour and always intended to be over by noon) and also behind the occasional appointment of a 'General Fast'. Detailed instructions for such fasts were issued in 1566 and were subsequently incorporated in the Book of Common Order. When a fast was proclaimed, on an occasion such as an outbreak of plague, strict observance was envisaged and sometimes enforced. What may seem odd to some is that Holy Communion was from time to time combined with the fast, but from some point it became a matter of routine to have a general fast before a celebration of Communion.

Possibly the Book of Common Order never gave universal satisfaction, for the reformers, who had come under various influences – Lutheran, Zwinglian and Calvinist as well as English – cannot have been in agreement. Divergence among them is indicated by the oft-quoted statement of the English ambassador in 1560 that, while some Scots were in favour of conformity with England, others were 'so severe in that they profess and so loath to remit anything of that that they have received' that they were not likely to agree.[19] Those who would have accepted the Prayer Book can hardly have been satisfied with its rival, and the Book of Geneva did not in practice wholly displace the Book of England. There is no trace of action to suppress the latter, copies of it were on sale in Edinburgh bookshops and there is evidence of its use. The latitude allowed by the Book of Common Order in the framing of some prayers would have made it perfectly legitimate for a minister to turn now and again to the words of the Prayer Book. When a Prayer for the King was inserted in the Book of Common Order in 1575, it differed in only three words from the prayer in Edward VI's Primer, a shortened version of which had been included in the Litany set forth by Queen Elizabeth. While it may be taken as proved that there were those who adhered to the Prayer Book, on the other wing Scots of puritan tastes were ready to disregard even the Book of Common Order. Very probably divergence between the two extreme opinions hardened with the emergence of controversy about church government. Although no real change had been made in the system of administration by superintendents, bishops and commissioners which originated in 1561, the Regent Morton (1572–78) was believed, probably with some reason, to be pressing for 'conformity with England', which might be taken to affect worship as well as government. The Presbyterian opponents of his policy, on their side, consorted with English puritans and adopted or shared their criticisms of the Prayer Book.[20] It was the Presbyterians who gained the ascendancy in the later 1580s and this meant distrust not only of bishops but of the forms of worship which the English bishops upheld.

Apart from serious argument about the respective merits of the two rival Books, it seems likely that the mere fact that the language and structure of the Book of Common Order were less rigid and formal than those of the Prayer Book may have encouraged a movement away from constraint, and, whatever the rubrics said and however much emphasis there was on 'reading', ministers may have felt stimulated to move towards compiling their own prayers or praying extemporaneously. Besides, the emphasis on preaching may have been a further incentive to disregard formal prayers. At any rate, changes occurred. Some abandoned the recitation of the Creed; the form for the Visitation of the Sick fell into disuse; and the term 'godfather' was replaced by 'witness'. Criticism of the Book, and modifications of it in practice, were not confined to such trends away from tradition, but included also a conviction that the Order for Communion was unduly bare and should include an explicit consecration prayer with an invocation or blessing on the elements and the action.[21]

However, the Book of Common Order was not deposed from its position as the official service-book. There are conflicting contemporary or near-contemporary assessments of the extent to which it was followed, but they reflect partisanship: those who were anxious to justify the liturgical policy followed by James VI in his later years brought themselves to allege that before that policy was initiated Scotland had 'no form of public prayer'; while those who opposed the royal policy, especially if they wrote after the reaction against liturgical worship set in in 1637, were equally eager to prove that the Book of Common Order had been a mere Directory. Calderwood's allegation that 'none are tied to the prayers of that book, but the prayers are set down as samplers' is only one degree less untrue than Samuel Rutherford's 'Our church never allowed read prayers, but men took them up at their own choice'. The latter at least is flatly contradicted by Alexander Henderson, who insisted that ministers had to conform themselves to the order of the Book and did not 'preach and pray what was good in their eyes'. There is certainly reliable evidence that the Book continued to be used. For example, its place as determining the normal forms of worship had been demonstrated in 1575, when the Prayer for the King was introduced; this would have been unnecessary if ministers had been in the habit of ignoring the Book. Besides, there is testimony that common prayers were still being publicly *read* every morning and evening.[22] Despite an attempt by the General Assembly in 1580 to abolish the office of reader, it continued, and the 'reader's service' retained its structure, as shown in an account of worship in the second decade of the seventeenth century, in the shape of a dialogue between a Protestant and a Roman Catholic visitor:[23]

> R.C. What is this the people are going to do?
>
> Prot. They bow themselves before the Lord, to make an humble confession of their sins, which you will hear openly read out by the public reader . . .
>
> R.C. But what go they now to do?
>
> Prot. Everyone is preparing (as you see) their Psalm Book, that all of them may sing unto the Lord . . . There is the psalm which the reader hath proclaimed . . .
>
> R.C. What doth the reader now?
>
> Prot. Yonder book which now he opens is the Bible. You will hear him read some portion of Holy Scripture . . .

If services still had a recognized, stereotyped structure, there were clearly foundations on which liturgical development could be based, and, while the situation was fluid, opinions were diverse enough to make it likely that almost any changes would find a measure of support from one side or another.

Movement for liturgical revision had been hinted at so early as 1584, when a commission to Archbishop Patrick Adamson referred to 'a uniform order in form of common prayer'. As Adamson was said to have used 'the English ceremonies' at a marriage and was accused of 'filthily adulterating the state of public prayer, with the simplicity of rites in ministration of the sacraments', the 'uniform order' of his commission surely meant a closer approximation to the English Prayer Book. Then in 1601, at the General Assembly, some alterations to the Book of Common Order were proposed, designed to excise obsolete prayers and introduce others more relevant, and the submission of additional prayers 'meet for the time' was invited, much as the Prayer for the King had been inserted in 1575.[24] Obviously if the Book had been habitually disregarded, this would have been a waste of time.

Nothing came of the 1584 proposal because the episcopal constitution of the church was soon undermined, and nothing came of the 1601 proposal because attention was for some years focused on the modifications in church government by which King James stage by stage revived the powers of the episcopate. There is, besides, nothing to suggest that before 1603 James wanted liturgical change, for, although he condemned 'vain proud puritans', his views reflected his Protestant upbringing. Thus, he rejected the Apocrypha, described the English Communion as 'an evil mass said in English', criticized the Litany's petition against 'sudden death' and even had doubts about using only prayer 'out of books'.[25] However, his views changed, and once he had obtained the approval of the Assembly (in 1610) and Parliament (in 1612) to his ingenious compromise between presbyters and episcopacy the way was open for liturgical experiment.

The king began his campaign in 1614 by ordering that Communion should be celebrated on 24 April (which was Easter Day) and next year an Easter celebration was ordained for all time coming. James next ordered colleges to observe the greater holy days and to use the Prayer Book in their services for the opening confession, the state prayers and the monthly round of the Psalter. Meantime the king consulted Archbishop Spottiswoode, who considered that some of the existing forms 'must be in some points helped' and that there should be greater uniformity, but insisted that the General Assembly must be involved in any changes. When an Assembly met (for the first time since 1610) at Aberdeen in August 1616 it recommended a new liturgy, the regular observance of Easter and the examination of children by bishops, and a committee of four was appointed to 'revise the Book of Common Prayer contained in the Psalm Book and to set down a common form of ordinary service to be used in all time hereafter'; the committee's work was to be subject to approval by a commission of bishops and ministers in December.

A first draft liturgy was drawn up, presumably in the later months of 1616.[26] It was no more than a revised morning service broadly on the lines of that in the Book of Common Order but with a more distinctly liturgical character and with rubrics which were mandatory and not permissive. Opening with the fourth commandment, the sentence 'Let the words of our mouths . . .' (Ps. xix, 14) and an exhortation to 'come boldly to the throne of grace', it proceeds to a long confession (with echoes of the Prayer Book). After Psalm xcii (prose) had been 'read or sung' and a prayer read for hallowing the Sabbath (concluding with the Lord's Prayer), there came 'a chapter of the gospel and another of the epistles, as they shall be by course' and a prayer for the blessing of the Word to the hearers. Next was to be read Psalm lxxxix, ciii or another, followed by the Creed. The prayer styled 'The Last Prayer', obviously meant to be preceded by the sermon, included intercession for 'the estate of the whole Kirk universal' and after it came a series of prayers 'meet for the time'. Some prayers in the Book of Common Order were retained as alternatives, and that book was apparently still to be used for sacraments and other rites. As the minister whose name is associated with this draft, Peter Hewat, was strongly critical of the further innovations soon proposed, the draft must represent a middle ground and may indicate the lines along which experiment had been proceeding in the parishes.

A second more ambitious draft, which can be assigned to 1617,[27] for a complete Prayer Book, professed to be merely 'The Old Leiturgie or Church Service used in the Church of Scotland explained and inlarged, wherein no change is maid as concerning the substance, only some prayers that were proper for their times, such as these which were used when the church was under the tyranny of strangers, are omitted and others meeter for this time placed in their room'. Outlines are given for services for the mornings and afternoons of four Sundays in a month, with such minor variants as the prescription of different psalms and the recitation of the Creed and the Commandments twice in the month. The 'reader's service' was reduced to a brief exhortation, confession, psalm, prayers, 'some plain and short portion of holy scripture if time serve' and a prayer for the congregation and those who minister to it. The minister's share was correspondingly upgraded: he was to use one of the confessions from the Book of Common Order 'or another as God shall please to move his heart to whom He has given the grace of prayer', a psalm was to be sung, a brief prayer led to the sermon, and the service closed with a psalm and blessing. A blank page after the sermon suggests that the great intercession was intended to be inserted at that point. The Communion Office provided that the deacons or others should set the elements on the Table, it reproduced a modified version of the invitation 'Ye that truly repent of your sins . . .' and its consecration prayer met the demand which had been expressed for something like an epiclesis: 'He . . . is given to us of Thy mercy a food for our souls in this sacrament; Lord bless it that it may be unto us an effectual exhibiting instrument of the Lord Jesus'. The words of institution were to be followed immediately by the distribution, during which the reader was to read 'the history of Christ's Passion' from St. John and Psalm ciii was to be sung while one group succeeded another at the Table. While this draft is as a whole more liturgical than the Book of Common Order, and while it includes a few more echoes of the Prayer Book (in the order for Baptism as well as elsewhere) and explicitly directs a congregational 'Amen' at the end of prayers and psalms, it was in the main in line with existing tradition and again may represent practice in some parishes.

Before a third draft appeared, circumstances had changed. In the face of strong opposition the king obtained from the Perth Assembly of 1618 approval of his 'Five Articles' – observance of the principal days of the Christian Year, permission for private administration of Baptism and Communion, Confirmation by bishops and kneeling at Communion. So far as the Christian Year was concerned, it is safe to say that, as there was no part of the reformers' programme which had met with less success than the attempt to suppress traditional festivals, this article may have been widely welcomed, if only because the king proclaimed that the holy days were also to be holidays. Arrangements for private administration of the sacraments in case of necessity may equally have been welcomed as meeting a real need. There is evidence that the sick had sometimes received Communion at home since the Reformation, and celebrations for small groups were held in churches on special occasions. Communion for invalids in their own homes was authorized by the Assembly in 1617, when it still withheld approval of the other Articles. The Reformed Church had tried to suppress private Baptism (as well as private marriage), but, although the 'preaching days' on which it could be administered would be frequent enough to meet most needs, there was a demand for something more, and the fact that a kirk session could censure a parishioner for allowing a child to die unbaptized shows that the possibility of private Baptism in case of urgency had not been ruled out. The harshness of the rules could be relaxed. The Assembly had conceded in 1602 that Baptism 'need not be delayed to certain particular days' and made a further concession in 1616. In 1638, when the Articles were collectively condemned, Baptism was allowed on any day when a preacher was available.[28] Episcopal Confirmation, the fourth Article, could hardly have been thought of as a revival of the practice of pre-Reformation times, when this rite had rarely been administered, and in any event it was not something that much affected the ordinary layman in his regular worship. The greatest hostility focused on the requirement to kneel at Communion. This had been an issue away back in the 1550s, and the 'Black Rubric' had been inserted – apparently at Knox's insistence – in the second English Prayer Book (1552) to overcome scruples. At the time the Articles aroused a furious storm, but now, after nearly four hundred years, they can be seen in a different perspective. Three of them – private Baptism and Communion and the Christian Year – were hardly novel then and have long been accepted by the Church of Scotland, which also has Confirmation, though by a minister and not a bishop. Kneeling at Communion was in 1618 condemned as popish, but Roman Catholics now habitually receive in a standing posture and indeed imitate Tudor puritans with 'a walking Communion', for the communicants walk up to receive and then walk away. Some twentieth-century historians have seen the justification for the opposition to kneeling in a contemporary fear that it implied belief in 'the real presence'; but this ignores that the Scots Confession of Faith of 1560 unambiguously proclaimed the real presence: 'In the Supper, rightly used, Christ Jesus is so joined with us, that He becomes the very nourishment and food of our souls. . . . The faithful, in the right use of the Lord's Table, so do eat the body and drink the blood of the Lord Jesus, that He remaineth in them and they in Him'. The objection was not to 'the real presence' but to the idolatry associated with the Mass. If the change of posture involved the administration of the elements by the minister to each individual communicant, this would have made a serious inroad on the anti-sacerdotal emphasis of the Reformation.

The Assembly which passed the Five Articles also approved of the preparation of a new liturgy and canons. The existing MS. of the second draft underwent revision, especially in its early pages, to bring it closer to the Prayer Book, and then the reviser evidently transferred his efforts to the preparation of a new liturgy.[29] The second and third drafts alike were attributed to William Cowper, Bishop of Galloway, and the third can therefore be assigned to a period between the Perth Assembly (August 1618) and Cowper's death (February 1619). No doubt work had been continuous since 1616, and possibly the main amendments made after August 1618 were to give effect to the Articles. The orders for Morning and Evening Prayer were now similar to Matins and Evensong, but there were no versicles and responses and although psalms were substituted for the morning canticles, no alternative psalms were offered for the evening canticles (familiar in metrical versions in the Book of Common Order). Yet the traditional reformed structure was preserved in that the Apostles' Creed at Morning Prayer was followed by something based on the Ante-Communion – the collect for due preparation, state prayers and a prayer 'for the whole estate of Christ's Church', one of the alternative versions of which was the Prayer for the Church Militant in the Prayer Book. On Sunday the Creed was to be followed immediately by the Commandments (with responses) and one of the confessions in the Book of Common Order. The Communion Office fits with the structure of the Sunday morning service, for it proceeds directly to the collect for due preparation and the words of institution, as confession, readings, sermon and intercession had already taken place before the minister came down from the pulpit and stood at the side of the Table. After the words of institution came the long exhortation (borrowing much from the Prayer Book), a short invitation, 'All ye that truly repent you of your sins . . .', the consecration prayer, administration and thanksgiving. The consecration prayer begins with a confession like that in the Prayer Book's Communion Office, goes on to echo the Prayer of Humble Access and introduces a sentence from the English consecration prayer petitioning that 'we receiving these Thy creatures of bread and wine . . . may be made partakers of His most blessed body and blood'. There follows a more specific epiclesis ('Send down O Lord Thy blessing upon this sacrament that it may be unto us the effectual exhibitive instrument of the Lord Jesus'), an abridgement of the oblation in the English Book, and the Lord's Prayer. Thereafter, rather oddly, the minister was to 'repeat the words of the institution for consecrating the elements', with the manual acts. A short prayer echoed the *Sursum Corda* and the elements were delivered 'to the people in their hands kneeling', with the words of the current English Book slightly modified. The narrative of the Passion was to be read during the Communion, and parts of Psalms ciii or xxxiv sung during the movement of the communicants, 'so by this intercourse of reading and singing the people shall be kept in a holy exercise till all have communicated'. Then came a post-Communion prayer (with very slight borrowing from the Prayer Book), Psalm cvi and the Blessing. The Table was to stand 'in that part of the church which the minister findeth most convenient', but other rubrics make it clear that there would still be a long table or tables around which the people would assemble, though now on their knees and evidently at such a distance that the minister could pass between them and the Table. The orders for Baptism and Confirmation were based on the English orders but omitted the sign of the cross.

This third draft received royal approval, a licence for printing it was issued in 1619, and an Ordinal was printed in 1620, but the Prayer Book never appeared. It seems that when the Five Articles were approved by Parliament in 1621 King James, who boasted that he 'knew the stomach of that people', gave an undertaking to press no more innovations on the Scots and that he kept his word. How far the Articles were observed is far from clear. The mere fact that some stern opponents decided to found schismatic congregations might suggest that parish churches were obeying the law, and this was to a certain extent true. Some of the main dates in the Christian Year were quite commonly observed, and Communion at Easter was not unpopular. The official authorization of private Baptism and Communion was no doubt welcome, and there is no evidence of the administration of Confirmation. As kneeling at Communion was not generally acceptable except in the conservative north-east, there were some unseemly ongoings elsewhere, but kirk session records indicate that the customary distribution by elders or laymen was still taking place, and suggest that the Article on kneeling was widely ignored. With the approval of Archbishop Spottiswoode, and for a time of Charles I, some clergy who had conscientious objections were not pressed to conform. Beyond the partial observance of the Articles and the likelihood that the English Prayer Book continued to be used in the chapel royal, some cathedrals and the university chapels, the main results of all James VI's policy can have been only indirect. How far the three draft liturgies circulated and how far the thought behind them was influential it is hard to say, but they may have stimulated liturgical revival, at a time when episcopal government prevailed and when Scots increasingly associated with an England where puritanism looked like a lost cause: after all it was in 1620 that the Pilgrim Fathers emigrated, and some Scots thought of imitating them. The third draft, at any rate, was not forgotten, for interest in it revived between 1629 and 1634. Nor can one wholly discount the influence of English visitors, like one in 1617, who despised their neighbours who 'christen without the cross, marry without the ring, receive the sacrament without reverence, die without repentance and bury without divine service'.[30] There is certainly evidence that the externals of worship were becoming more seemly. In the years before and after 1560 there had been many complaints about the state of church buildings, but in the early seventeenth century there was much renovation and some new building. An Act of Parliament of 1617 required every parish church to have its own communion plate, and there is evidence of the provision of some fine silver work, bells and candelabra.[31] There are indications that the long tables customary for Communion were being supplemented by a small permanent Table at which consecration took place. An English visitor of 1629 commented very favourably on 'a very pretty church . . . two fairer churches for in-work than any I saw in London . . . seven great bells . . . and chimes . . . many candlesticks . . . the finest seats I have seen anywhere and the orderliest church'.[32] The excellence of the 'Aberdeen Psalter' of 1635 reflected the interest which both James and Charles took in fostering church music.

Such outward material signs may well have indicated inward spiritual growth, for individuals of deep religious convictions developed a novel devotion to Holy Communion. Archibald Johnston of Wariston, who was to become a framer of the National Covenant, a scourge of episcopacy and a leader of the most radical of the Covenanters, was an assiduous communicant under the Episcopalian regime and in 1637 communicated at least five times between 16 April and 4 November. Not only so, but he derived spiritual comfort from the sermons of bishops, including that very 'high' churchman Sydserf of Galloway, and of Dean Hannay, at whom, according to legend, Jenny Geddes later threw her stool.[33] The extent of dissatisfaction with the regime of the later years of King James and the earlier years of Charles, and the depth of division, have clearly been exaggerated.

Yet if there was a chance that gradual modifications in worship, along lines indicated in the draft liturgies, would have become generally acceptable, that chance was abruptly terminated by Charles I. The proceedings of the years 1633 to 1637, culminating in the first Scottish Prayer Book, are well documented and are worthy of examination as part of the story of the rebellion, but have little relevance to the history of Scottish worship at this point, influential though the Book became when a liturgical revival began among Episcopalians in the eighteenth century.

In 1629 Charles asked to see the third of the draft liturgies, and some further work was done on that basis, but in 1633, when the king came to Scotland and among other things prescribed the use of the surplice, it was evident that he wanted Scotland simply to accept the English Prayer Book. The older Scottish bishops insisted that a Scottish Book must make concessions to Scottish usage and prejudices, while more recently appointed bishops, especially Wedderburn of Dunblane, seem to have fallen under the spell of the First Book of Edward VI, that most conservative of Anglican liturgies. Ultimate decision among conflicting

views lay with the king, who was sensitive about his prerogative and
royal dignity and was much attached to trivia.

While revision was proceeding, a Code of Canons[34] was published
early in 1636. This required approval of a 'Book of Common Prayer and
Administration of the Sacraments, the Rites and Ceremonies of the
Church' although the Book had not yet taken final shape. One Canon
forbade ministers to 'conceive prayers *ex tempore*', but another suggests
that there was to be some latitude, with episcopal authority. A font was
to be placed 'somewhere near the entry of the church' and 'a comely
and decent table for celebrating the Holy Communion' was to be set 'at
the upper end of the chancel or church'. One of the final canons
expressly authorized private confession and absolution.

The Prayer Book which appeared in 1637 was by no means devoid of
concessions to existing Scottish practice and tradition, such as the
almost complete elimination of the Apocrypha, the substitution of
'presbyter' for 'priest' and the inclusion of an epiclesis, which the
English Book lacked. But the effect of such concessions was nullified
by features which were quite unacceptable, inserted mainly on the
insistence of the king personally. Prefixed to the liturgy was a
proclamation commanding its use by royal prerogative alone; the
Calendar, far from being simplified, was expanded; there were still
twelve lessons from the Apocrypha; there was a reference to 'ornaments
to be prescribed'. Perhaps most objectionable of all was the rubric on
the position of the celebrant at Communion. At the penultimate stage
the proposed formula was: 'During the time of consecration the
presbyter who consecrates shall stand in the midst before the altar, that
he may with the more ease and decency use both his hands, which he
cannot so conveniently do standing at the north side of it'; the final
version was 'shall stand at such a part of the Holy Table where he may
with the more ease and decency use both his hands', but this was no less
offensive in so far as it raised in suspicious minds fears not only of the
eastward position but of an elevation and seemed to fly in the face of all
that the reformers had advocated.

The hostile reception which the new service-book met when it was
read for the first time on 23 July 1637 is well known, and although every
parish minister was supposed to acquire two copies it is unlikely that it
was much used. John Maxwell, Bishop of Ross, who had been one of
the chief authors, used it in his cathedral at Fortrose for some months
and the Bishop of Brechin showed more determination than some of his
fellows when he read the Book under the protection of a brace of pistols.
The National Covenant, at the end of February 1638, committed the
signatories to reject both canons and liturgy until they had been
approved 'in free assemblies and in parliaments' and in the following
November a General Assembly at Glasgow condemned the service-
book 'both in respect of the manner of the introducing thereof and in
respect of the matter which it containeth'. The decisions of that

Assembly were ratified by Parliament in 1639, after the king's government had collapsed and the Covenanters were in complete control. The Archbishop of St. Andrews remarked sadly that 'now all that we have been doing these thirty years past is cast down at once', but these events were to prove the end not only of James' and Charles' innovations but of the ways of worship of the first reformers.

NOTES

1. *Acts of the Parliaments of Scotland*, II, pp. 415, 485; *Letters and Papers of Henry VIII*, XVIII (1), 324; *Extracts from the Council Register of Aberdeen* (Spalding Club), I, p. 189; John Knox, *History of the Reformation in Scotland*, ed. Dickinson (Edinburgh, 1949), I, p. 45; *Hamilton Papers*, ed. Bain (Edinburgh, 1890–92), I. p. 445; D. Patrick, ed., *Statutes of the Scottish Church* (Scot. Hist. Soc.), pp. 101, 136.
2. Knox, I, p. 148, II, pp. 277, 321.
3. G. C. Butterworth, *The English Primers 1529–45* (Philadelphia, 1953); H. Maynard Smith, *Henry VIII and the Reformation* (London, 1948), pp. 394–399.
4. *Hamilton Papers*, I, p. 445; *cf. Calendar of State Papers relating to Scotland and Mary, Queen of Scots*, I, no. 74.
5. *Register of the Privy Seal of Scotland*, III, no. 2513; *Historical MSS. Commission Report*, II, p. 187; *Spalding Club Miscellany*, IV, p. 120; Patrick, *op. cit.*, p. 187.
6. Knox, I, pp. 137–138; Patrick, *op. cit.*, p. 158; *Cal. S.P. Scot.*, I, p. 289.
7. G. Donaldson, *The Making of the Scottish Prayer Book of 1637* (Edinburgh, 1954), p. 14; there is plenty more evidence.
8. Some additions to the better known instances are given by G. J. Cuming, *Liturgical Review* 10:2 (November, 1980), 80–81.
9. W. McMillan, *The Worship of the Scottish Reformed Church 1550–1638* (London, 1931), pp. 77–80; Kenneth Elliott, 'Scottish Music of the Early Reformed Church', *Transactions of the Scottish Ecclesiological Society* 15:2 (1961) 18–32; Millar Patrick, *Four Centuries of Scottish Psalmody* (Oxford, 1949), chapter vi.
10. McMillan, *op. cit.*, pp. 169, 223.
11. *Register of Privy Seal*, VI, nos. 111, 997, 2044; G. Donaldson, *The Scottish Reformation* (Cambridge, 1960), p. 84.
12. McMillan, *op. cit.*, pp. 233–236, 242–243.
13. *Ibid.*, pp. 218–219.
14. See note 28 below.
15. McMillan, *op. cit.*, p. 371, where no source is given.
16. E.g., *Acts of the Parliaments of Scotland*, III, pp. 32, 104, 376, 447, V, pp. 266, 594–595, VIII, p. 586, IX, p. 196.

17. E.g., *Register of Kirk Session of St. Andrews* (Scot. Hist. Soc.), I, p. xlviii; *Stirling Presbytery Minutes* (Scot. Hist. Soc.), p. 137.
18. *Acts of the Parliaments of Scotland*, III, p. 453; Donaldson, *Scottish Prayer Book*, p. 18 and n; *Stirling Presbytery Minutes* (Scot. Hist. Soc.), p. 64.
19. *Cal. S.P. Scot.*, I, no. 891.
20. Donaldson, *Scottish Prayer Book*, pp. 24–26; Donaldson, 'Scottish Presbyterian Exiles in England', *Records of Scottish Church History Society* 14 (1962), 67–80.
21. Nat. Lib. Scot., Wodrow MSS., fol. vol. xliv, no. 24, printed in Donaldson, *Prayer Book*, p. 29; McMillan, *op. cit.*, p. 170.
22. E.g., *Register of Kirk Session of St. Andrews*, II, pp. 829–830; *South Leith Records*, ed. D. Robertson (Leith, 1911), p. 5; *Stirling Presbytery Minutes*, p. xxv.
23. William Cowper, *Works* (1629), p. 680.
24. D. Calderwood, *History of the Church of Scotland* (Wodrow Soc.), IV, pp. 145, 163; *Wodrow Soc. Misc.*, I, p. 417; *Acts and Proceedings of the General Assemblies of the Kirk of Scotland* (Bannatyne and Maitland Clubs), III, pp. 970–971.
25. Donaldson, *Scottish Prayer Book*, pp. 27, 30, 62n, 74.
26. In G. W. Sprott, ed., *Scottish Liturgies of James VI* (Edinburgh and London, 1901).
27. In *Scottish History Society Miscellany*, X. This was overlooked in the Introduction to *The Making of the Scottish Prayer Book of 1637*.
28. McMillan, *op. cit.*, chapter xvii, pp. 259–260, 264–265; Calderwood, VII, pp. 285–286; *Register of the Kirk Session of St. Andrews*, I, p. 302; *Stirling Presbytery Minutes*, pp. xxv, 50–51; Donaldson, *Scottish Prayer Book*, pp. 77–78; P. Hately-Waddell, *An Old Kirk Chronicle* (Edinburgh, 1893), pp. 19, 46, 59.
29. In G. W. Sprott, ed., *Scottish Liturgies of James VI*.
30. P. Hume Brown, *Early Travellers in Scotland* (Edinburgh, 1891), p. 101.
31. C. A. Ralegh Radford and G. Donaldson, 'Post-Reformation Church at Whithorn', *Proc. Soc. Antiq. Scot.*, 85 (1953), 125–133; G. Donaldson, *Scotland: James V to James VII* (Edinburgh, 1965), p. 274; *Transactions of the Aberdeen Ecclesiological Society* 3 (1894–1896), 207 sqq.; McMillan, *op. cit.*, pp. 240–241.
32. Quoted in Agnes Mure Mackenzie, *Scottish Pageant 1625–1707* (Edinburgh and London, 1949), p. 100.
33. Archibald Johnston, *Diary 1632–39* (Scot. Hist. Soc., 1911), pp. 55, 63, 89, 100, 114, 198, 248, 250, 256, 261, 269, 272.
34. In William Laud, *Works* (Oxford, 1847–60), V, part 2, pp. 586 sqq.

BIBLIOGRAPHY

Burnet, George B., *The Holy Communion in the Reformed Church of Scotland 1560–1960* (Edinburgh and London, 1960).

Donaldson, Gordon, *The Making of the Scottish Prayer Book of 1637* (Edinburgh, 1954).

Donaldson, Gordon, *The Scottish Reformation* (Cambridge, 1960).

Donaldson, Gordon, ed., 'A Scottish Liturgy of the Reign of James VI', *Scottish History Society Miscellany* 10 (1965), 87–117.

Elliott, Kenneth, 'Scottish Music of the Early Reformed Church', *Transactions of the Scottish Ecclesiological Society* 15:2 (1961), 18–32.

McMillan, William, *The Worship of the Scottish Reformed Church 1550–1638* (London, 1931).

Patrick, Millar, *Four Centuries of Scottish Psalmody* (Oxford, 1949).

Sprott, G. W., ed., *Scottish Liturgies of the Reign of James VI* (Edinburgh and London, 1901).

Chapter Four

COVENANT TO REVOLUTION

Gordon Donaldson

The direction which English high-churchmanship had given to liturgical reform in Scotland terminated abruptly in 1638. But there was to be no escape from English influence. After the civil war between the king and his English parliament started in 1642 the Scottish Covenanters sent an army to help Parliament on the understanding that an endeavour would be made 'to bring the Churches of God in the three kingdoms to the nearest conjunction and uniformity in religion, Confession of Faith, Form of Church Government, Directory for Worship and Catechism'. Already before this alliance had been formulated in the Solemn League and Covenant the English parliament had inaugurated the Westminster Assembly of Divines and had arranged for the Scottish General Assembly to send representatives. Eight Scots – five ministers, an earl, a baron and a knight – were authorized to attend a gathering of about 150 Englishmen to treat 'in all matters which may further the union of this island in one form of kirk government, one Confession of Faith, one Catechism, one Directory for the Worship of God'. The Scots, though few, had considerable influence, but they were not incorporated in the Assembly, and its productions were issued as those of 'The Assembly of Divines at Westminster, with the assistance of Commissioners from the Church of Scotland'.

The Westminster Directory for Public Worship was approved by the Scottish Parliament and General Assembly in February 1645. It had been expressly designed to supersede the English Prayer Book, which, in a Preface, it roundly denounced as an 'idol' (a term which appealed to one of the Scottish commissioners, Robert Baillie[1]) and as an 'offence', with its prescribed prayers, its 'set forms' and its 'unprofitable and burdensome ceremonies'. The Directory therefore stands in sharp contrast to the English and Scottish Prayer Books, but it also contrasts with the Book of Common Order, for, although there are lengthy passages designed as guidance to the contents of the prayers which were to be used, there were hardly any 'set forms' of words except the formulae for Baptism, for the administration of Communion – 'Take ye, eat ye, this is the Body of Christ which is broken for you; do this in remembrance of Him' – and for the marriage vows. These apart, the one feature of traditional worship which was to be retained was the Lord's Prayer: 'And because the prayer which Christ taught his disciples is not only a pattern of prayer, but itself a most comprehensive prayer, we recommend it also to be used in the prayers of the Church'. There was not even a 'set form' for a Blessing such as the Book of Common Order had provided.

There was no mistaking the centrality and dominance of the sermon. Out of twelve pages describing the normal Sunday service, ten are taken up with 'Public Prayer before the Sermon', 'Of the Preaching of the Word' (designed to instruct the minister in the structure of his sermon) and 'Of Prayer after Sermon'. The only other elements in the services were to be the reading of the scriptures (preferably a chapter from each Testament, the books being read through in order) and the singing of psalms. The one place specified for a psalm was at the end of the service, following the Prayer after Sermon: 'The prayer ended, let a psalm be sung if with conveniency it may be done.' But the Directory concluded with a few sentences emphasizing the duty of Christians 'to praise God publicly by singing of psalms together in the congregation, and also privately in the family'. It gave some general directions and urged that everyone who could read should have a psalm-book, but added that 'for the present, where many of the congregation cannot read, it is convenient that the minister, or some other fit person appointed by him and the other ruling officers, do read the psalm line by line before the singing thereof'. It has been remarked that this was hardly necessary in Scotland, where so many people could read and where they had been accustomed since the Reformation to handle a 'Psalm Book' usually containing tunes as well as words, for all to see, and that this concession to an illiterate English populace resulted in foisting on the Scots what has been called 'the detestable practice of lining out', which rendered agreeable musical standards impossible. The Psalter which had been prepared in Scotland in the 1560s had hitherto held the field. A new version – 'The Psalms of King David translated by King James' but owing a good deal to Sir William Alexander, Earl of Stirling – had been printed in 1631. This was in much more polished verse, but it was thought to be a less accurate translation and to be too ornate, and any prospects that it ever had of prevailing vanished when it was printed with the Prayer Book of 1637. A fresh revision went ahead in the era of the Westminster Assembly. Again there was an English basis, in the work of the Cornishman Francis Rous, which had been heavily revised by the Westminster Assembly, but the Scots made further substantial changes, to produce the metrical Psalter still in use today.

It would appear that the structure of the service envisaged by the Directory for an ordinary Sunday morning service would, at its best, have been: Summons to Worship; Prayer of Approach to God; readings and psalms; Confession; Sermon; Great Intercession, concluding with Lord's Prayer; Blessing. The Communion, when it was celebrated, would follow on that service. It seems to be implied that the elements would be brought in before the minister gave an exhortation, which preceded the reading of the Words of Institution. The Prayer of Consecration, which followed, included an epiclesis in the form of a petition that God would 'vouchsafe His gracious presence and the effectual working of His Spirit in us and so to sanctify these elements both of bread and wine and to bless His own ordinance that we may receive by faith the Body and Blood of Jesus Christ'. Then came the fraction, the administration and a post-Communion prayer. The Directory gives guidance also for Baptism, Marriage, the Visitation of the Sick and the Burial of the Dead. By laying down that marriages were not to be on Sunday the Directory took a line flatly contrary to that of the reformers. The directions for Burial are of a very negative nature, and funeral sermons, which had been known since the Reformation, had been forbidden by the General Assembly in 1638. The Directory seems to have intended the elimination of the reader (although his office had been approved by the General Assembly so recently as 1642), for only ministers and (occasionally) candidates for the ministry were intended to read even the lessons.

   The Directory, because of the very latitude it offered, need not have been wholly fatal to the ways of worship customary since the Reformation and authorized by the Book of Common Order, any more than the Book of Common Order, when it was introduced, necessarily eliminated the use of prayers from the Prayer Book. Ministers could, for example, have continued to use a confession from the Book of Common Order as part of the prayer before sermon and to use its great intercession before or after sermon. Nor did the Directory expressly forbid the use of the scriptural canticles associated with Evensong and printed with the Book of Common Order, or even expressly forbid the Doxology or the Creed (though both of those might have been taken to fall under the general condemnation of 'set forms'). After all, the whole orientation of the Directory was English, shaped by a hostile attitude towards the English Prayer Book, and there is no reason to believe that the majority of the Scots, if left alone, would have voted for the abandonment of the Book of Common Order. The General Assembly's approval of the Directory was qualified: it was to be 'no prejudice to the order and practice of this kirk, in such particulars as are appointed by the books of discipline and acts of the General Assemblies and are not otherwise ordered and appointed in the Directory'. However, the Book of Common Order was not printed again after 1644 and the indications are that the Scots, whether they wanted to or not, were under some pressure to conform to the ways of the English puritans and that the interpretation put on the Directory, despite the Assembly's qualification, was that what it did not expressly sanction was forbidden. Thus, the use in public worship of the Doxology, the Creed and the Ten Commandments (which it did not positively sanction) was laid aside, but with them went the Lord's Prayer (which the Directory actually commended). Besides, already in 1640, before the Directory, objection had been voiced, apparently for the first time, to the reading of 'any set prayer'.[2] Not only so, but the emphasis came to be more and more almost exclusively on preaching. Partly on the argument that people ought to read the Bible for themselves at home, the public reading of passages of Scripture gave way to 'lecturing' or exposition which amounted to an additional sermon, and at Communion services there were 'table addresses' to each group of communicants as well as the main sermon. Even psalmody went by the board: in Edinburgh 'in the year of God 1645 the reading of chapters in the kirk by the common reader and singing of psalms were discharged and in place thereof come in the lectures'. In the turmoil of the later 1640s and during the English occupation in the 1650s, when radical Covenanters were collaborating with English Independents and when various separatist congregations appeared in Scotland, practices developed which would probably have appalled not only the reformers but even the compilers of the Directory. A contemporary noted that 'in these separated meetings, nothing is to be had but a long preachment'.[3] Partly because of the animosities among the Covenanters and their associates, celebration of Communion became infrequent: in parish after parish, five, six or even nine years passed without the people assembling round the Lord's Table. On the other hand, the very occasional joint Communion, in which people from several parishes joined, first became common among the extremists at this period, and the fast before the Communion became a more regular feature.

The innovations of the Directory and its sequels encountered a good deal of opposition, and not only in the conservative north-east where King James' programme had met with most acquiescence. Leading Covenanters were as critical as any. Alexander Henderson, who helped to frame the Covenant and was Moderator of the Glasgow Assembly of 1638 which rejected the Prayer Book and episcopacy, had declared in 1642 that he could not 'take upon me . . . to set down other forms of prayer than we have in our Psalm Book, penned by our great and divine reformers'. Robert Baillie was as much exercised in 1643 about the 'novations' of English puritans or Brownists as he had been about the 'novations' of Charles I five years earlier and especially deplored the dropping of the Creed, the Doxology and the Lord's Prayer. And it has often been related how David Calderwood, stout Presbyterian though he was, pled for the retention of the Doxology and, when he was overruled, consoled himself with the hope that he would sing it in heaven. But popular feeling too was strong, for the introduction of 'lectures' in Edinburgh 'did not content the people, because there was no reading of chapters nor singing of psalms on the Sabbath day', and, although the Directory did not provide for godparents, people persisted in retaining them.[4] The Scots, or at any rate the less radical among them, were well aware that they were surrendering some of their own treasured practices for the sake of the prospect – which proved illusory – of Anglo-Scottish conformity. Thus it had been a decent custom in Scotland for people and minister alike to 'humble themselves' – that is, bow or kneel – in personal devotion on entering the church or before the beginning of the sermon, and to visit churches for private prayer outwith the hours of service. The Westminster divines looked unfavourably on such practices, possibly because they thought them ostentatious, possibly because they wanted to dissociate any particular sanctity from the stone and lime of a church building. But when the Scots gave in on the issue of the minister's private prayer before the sermon they expressly declared that it was 'for satisfaction of the desires of the reverend Divines in the Synod of England and for uniformity with that kirk, so much endeared to us'. The General Assembly at first forbade 'all condemning . . . such lawful things as have been . . . practised since the first beginning of reformation' and 'took in very ill part' the disuse of the Lord's Prayer and the Doxology.[5] It is difficult to believe that all this resentment could die down in a few years or that a return to the ways of earlier generations would not, in due course, be welcomed by many.

When the king came back, in 1660, there was no governmental action in respect of worship to parallel the change made in administration by the restoration of episcopacy. Although Charles II himself was credited with the expression of his 'will' in this field, the one Act of Parliament which could have been held to be relevant to worship was the Act Rescissory, which cancelled all legislation since 1633, but its effects were far from clear-cut. Thus, Parliament's approval of the Directory was annulled, but it could have been argued that the approval given to it by the General Assembly (which had not met since 1653, when Cromwell's men sent it packing, and was not to meet again until 1690) still stood. At the same time, only fifteen years had passed since that approval had been given, and those who had opposed it then, as well as others who had not become reconciled to the later 'novations', presumably welcomed the prospect of reviving the Book of Common Order. The Act Rescissory – if its bearing on worship had been thought out at all, which may be doubted – indicated an intention to revert to the position which had obtained not only before the revolutionary interlude of the 1640s but also before King Charles I's unpopular innovations of 1633–37. However, the reaction went much farther than that, for although the Five Articles of Perth, approved by Parliament in 1621, now once more became, in terms of the Act Rescissory, technically the law of the land, it is quite clear that the government did not consider it to be its business to enforce them and they had even less force now than they had when they were first passed. If the official liturgical standard of the Restoration Church is to be defined in chronological terms then it was broadly the pre-1618 standard, though practice turned out to accord much more with the Westminster standard.

The evidence which survives for five of the dioceses – Edinburgh, St. Andrews, Dunblane, Galloway and Aberdeen – suggests that, although there was neither central nor provincial direction, the bishops were acting in concert and the diocesan regulations have so much similarity that they can be treated as a single code. What was in mind was to eliminate the novelties which had come in the later 1640s and to ignore the innovations made by James VI in his later years and by Charles I, so returning to what Alexander Henderson would have called the practice of 'our great and divine reformers'. 'Lecturing' was to be abandoned and the reading of the scriptures – usually at least one chapter from each Testament – restored. The office of reader was to be revived, in every congregation if possible, and his function, as of old, was to read 'a set form of prayer', psalms and lessons. The Lord's Prayer was to be used, the Doxology added to the psalms, the Apostles' Creed recited and the Commandments read.[6] The Lord's Prayer had been commended in the Directory, the Creed had been expounded in the Westminster Confession and printed at the end of the Catechisms, the Commandments were canonical Scripture, so the Doxology alone was contrary to the Westminster standards.

Although readers were to use 'a set form of prayer', what it was to be does not appear. The Directory was to be 'laid aside and not used' and 'the liturgy in the old Psalm Book' (that is, the Book of Common Order) was to be 'practised', but although the old 'liturgy' was thus authorized it was never reprinted after 1644. Nor was the Westminster Directory reprinted, but as it was a book for the minister, not a book for the people, few copies were needed. What is more significant is that the Westminster Confession, with the Larger and Shorter Catechisms, the Lord's Prayer and the Creed, was several times published (1669, 1671, 1673, 1675, 1678, 1683, 1685). A reference in official church records to the 'Confession of Faith of the Reformed Church of Christ in Britain and Ireland'[7] can mean only the Westminster Confession. Clearly the Westminster standards were to some extent being upheld or at any rate exerting some influence, and on this ground alone it would seem very doubtful if the Directory was entirely 'laid aside'.

Sir Walter Scott depicted in *Old Morality* a regime in which people were being dragooned into the parish churches to take part in Prayer Book worship, a howler for which he was mercilessly attacked by that doughty and thorough Presbyterian scholar Thomas McCrie.[8] But errors are more easily spread than eradicated, there are still writers who think they know better than contemporaries did how worship was conducted, and it is too often assumed or implied that because the Church's government was episcopal the people were being coerced into attending services with prayer book, altar and surplice. Not illogically, on this premiss, we are sometimes told that 'All the Covenanters wanted was freedom to worship God in their own way'. But how men worshipped God was not then the issue, and freedom was the last thing that the

Covenanters upheld (pledged as they were to the Solemn League). By a curious paradox, there was in that period a freedom in the Church of Scotland hard to parallel anywhere, for no service-book was even authoritatively maintained, let alone enforced.

Warned by the fates of Charles I and Archbishop Laud, each of them beheaded, neither Charles II nor his archbishops took the risk of introducing a service-book to Scotland. There were, as always, those who favoured the Prayer Book, notably Robert Leighton, Bishop of Dunblane, Alexander Burnet, Archbishop of Glasgow, and Gilbert Burnet, minister of Saltoun and later Bishop of Salisbury. Here and there a minister used the book in church, more likely by simply saying the prayers from memory (as Gilbert Burnet did) than by reading them. Not only English Prayer Books, but also the 1637 Scottish Book (of which such a large edition seems to have been printed that even now it is not exactly a rare book) were readily available and were used by both minister and laymen in study, private devotion and family worship.[9] But the Prayer Book was so far from being officially recognized for use in public worship that an act of council was considered necessary to legalize the use of the English Book even in private families, and that not until 1680.[10] It was remarked in 1681 that many copies of the Prayer Book were being sold in Edinburgh, but that was hardly a novelty.

There was some talk in 1666 of preparing a liturgy, and Archbishop Alexander Burnet seems to have taken a lead, but it emerged that there was a clear preference for nothing more ambitious than the 'third draft' of 1618–19, that extremely simplified version of the Prayer Book, which had been submitted to Charles I in 1629, and even this modest proposal was not proceeded with.[11] All that was ever done was even more modest. Morning and evening prayers drawn up for Aberdeen Cathedral consisted only of a confession, lessons and a prayer of thanksgiving and intercession concluding with the Lord's Prayer; the Creed was not included but in the morning the Commandments were read and in the evening a portion of the *Te Deum*.[12] When in 1683–85 a committee of the synod of Aberdeen prepared a kind of manual,[13] it was merely a collection of prayers, with a lectionary, to be used within the existing structure of worship, and even this was apparently not printed. A complaint in 1678 by a minister in Dunblane diocese of 'private assayes' to impose 'ane unwarrandable liturgie of unsound and lifeless form' may point to some projected unofficial compilation, but there is nothing to substantiate his grievance.[14]

Not only was there no liturgy, but the meagre requirements put forward in 1662 met with little compliance and had to be repeated again and again, apparently with only limited effect. In Galloway the synod learned in 1664 that 'some of the brethren . . . have not been careful to practise these duties' and in Dunblane one or more of the enactments on reading the scriptures, the use of the Doxology, the Lord's Prayer, the Creed and the Commandments were repeated almost annually until

1668. Possibly at that point the struggle was given up in despair, for so late as 1688, on the eve of the overthrow of the Restoration settlement, the Creed, Lord's Prayer and Doxology were still not in general use in the presbytery of Inverness and Dingwall.[15] In the intervening years there is evidence from various other places of failure to achieve uniformity.[16] In particular, it seems to have proved so difficult to check ministers' persistence in 'lecturing' that the bishops had to call in the privy council to condemn this novelty in 1670, and even then means were found of evading the prohibition.[17]

There appears to have been a good deal of unseemly behaviour. While some people uncovered their heads for prayer, and knelt, others (even in Aberdeenshire) sat with their heads covered, despite exhortations to kneel or stand, and it is unlikely that the order given to the ministers of Dunblane diocese to teach the people to return to kneeling or standing at prayer, in place of 'their most indecent practice of sitting' had much effect. Some stood for the Doxology, others declined to sing it at all, so that in one parish 'you may hear the Doxology Christianly, but in the next parish church no mention of it; . . . yea, and too often in the same Church Assembly, . . . when it comes to the closing Psalm some sing the Doxology decently, others sitting by who did sing the Psalm intently turn silent at the Doxology, yea, some are worse, deriding and scoffing the singers of it'.[18] In Aberdeen, at least, it was expected that people would stand for the Creed, but it is not likely that this expectation was fulfilled either. The Article of 1618 which had required kneeling at Communion was generally disregarded, though kneeling was not entirely unknown, but this particular question was hardly significant, as Holy Communion was a very rare event. While a good many ministers, especially in the north-east at least, did manage to celebrate at Easter and some on Whitsunday, attempts to secure even an annual celebration, whether at Easter or any other time, had only limited success. There were parishes where twelve, eighteen or even twenty-four years passed without a celebration. It is hard to believe that the posture of communicants was a burning issue.

The prevailing freedom in worship meant not only that the puritanically minded could have their way but that traditionalists also had a certain latitude. Thus, although godparents were said not to be required[19] – which again might suggest the use of the Directory rather than the Book of Common Order – baptismal registers show that they were not unknown. Some once well-established and popular features in worship which had been eclipsed for some years, such as the singing of the psalms and 'the exercise of the Catechism', were restored.[20] Equally, there was a certain revival of the observance of the Christian Year, for Epiphany, Good Friday, Easter, Ascension, St. Andrew's Day and Christmas were marked in one way or another in some places, but there was no more consistency in this than in anything else, though the prohibition (for secular reasons) on eating flesh in Lent, abandoned in

1640, was resumed. The synod of Aberdeen ordered that private Baptism and Communion should not be denied to those who sought them, and, like the Prayer Book, laid down that preferably there should be two or three to communicate with 'the person desiring the same'.[21] Such permission no doubt met a certain need, as it had done between the Reformation and the Covenants, but now there was the complication that the authorities, who were concerned to suppress Baptism by nonconforming preachers, had to be wary on private Baptism. Funeral services and sermons, which had been forbidden in 1638, seem to have become once more not uncommon, though our information is mainly for persons of rank.[22]

It hardly makes sense in this period to speak of 'permissible deviations' for there were few standards from which men might deviate. While it seems that each minister very largely did what was right in his own eyes, layfolk whose tastes were either more traditional or more radical than their minister's may often have felt aggrieved. There must therefore have been a good deal of irritation, but it is hard to believe that official policy – where there was official policy – can have caused general resentment. The numerous covenanting manifestos collected by Robert Wodrow contain no allusions to liturgical disagreement as a reason for schism: he evidently did not reckon the feeble attempts to secure uniformity of worship as among 'the sufferings of the Church of Scotland'. All the emphasis in the contest with nonconformity was on the political issue of the royal supremacy and the administrative issue of episcopacy. An English nonconformist visitor saw it quite clearly: 'The public worship in the churches . . . is in all respects after the same manner managed as in the Presbyterian congregations in England, so that I much wondered why there should be any dissenters here, till I came to be informed of the renunciation of the Covenant enjoined, and the imposition of the hierarchy'.[23] On one side, the government never laid down requirements in worship except in the act of council condemning 'lecturing'; when the Court of High Commission was revived it received no powers relating to conformity in worship;[24] and the bonds which so many people had to give for their good behaviour never promised conformity in worship. On the other side, the malcontents, in the many documents giving their reasons for dissent, never mentioned dissatisfaction with church services among their reasons for staying away from them.[25] It is significant of the whole emphasis that some ministers were in trouble for not observing the king's birthday on 29 May but none for failing to observe their Saviour's birthday on 25 December.

The opposition must have realized that it was in a hopelessly illogical position. The Solemn League, to which they so loudly proclaimed their adherence, committed its signatories to the Directory, and a petition in 1661 had asked that Parliament should ratify *inter alia* the Directory. But in practice the malcontents repudiated the Directory when they insisted on lecturing, when they laid aside the psalms and when they rejected the Lord's Prayer. In the last particular it was the bishops who were upholding the Directory. Thus the Pentland rebels, in 1666, did remark that the king, at his coronation (in 1651) had undertaken to establish the Directory, but they did not give his failure to do so as one of the reasons for their rebellion. And when James Renwick made his profession of faith before his execution in 1688 he listed among the standards he 'owned' the Directory for Family Worship but not the Directory for Public Worship.[26]

The buildings which were the scene of worship were, some of them, no more seemly than the conduct of many of the worshippers. Country churches, it was remarked by a visitor, were 'poor and mean', and official reports show that even within a single presbytery there was great variation. There were churches in the Highlands which, with neither doors nor roofs, with defective thatch or unglazed windows, looked like relics from medieval times and must have made it seem as if no Reformation had ever taken place. Inside there was, of course, no altar or liturgical chancel, and communicants, as of old, sat at long tables in the body of the church or in the structural chancel on the rare occasions when Communion was celebrated. Baptism was administered not from a font but from a basin attached to the pulpit – one survival at least of the reformers' stress on the indissoluble link between Word and sacraments. The pulpit itself was sometimes a kind of three-decker, incorporating the reader's desk below the minister's compartment and lower still the 'stool of repentance, or rather a bench for five or six to sit on, to be seen by the congregation and bear the shame of their crimes'.[27] Communion vessels seem to have been scarcer than they had been before 1638: perhaps some had been melted down to pay the armies of the Covenant, some may have been carried off by incumbents dispossessed in 1662. Musical standards must have been deplorable, for when a collection of tunes to accompany the 1650 Psalter was first issued (and that not until 1666) it contained only twelve tunes, all in common metre, and they came to constitute a fixed canon. Reviewing the behaviour of worshippers, their environment when they worshipped, and the infrequency of Holy Communion, it is hard to avoid the conclusion that standards of devotion were lower than they had been before 'the troubles' began with the revolt against Charles I. Only the writings of Robert Leighton and Henry Scougal's Life of God in the Soul of Man remind us that there were some souls who were not preoccupied by ecclesiastical politics.

There are three contemporary accounts of Scottish worship in this period which are often quoted. Sir George Mackenzie, in his A Vindication of the Government in Scotland during the reign of King Charles II (1691), wrote: 'The way of worship in our church differed nothing from what the presbyterians themselves practised (except only that we used the doxology, the Lord's Prayer and in Baptism the Creed, all which they rejected). We had no ceremonies, surplice, altars, cross in baptisms, nor the meanest of those things which would have been allowed in England by the dissenters in way of accommodation'.[28] The author of *The Case of the Present Afflicted Clergy in Scotland*, written as a defence of the Episcopalians in 1690, made much the same points: 'As to the worship, it's exactly the same both in the church and conventicle; in the church there are no ceremonies at all enjoined or practised, only some persons more reverent think fit to be uncovered which our presbyterians do but by halves even in the time of prayer; we have no liturgy nor form of prayer, no not in the cathedrals, the only difference in this point is, our clergy are not so overbold nor fulsome in their extemporary expressions as the others are ... and we generally conclude one of our prayers with that which our Saviour taught and commanded, which the other party decry as superstitious and formal; "Amen" too gives great offence, though neither the clerk nor people use it, only the minister sometimes shuts up his prayer with it. The sacraments are administered after the same way and manner by both: ... in Baptism neither party use the cross'.[29] Perhaps most familiar of all is the description given by Thomas Morer, an English army chaplain stationed in Scotland in 1690: 'The Episcopalian Church have hitherto used no liturgy at all, no more than the Presbyterians who now govern, and their whole service on the Lord's day ... depends on these particulars: First, the precentor, about half an hour before the preacher comes, reads two or three chapters to the congregation of what part of Scripture he pleases or as the minister gives him directions. As soon as the preacher gets into the pulpit, the precentor leaves reading, and sets a psalm, singing with the people till the minister, by some sign, orders him to give over. The psalm over, the preacher begins, confessing sins and begging pardon, exalting the holiness and majesty of God and setting before Him our vileness and propensity to transgress His commandments. Then he goes to sermon, delivered by heart, and therefore sometimes spoiled by battologies [futile repetitions], little impertinences and incoherence in their discourses. The sermon finished, he returns to prayer, thanks God for the opportunities to deliver His word; prays for all mankind, for all Christians, for that particular nation, for the sovereign and royal family without naming any, for subordinate magistrates, for sick people, especially such whose names the precentor hands up to him, then concludes with the Lord's Prayer, to sanctify what was said before. After that another psalm is sung, named by the minister, and frequently suited to the subject of his sermon; which done, he gives the benediction, and dismisses the congregation for that time. . . .' The difference between Episcopalians and Presbyterians, Morer repeats, can scarcely be discerned in their worship: 'Their singing of psalms, praying, preaching and collection are the same, and 'tis the whole of their worship in both congregations. They both do it after the same manner, saving that after the psalm the Episcopalian minister uses the doxology, which the other omits, and concludes his own prayer with that of the Lord, which the Presbyterian refuses to do.'[30]

While these accounts are not to be dismissed, it is quite clear from ample evidence that they are misleading in so far as they imply that there was uniformity in practice: even the Lord's Prayer, the Doxology and the Creed, though held out as the distinguishing marks of Episcopalian worship, were very far from universal. Morer's account is valuable in so far as it indicates what has been called the 'traditional structure' of Sunday worship and (leaving aside the place of the 'precentor' or reader, with functions rather more limited than had been the custom before the Covenanting period) the outline Morer gives looks more like the Directory than the Book of Common Order. Morer also reminds us that presbytery and episcopacy might come and go but the kirk session discipline went on and the public denunciation of offenders continued to enliven public worship.

NOTES

1. Robert Baillie, *Letters and Journals* (Bannatyne Club, 1841–42), II, p. 117.
2. W. McMillan, *The Worship of The Scottish Reformed Church, 1550–1638* (London, 1931), p. 115.
3. J. Nicoll, *Diary* (Bannatyne Club, 1836), pp. 114–115; Gilbert Burnet, *Vindication*, p. 200.
4. Baillie, II, pp. 2, 46, 51, 69–71, 76, 94, 427; John Hunter, *Diocese and Presbytery of Dunkeld* (London, 1871), p. 65 n. 1; Nicoll, p. 115; G. Donaldson, *The Making of the Scottish Prayer Book of 1637* (Edinburgh, 1954), p. 18 n.
5. *Acts of the General Assembly of the Church of Scotland* (Church Law Society, 1843), p. 121; Burnet, *Vindication*, p. 182.
6. Hunter, *Diocese and Presbytery of Dunkeld*, I, pp. 60–65 (for St. Andrews and Edinburgh); *Ecclesiastical Records of Aberdeen* (Spalding Club 1846), pp. 262–264; *Register of the Synod of Galloway 1664–71* (Kirkcudbright, 1875); *Records of the Exercise of Alford* (New Spalding Club, 1897), pp. 1–3; *Register of the Diocesan Synod of Dunblane* (ed. John Wilson, Edinburgh and London, 1887), pp. 2–4.
7. *Inverness and Dingwall Presbytery Records* (Scot. Hist. Soc.), p. 60.
8. Thomas McCrie, *Miscellaneous Writings* (Edinburgh, 1841), pp. 276–279.
9. R. S. Rait, 'Walter Scott and Thomas McCrie', in H. Grierson, *Sir Walter Scott Today* (1932); G. D. Henderson, *Religious Life in Seventeenth-Century Scotland*, p. 237.
10. *Register of the Privy Council of Scotland*, 3rd. ser., VI, p. 388.

11. *Lauderdale Papers* (Camden Soc. New Series, 1884–85), II, App. pp. xxx, xxxiii.
12. Henry Scougal, *Life of God in the Soul of Man*, ed. James Cooper (1889), pp. 123–133.
13. *Records of the Exercise of Alford*, p. 366..
14. *Register of the Synod of Dunblane*, pp. xiv, 146–151.
15. *Inverness and Dingwall Presbytery Records*, p. 133.
16. I. B. Cowan, 'Worship and Dissent in Restoration Scotland', *Scotia*, 2 (1979), 62–63.
17. *Register of the Privy Council of Scotland*, 3rd. ser., III, p. 123.; Alexander Kirkton, *Secret and True History of the Church of Scotland* (1817), pp. 291–292.
18. Nicoll, *op. cit.*, p. 382; Hunter, *op. cit.*, I, p. 63.
19. Walter R. Foster, *Bishop and Presbytery* (London, 1958), p. 126.
20. Nicoll, *op. cit.*, pp. 115, 382.
21. *Ecclesiastical Records of Aberdeen*, p. 264.
22. E.g., Robert Wodrow, *The History of the Sufferings of the Church of Scotland* (Edinburgh, 1721–22), I, pp. 189, 190, 219.
23. D. Butler, *The Life and Letters of Robert Leighton* (London, 1903), p. 485.
24. Wodrow, I, pp. 192–193, 318–319.
25. E.g., Wodrow, I, p. 159.
26. *Ibid.*; I, pp. 32, 246; II, p. 637.
27. Foster, *op. cit.*, pp. 122–123.
28. Mackenzie, *Vindication* p. 9; *cf.* David Reid, *The Party-Coloured Mind* (Edinburgh, 1982), p. 184.
29. Foster, *op. cit.*, pp. 125–126.
30. This account by Morer, from which extracts are given by Foster, is printed in *Ecclesiastical Records of Aberdeen*, pp. lxv–lxix.

BIBLIOGRAPHY

Burnet, George B., *The Holy Communion in the Reformed Church of Scotland 1560–1960* (Edinburgh and London, 1960).
Burnet, Gilbert, *A Vindication of the . . . Church and State of Scotland* (Edinburgh, 1673).
Donaldson, Gordon, 'Scottish Ordinations in the Restoration Period', *Scot. Hist. Rev.*, 33, 169–175.
Foster, Walter R., *Bishop and Presbytery* (London, 1958).
Henderson, G. D., *Religious Life in Seventeenth-Century Scotland* (Cambridge, 1937).
Hunter, John, *Diocese and Presbytery of Dunkeld* (London, 1871).
McMillan, William, *The Worship of the Scottish Reformed Church 1550–1635* (London, 1931).

Morer, T., *A Short Account of Scotland* (London, 1702). (Reprinted in *Ecclesiastical Records of Aberdeen* [Spalding Club, 1846], LXV–LXIX.)

Patrick, Millar, *Four Centuries of Scottish Psalmody* (Oxford, 1949).

Wodrow, Robert, *The History of the Sufferings of the Church of Scotland* (Edinburgh, 1721–22).

Chapter Five

REVOLUTION TO DISRUPTION

Henry Sefton

The worship of eighteenth-century Scotland has been little esteemed. This poor opinion has been reinforced by the use of the term renascence[1] to describe developments in the nineteenth century. But this is to do less than justice to the worship of the Established Church and to ignore other interesting and significant developments in worship during the period between the Revolution of 1688 and the Disruption of 1843.

At the Revolution there was no legislation on worship. The Parliament of 1690, having heard the *Confession of Faith* read aloud, declined to listen to the *Catechism* or the *Directory for Public Worship*[2] and so the parliamentary act which 'established ratified and confirmed' the Presbyterian church government and discipline as established in 1592 to be 'the only government of Christ's Church within this Kingdom' made no provision for the regulation of worship. It is the more interesting therefore that it was a controversy relating to worship which led to a substantial modification of the 1690 Act[3] by the Parliament of Great Britain.

The Greenshields affair began in 1709 when James Greenshields, a clergyman who had received ordination from the deprived Bishop of Ross, opened a meeting-house near St. Giles' in Edinburgh in which he read the services of the *Book of Common Prayer* of the Church of England. This was a novelty in Scotland both for Episcopalians and Presbyterians since no Prayer Book had been imposed during the second episcopal period. Greenshields was summoned before the Presbytery of Edinburgh and ordered to desist. When he refused the magistrates of Edinburgh put him in prison. Greenshields appealed to the Court of Session and when unsuccessful before that court took his case to the House of Lords. The Lords reversed the decision of the Court of Session and awarded costs against the magistrates of Edinburgh.[4] In 1712 the Parliament of Great Britain clearly had Greenshields' case in mind when it passed *An Act to prevent the Disturbing of those of the Episcopal Community in that part of Great Britain called Scotland in the exercise of their Religious Worship and in the use of the Liturgy of the Church of England.*[5] This Act, commonly known as the Toleration Act, in effect recognized two Churches in Scotland and for the first time ever gave legal sanction to worship other than that of the Established Church. The courts of the Established Church were deprived of the support of the civil magistrates in the execution of their judgements such as they had had in the Greenshields case. Episcopal ministers were to be permitted to baptize and to conduct marriages and an Act of the Scottish Parliament forbidding this was repealed. This toleration was, however, only extended to those clergymen who were prepared to take the oath of allegiance to Queen Anne and the oath of abjuration of the exiled Stuarts and to pray explicitly for Queen Anne and the Electress of Hanover in the course of divine worship. Thus in the course of the eighteenth century there were established in many of the towns of Scotland 'qualified' chapels in which the English liturgy was used and the Hanoverian kings were prayed for by name. Because many of those attending these chapels were English expatriates they were commonly known as English chapels.[6]

Many of the native Scottish Episcopalians refused to take the oaths and pray for the ruling dynasty. For their benefit the 1637 Book of Common Prayer was reprinted verbatim by George Seton, 5th Earl of Winton, in 1712.[7] But as this edition was relatively expensive the Communion Office of 1637 was reprinted separately in a series of 'wee bookies' from 1722 onwards.[8] In the north-east of Scotland the Episcopalian clergy at the instigation of Bishop James Gadderar were in the habit of transposing the various parts of the office so that the prayer for Christ's Church was taken from a place immediately after the Offertory and inserted immediately after the conclusion of the prayer of Consecration; the Invitation, Confession, Absolution and Comfortable Words were placed immediately before the prayer of Humble Access instead of before the *Sursum Corda*.[9] These alterations, which in the opinion of Gadderar and his clergy represented the 'proper and true order' in which the office ought to be said, were incorporated in an edition of the Wee Bookie printed in 1735.[10]

Bishop Gadderar also seems to have been involved in the publication in 1718 of a Communion Office for the Nonjurors in England.[11] This was entitled *A Communion Office taken partly from the Primitive Liturgies and partly from the first English Reformed Common-Prayer-Book* and while intended for use in England was also used in the private chapel at Craighall, the residence of a Perthshire laird, Thomas Rattray. Rattray was ordained when of mature age and was consecrated as Bishop of Brechin in 1727, becoming Bishop of Dunkeld in 1731 and Primus of the Episcopal Church in 1739. Despite this busy life he devoted himself to the study of the Eastern Liturgies and more especially of the Liturgy of St. James. The fruit of this was his edition, published posthumously in 1744, of *The Ancient Liturgy of the Church of Jerusalem, being the Liturgy of St. James, Freed from all Latter Additions and Interpolations of whatever kind, and so restored to its Original Purity*. The method used to free the Liturgy of St. James from later interpolation was to compare it with the Clementine liturgy, 'which never having been used in any Church since it was inserted into the Apostolic Constitution has none of those Additions which were afterwards introduced into the other Liturgies.' Rattray's thoroughness is shown by a detailed comparison also with St. Cyril's *Sixth Mystagogical Catechism* and the liturgies of saints Mark, Basil and John Chrysostom. Appended to this is an adaptation of the *Liturgy of St. James* intended for actual use. This was entitled *An Office for the Sacrifice of the Holy Eucharist* and was also published separately in 1748.[12]

It is doubtful if this office was actually used elsewhere than at Craighall but in the opinion of Bishop John Dowden it is to Rattray's work that the Episcopal Churches in Scotland and in the United States of America 'owe the most characteristic features of their respective liturgies'.[13] The most important of these is the order of the prayer of Consecration in which the recital of the history of the institution immediately precedes the oblation which in its turn precedes the invocation of the Holy Spirit upon the elements. This order was followed in an edition of the Communion Office issued in 1755 by Bishop William Falconar and thus in turn served as a model for the Communion Office of 1764 which by the end of the century was generally accepted by the Scottish Episcopalians. It was this rite which was used at the consecration in 1784 of the first bishop of the American Episcopal Church, Samuel Seabury, and which he promised to commend to his brethren in the United States on his return.[14] One of Seabury's successors as Bishop of Connecticut has commented: 'In giving the Consecration Prayer to us Scotland gave us a greater boon than when she gave us the Episcopate.'[15]

The Established Church gave no welcome to these liturgical developments. The General Assembly of 1707 passed an Act against Innovations in the Worship of God and the Presbytery of Edinburgh took action against Greenshields. In 1712 one of the ministers of Brechin, John Willison, published *Queries to the Scots Innovators in Divine Service. . . . Being a Compendious Collection of the Choicest Arguments against the present INNOVATIONS. By a Lover of the Church of Scotland.* In Willison's view, Christ the great King and Lawgiver in His Church has the sole power of appointing the method and manner of His own worship. Willison interprets this to mean that whatever is not contained in Scripture is unlawful and forbidden and so he asks the 'innovators': 'What Warrand have ye then from this Rule for these innovations in Worship, did Christ or his Apostles enjoyn or practise any such?' On this basis his attacks 'Altars, bowing thereto, keeping Saints Days, the sign of the Cross, kneeling at the Sacrament'. Following Act X of the General Assembly of 1690 he opposes the dispensing of the sacraments in private places. Willison is also unhappy at the use of the terms like Sunday (instead of Lord's Day or Sabbath) and Advent Sunday, Epiphany and Easter and pours scorn on the alleged scriptural authority for the rite of Confirmation which he describes as 'one of the Papists bastard Sacraments'.[16]

Willison is even more critical of what is deemed sufficient preparation for Confirmation and admission to Communion. A child of five could repeat the catechism which is provided. 'Ought their doing this be reckoned a sure Mark of their being in a regenerate and pardoned state?' The evidence is rather to the contrary in that many children and others who can repeat the catechism 'shew no liking to Godliness but instead thereof discover most vitious Inclinations and break out into gross sins which are small Evidences of their Regeneration and Forgiveness'. He is also worried by the requirement that every parishioner should communicate at least three times in the year as stated in the rubric at the end of the Office for the Communion. It is not the frequency which concerns him – he was later to plead for greater frequency in communicating – it is the fact that there is no exception of the ignorant or scandalous and no compassion for 'any poor Melancholy, doubting Christian that dare not adventure to this Ordinance so oft or at such precise Times.'[17]

Some time later during his ministry at Dundee, Willison expressed concern about the qualifications the Independents required for Church membership and for admission to the Lord's Supper. They were requiring not only knowledge and a holy life but also definite signs of conversion and spiritual experience. Willison was not one to take lightly the matter of preparation for the Lord's Table but in his *Defence of National Churches . . . against the cavils of Independents*, published in 1729, he feels that bad consequences can result from this kind of discipline. It is a usurpation of God's privilege of judging the hearts of men. There are those who know and profess the Truth but who cannot produce evidences of grace; are they to be excluded from pastoral care and exposed to Satan? There are many gracious people who have doubts but who have a better right to Church membership than those who would thus exclude them.[18]

Willison named no names but John Glas, the former minister of Tealing near Dundee responded forcefully to his pamphlet.[19] Believing that the whole idea of a national Church was sinful, Glas and some of his parishioners had formed their own church on what they believed was a more spiritual New Testament pattern. This led them to adopt what the historian Robert Wodrow calls 'surprising novelties'. Wodrow notes the holy kiss, saying amen, and the use of the Lord's Prayer and he sarcastically expresses surprise that Glas has not thought of giving the Eucharist to infants.[20] Wodrow, however, does not mention the Glasite practice of weekly celebration of the Lord's Supper or the Agape meal which gave them the nickname of 'The Kail Kirk'. This meal was served between the morning service and the afternoon service and was an opportunity for the rich to share with the poor as a sign of brotherly love.[21] The Lord's Supper was observed at the close of the afternoon service each Lord's Day.[22]

Many of Willison's published writings are directed towards a more frequent observance of the Lord's Supper within the Church of Scotland. It is probable that this concern of his dates back to his ministry at Brechin for when he celebrated the sacrament there on 3 August 1707, it was the first observance for fifteen years.[23] His *Sacramental Directory* published in 1716 includes this comment: 'It is not sufficient to commemorate His love once a year; there ought to be a constant and habitual remembering of our Redeemer's death, and this habit must be acquired by frequent and reiterated acts of communicating.'[24]

In this Willison was echoing recommendations of the General Assembly. Act XIX of 1701 recommends to presbyteries to take care that the Lord's Supper be more frequently administered within their bounds and that the number of ministers to serve thereat be restricted so that neighbouring churches be not thereby cast desolate on the Lord's Day. Act VI of 1711 recommends to presbyteries to do what they can to get it so ordered that the sacrament of the Lord's Supper may be administered in their bounds through the several months of the year and not only in the summer season. Act XI of 1712 enjoins all presbyteries to enquire if the Acts appointing more frequent celebration of the sacrament of the Lord's Supper be duly observed by all the brethren. In the case of any minister neglecting to celebrate the sacrament for a whole year the presbytery was to call for an account of the reasons of his omission of 'that great and solemn duty and ordinance'. Twelve years later the General Assembly admits that the Act of 1711 has not had its full effect and re-enacts it. Act VI of 1724 goes on to enjoin kirk sessions and presbyteries to take care that on the Lord's Day upon which the sacrament is to be administered the neighbouring congregations be supplied with a sermon. Ministers are also enjoined to give warning on the preparation day that if any disorders shall be committed on the Lord's Day those guilty will be censured according to the degree of their offence. The General Assembly of 1751 re-enacts Act XI of 1712.

The careful records of Communion seasons in the parish of Kinneff in the Mearns kept by the Rev. James Honyman who was minister there from 1733 to 1780 show both the strengths and the weaknesses of the elaborate arrangements for the observance of the Lord's Supper in eighteenth-century Scotland. Preparations for one such season began on 25 November 1733 when Honyman intimated that he was to begin his examination of the parish. This catechizing continued until 10 February 1734. Apparently the response was not to the minister's liking for on 17 March he began a series of afternoon meetings in the church for catechetical doctrine. On 21 April 1734 he intimated a visitation of the families of the parish and this continued until 21 July. It was not until 25 August that he intimated that the sacrament would be celebrated on 29 September and that he would be preaching sacramental doctrine until then. On 8 September the sacrament was intimated again and notice was given that the minister 'was to go through the parish in order to Distribute Tokens and desired the people of Different towns to attend on several days at their respective places this week for that end'. The distribution of the tokens (which gave admission to the sacramental table) was continued a second week and on Sunday, 22 September, the Fast Day was intimated for the following Wednesday on which day young communicants were 'to discourse with the minister'.

There were two sermons on the Fast Day on which the Preparatory Service on Saturday was announced when young communicants would receive their tokens. Then the kirk session met and the elders were assigned 'their respective posts on this occasion for the more orderly celebration of the Sacrament'. There were again two sermons on the Saturday and the climax was reached on 29 September when it is recorded: 'This Sabbath the Sacrament of the Lord's Supper was orderly and gravely celebrate in this Congregation.' Honyman was assisted by the ministers of Fetteresso and Bervie. After the sacrament there was an afternoon service and at the Thanksgiving on the Monday there were again two sermons.[25]

An account similar to that of the minister of Kinneff is given in *Peter's Letters to His Kinsfolk* by J. G. Lockhart. This purports to be the observations of a young Englishman travelling in Scotland early in the nineteenth century and includes the following description of the actual service of the Lord's Supper:

> Here the sacramental symbols were set forth at the upper extremity of a long table covered with a white cloth, which extended the whole length of the church, from the pulpit to the gate. At the head of this table, around which as many were already seated as it could at once accommodate, the minister of the place took his seat also; after his sermon was concluded and he had read aloud several chapters of the Bible, which are pointed out for this purpose in the Directory of the Scottish Church as containing words suitable to the occasion – words of encouragement to the worthy and of warning to the presumptuous communicant. He then craved a blessing, and having broken pieces of bread, and given of it to those immediately beside him, large loaves, cut into slices were carried around the table and distributed to all who sat at it by two or three of the lay-elders. The cup in like manner was sent round shortly afterwards . . .

Almost in spite of himself Peter is impressed but he is critical of the address given by the minister during the distribution of the bread and wine – 'Silence surely is the only proper accompaniment to so awful a solemnity' – though he concedes the 'noble warmth and tenderness of feeling' of the minister. His account continues:

> After the address was terminated those who had been its immediate objects withdrew and left their seats free for the occupation of another company, and

so in the same manner did company succeed company throughout the whole of the day – minister succeeding minister in the duty of addressing them – which is called in their language serving the tables.

Peter goes on to contrast the scene in the church with the scenes in all the alehouses of the village and in many of the neighbouring fields. He 'was quite scandalized to find such a deal or racketting going on so near the celebration of such a ceremony, regarded and conducted by those engaged in it with a feeling of reverence so profound and exemplary.'[26] Clearly Act VI of 1724 was still honoured as much in the breach as the observance.

An entry in the record of the kirk session of Kinneff for 11 January 1736 recalls an aspect of public worship characteristic of seventeenth- and eighteenth-century Scotland:

George Watson represented to the Session that he had now appeared in sackcloth upon the public place of repentance eight sabbaths, and been rebuked and testified his sorrow for the sin and scandal of adultery and that no body would fee or hire him to work while under Church censure whereby his family was reduced to straits, therefore petitioned for Absolution. The Session agree he may be absolved if the Presbytery thinks proper upon a satisfying appearance next Lord's Day and ordered him to attend the Presbytery for that end this week.

Watson was indeed absolved the following Lord's Day probably in a form not unlike that in the 1567 Order of Excommunication and Public Repentance which is:[27]

In the name and authority of Jesus Christ, I minister of his blessed Evangel, with consent of the whole ministry of the Church absolve thee, N, from the sentence of excommunication, from the sin by thee committed, and from all censures laid against thee for the same before, according to thy repentance; and pronounce thy sin to be loosed in heaven and thee to be received again to the society of Jesus Christ, to his body the Church, to participation of his sacraments and finally to the fruition of all his benefits; in the name of the Father, the Son and the holy Spirit. AMEN.

Despite the fact that the Church courts were debarred by the Toleration Act of 1712 from calling on the civil magistrate to compel attendance or to execute their sentences, public repentance of this kind continued to the end of the eighteenth century as the well-known case of Robert Burns testifies.[28]

When a man under discipline desired Baptism for a child the common rule was to defer the Baptism until the scandal of the parent was removed.[29] Act IV of the General Assembly of 1712 declares that it is the duty of Christian parents to dedicate their children to God in baptism and to covenant for their education in the faith of Christ. No other sponsor is to be taken 'unless the parents be dead, or absent, or grossly ignorant, or under scandal, or contumacious to discipline'. But if either parent should give evidence of repentance, whether father or mother, that parent should be allowed to present the child. Act X of 1690 had again condemned private Baptism 'in any place, or at any time, when the congregation is not orderly called together to wait on the dispensing of the Word' but it is clear that during the eighteenth century the Act was frequently not observed.[30]

A curious feature of Presbyterian worship in this period is that the reading of Scripture was almost completely superseded by 'lecturing'. According to the historian Wodrow, the practice of lecturing could be traced back to the 1630s when some of the ministers of Edinburgh objected to the reading of chapters of Scripture in the course of daily prayers by readers. The six ministers of the city decided to take over this duty themselves, dividing up the week between them. It was agreed that there should be short notes given on the passages of Scripture which were read. This was done for some years but when this duty was found more burdensome than they had expected it ceased to be a daily observance and was first confined to three days and eventually transferred to the forenoon service on the Sabbath.[31] Lecturing was criticized by Robert Baillie on the grounds that 'if all this work be laid on the minister before he preach we fear it put preaching in a more narrow and discreditable roume than we would wish'.[32] Bishop Leighton persuaded the clergy of Dunblane to give up the practice.[33]

The General Assembly of 1694 gave official approval to lecturing but Act IX stipulates that in doing so ministers 'shall in their exercise of lecturing read and open up to the people some large and considerable portion of the Word of God'. Clearly the emphasis was intended to be on the reading of Scripture rather than on the exposition of it but in practice the lecture seems to have become a kind of preliminary sermon. It is significant that Act IX of 1812 commends the action of the Synod of Aberdeen in reviving the practice of reading the Word in the congregation and recommends to all ministers to read at one of the meetings for public worship such portion of the Old or New Testament or of both as they may judge expedient. It is expressly stated, however, that this recommendation shall not supersede the exercise of lecturing.

Another early concern of the General Assembly after the Revolution Settlement was psalmody. Act XI of 1690 recommended to the ministers concerned in the Highlands to dispatch the whole paraphrase of the Irish (i.e. Gaelic) psalms to the press while Act XX of 1694 commanded that this version of the psalms be used in public worship where the preaching and prayers were in Irish. Several revisions of this translation were made during the eighteenth century but it was not until 1826 that a definitive Gaelic Psalter received the full authority of the General Assembly.[34]

The possibility of including other scriptural songs in the worship of the Church was considered by the General Assemblies of 1706, 1707 and 1708 but the project seems to have rested until 1745 when the printing of some pieces of 'Sacred Poesy' was authorized, pending a decision on their suitability for public worship. According to Millar Patrick the collection was too evangelical in tone for the liking of the Moderates and so the matter was remitted year after year.[35] It was not until 1781 that the *Translation and Paraphrases, in verse, of several Passages of Sacred Scripture* appeared and even then the collection received only interim approval by the General Assembly. Other Christian bodies were more adventurous. Spiritual songs were in use among the Glasites and Glas himself composed a paraphrase of Revelation 5 which was sung at the close of the Communion service.[36] In 1794 the Relief Synod agreed to enlarge their psalmody by literal versions of particular portions of Scripture and also by hymns agreeable to the tenor of the Word of God.[37]

The General Assembly also had something to say about the manner of singing psalms. Act VIII of 1746 recommended that in family worship the praises of God should be sung without the intermission of reading each line. Schoolmasters were also to be careful to instruct the youth in singing the common tunes. The practice of 'lining' is said to have been introduced from England shortly after the publication of the revised metrical Psalter in 1650.[38] It grew out of the need to help the illiterate and consisted of the precentor reading or singing one line of a metrical psalm after which the line was sung by the people. Despite the hint given by the General Assembly 'lining' continued throughout the eighteenth century and even today has not entirely died out among Gaelic-speaking congregations.[39] The common tunes were tunes which could be set to any metrical psalm in common metre. There were traditionally only twelve of these but in practice even fewer were in use in many parishes.[40]

There were several unofficial attempts at improving the quality of the music of the Church. The 'Choir Movement' began in the Aberdeenshire parish of Monymusk under the inspiration of the local laird Sir Archibald Grant and under the instruction of an English infantryman, Thomas Channon, who was stationed in Aberdeen. Some members of the Synod of Aberdeen secured the discharge of Channon from the army in 1753 so that he could devote his full time to training choirs and he seems to have made a considerable impact on the singing of the psalms in the north-east, managing to dislodge the practice of 'lining' in many parishes there. The movement spread to the south and was carried forward by men like Cornforth Gibson and Robert Bremner.[41] New psalm tunes were written and others were brought back into use. Andrew Thomson, minister of St. George's, Edinburgh, is said to have composed 178 tunes of which the one named after his church is still in common use.[42] Attempts to improve the quality of praise by employing musical instruments were frustrated by popular opposition. There were those who objected to Channon's use of a pitch-pipe at choir practice[43] and the attempt to introduce a small organ into

St. Andrew's Church, Glasgow, in 1807 failed after considerable judicial proceedings.[44]

There is nothing in the Church of Scotland to compare with the liturgical activity of the Scots Episcopalians. As we have seen, the *Directory for Public Worship* did not have its statutory authority restored in 1690 but Act X of the General Assembly of 1705 'seriously recommends to all ministers and others within the National Church the due observation of the Directory for the Public Worship of God'. Subsequent General Assemblies drew attention to particular requirements of the *Directory*. Act IV of 1709 recommends persons of all ranks to 'forbear bowing and other expressions of civil respect and entertaining one another with discourses while divine worship is performing and holy ordinances are dispensing'. It was not until late in the eighteenth century that most churches were provided with fixed seating.[45] People either stood or brought stools and so there was much more room to move about. When a church was rebuilt, lofts were inserted for the lairds and space was allocated to them according to the value of the land they owned in the parish.[46] It was the custom for the minister on entering the pulpit to bow to the several lairds in order of social precedence who rose to bow in return.[47]

The order of service seems to have followed the lines laid down by the *Directory* except that the lecture superseded the reading of Scripture. A psalm led by the precentor until the minister entered the pulpit was followed by a prayer and a lecture on a passage of Scripture commented on verse by verse; another prayer was followed by the sermon; a prayer after sermon, the singing of a psalm and the benediction concluded the service. The same order was followed in the afternoon with the omission of the lecture. During the interval 'between sermons' those living nearby went home for bread and ale, others went to the inn while others remained in church. Some lairds had a retiring-room built behind their loft where they could be warmed and fed.[48]

The General Assembly of 1736 drew attention to the *Directory*'s requirements regarding preaching. Act VII recommends ministers to 'make it the great scope of their sermons to lead sinners from a covenant of works to a covenant of grace for life and salvation and from sin and self to precious Christ'. The context of this Act is the attempt to conciliate Ebenezer Erskine and his fellow Seceders and the report of a committee for purity of doctrine in the case of the alleged heresy of Professor Archibald Campbell of St. Andrews. The Act is, however, responding to a tendency in sermons to defend the Christian faith against the 'infidelity' of the time by insisting on its useful and improving character.[49] In the course of the century preachers took great pains over the composition of their sermons and discarded the enormous number of 'heads' favoured by their predecessors. Conservatives like Wodrow dismissed this as 'harranging' and complained that without heads the people would retain nothing of the sermon.[50]

It is difficult to know how far the detailed guidance of the *Directory* was followed in the offering of prayer but the lack of a liturgy did not necessarily mean that prayers were lacking in dignity and beauty. When one of the royal chaplains, Dr. Robert Wallace, said prayers at the 1754 election of Scottish representative peers to sit in the House of Lords, an English visitor remarked: 'The liturgy of the Church of Scotland seems to be very beautiful.'[51] It is clear that Wallace's high standard was not always attained but for many it was a matter of pride that the Church of Scotland was not bound by a liturgy. Lecturing to his students at St. Andrews, Principal George Hill commented:

> The Church of Scotland, in adopting a Directory instead of a Liturgy, considers its ministers as men of understanding, of taste, and of sentiment, capable of thinking for themselves, who without being confined to the repetition of a lesson that has been composed for them may be permitted to exercise their talents, with a becoming independence upon Divine aid, in the sacred and important office of leading the devotions of Christian worshippers.[52]

But there was another less sanguine view being expressed at about the same time. In a preface explaining the reason for the publication of *The Scotch Minister's Assistant* that anonymous writer[53] remarks:

> It has often been complained of as a considerable disadvantage, that there are no Forms prescribed by the Church of Scotland for celebrating Marriage, Baptism and the Lord's Supper. Every Clergyman is left to exercise his own talents upon such occasions, with no other assistance than a few general instructions laid down in the Directory annexed to the Confession of Faith.

It was because no attempt had hitherto been made by any minister of the Church of Scotland 'to remedy this obvious inconvenience' that the author hoped that his work would be favourably received by his younger brethren for whose use it was chiefly intended. Forms were provided for marriage services, Baptism and Communion services and for an ordination prayer and family devotions.

The Scotch Minister's Assistant envisaged Communion services not unlike that we have already described. But in 1824 an important change was made in the service at St. John's Church in Glasgow. Instead of the people coming forward to sit at the tables as formerly, the elders distributed the bread and wine to the people who remained seated in pews the desks of which were covered with white linen cloths. This was the commonly accepted method of administration in the Congregational churches in England but it was not unknown in the Church of England. The innovation was roundly condemned by the General Assemblies of 1825 and 1826 and also in various pamphlets and treatises, but general opinion favoured the practice and it gradually spread.[54]

It is remarkable, however, that another book of forms for worship published in 1843 not only assumes that communicants will come forward to the Table for the sacrament but also provides specimen lectures. *The Service of the House of God*, compiled by the Rev. William Liston, minister of Redgorton, is intended chiefly 'to assist the devotion and direct the meditations of those who are necessarily detained from public worship' but is also offered as 'a directory to young clergymen on their first entering their official duties'. But despite its wider intended readership this volume is no more a liturgy than *The Scotch Minister's Assistant*.

It would be idle to claim that the eighteenth century saw great advances in the public worship of the Church of Scotland but to dismiss it as a period of decadence is less than fair.[55] The Episcopal Church exercises an influence well beyond Scotland in liturgical matters and the Glasites show a readiness to adapt their worship in accordance with their understanding of Scripture.

NOTES

1. E.g., John Kerr, *The Renascence of Worship* (Edinburgh, 1909). Charles G. McCrie, 'The Modern Renaissance' in *The Public Worship of Presbyterian Scotland* (Edinburgh and London, 1892), pp. 310–358.
2. A. Ian Dunlop, *William Carstares and the Kirk by Law Established* (Edinburgh, 1967), p.72.
3. *Act Ratifying the Confession of Faith and Settling Presbyterian Church Government*, 1690 cap. 5.
4. A. I. Dunlop, *op. cit.*, pp. 126–127, 130.
5. 10 Annae c.X.
6. F. Goldie, *A Short History of the Episcopal Church in Scotland* (2nd edn.) (Edinburgh, 1976), pp. 41, 45.
7. John Dowden, *The Annotated Scottish Communion Office* (Edinburgh, 1884), p. 56. Alan C. Don, *The Scottish Book of Common Prayer 1929* (London, 1949), p. 21.
8. A. C. Don, *op. cit.*, pp. 35, 37.
9. *Ibid.*, p. 36.
10. *The Communion Office for the use of the Church of Scotland, as far as concerneth the Ministration of that Holy Sacrament*. Authorized by K. Charles I Anno 1636. All the Parts of this Office are ranked in the natural order (Printed in the Year of our Lord 1735).
11. Dowden, *op. cit.*, pp. 72–73; Don, *op. cit.*, pp. 27–28.
12. Don, *op. cit*, pp. 41–44; Dowden, *op. cit.*, pp. 88–93.
13. Dowden, *op. cit.*, p. 93.
14. Dowden, *op. cit.*, pp. 108–117; Don, *op. cit.*, pp. 51–52.
15. *American Church Review* 39 (New York, July 1882), 18.
16. John Willison, *Queries* . . . (n.p. 1712), pp. 15, 17.
17. *Ibid.*, pp. 21, 138.

18. John Willison, *A Defence of National Churches* . . . (Edinburgh, 1729), pp. 148, 162–164.
19. John Glas, *A Further Continuation of Mr. Glas's Narrative* (Edinburgh, 1729).
20. Robert Wodrow, *Correspondence* (Edinburgh, 1843), III, pp. 458–460.
21. John Glas, *Works* (Perth, 1782), III, p. 447. Derek B. Murray, *Social and Religious Origins of Scottish Non-Presbyterian Protestant Dissent* (St. Andrews Ph.D. thesis, 1977), p. 193.
22. John Glas, *Works,* III, p. 441, V, pp. 9–10.
23. David B. Thoms, *The Kirk of Brechin in the Seventeenth Century* (Brechin, 1972), pp. 140–141.
24. John Willison, *A Sacramental Directory* (Edinburgh, 1798), p. 63.
25. *Minutes of the Kirk Session of Kinneff 1733–1748* (S.R.O. CH2/218).
26. John G. Lockhart, *Peter's Letters to his Kinsfolk,* ed. William Ruddick (Edinburgh, 1977), pp. 185–186.
27. *The Book of Common Order of the Church of Scotland,* ed. G. W. Sprott (Edinburgh, 1901), p. 71.
28. For a fuller account see W. D. Maxwell, *A History of Worship in the Church of Scotland* (Oxford, 1955), pp. 145–155.
29. Andrew Edgar, *Old Church Life in Scotland: Second Series* (Paisley and London, 1886), p. 223.
30. W. Mason Inglis, *An Angus Parish in the Eighteenth Century* (Dundee, 1904), p. 134. Andrew Edgar, *op. cit.,* p. 209.
31. Robert Wodrow, *Analecta* (Maitland Club, 1842), II, pp. 290–291, 368.
32. Robert Baillie, *Letters and Journals* (Bannatyne Club, 1841), II, p. 122.
33. George Grub, *An Ecclesiastical History of Scotland* (Edinburgh, 1861), III, pp. 201–205.
34. Thomas Young, *The Metrical Psalms and Paraphrases* (London and Edinburgh, 1909), pp. 122–123.
35. Millar Patrick, *Four Centuries of Scottish Psalmody* (Oxford, 1949), p. 212.
36. S. Pike, *A Plain and Full Account of the Christian Practices Observed by the Church Assembling in St. Martin's-the-Grand, London* (London, 1766), pp. 7–8.
37. Gavin Struthers, *The History of the Relief Church* (Glasgow, 1843), pp. 374–375.
38. W. D. Maxwell, *op. cit.,* p. 110.
39. M. Patrick, *op. cit.,* pp. 129, 141–146, 191.
40. *Ibid.,* pp. 55, 66, 68, 110–111, 123, 144.
41. *Ibid.,* pp. 139, 149–163, 169, 191.
42. C. G. McCrie, *op. cit.,* pp. 318–319.
43. M. Patrick, *op. cit.,* p. 152.

44. C. G. McCrie, *op. cit.*, pp. 315–317.
45. George Hay, *The Architecture of Scottish Post-Reformation Churches 1560–1843* (Oxford, 1957), p. 198.
46. *Minutes of the Kirk Session of Kinneff 1733–48*, pp. 293ff.
47. Henry G. Graham, *The Social Life of Scotland in the Eighteenth Century* (London, 1906), p. 290.
48. *Ibid.*, pp. 290–291. G. Hay, *op. cit.*, p. 53.
49. This is obvious in many of the sermons preached on behalf of the Society in Scotland for Propagating Christian Knowledge and in some Synod sermons.
50. R. Wodrow, *Analecta* II, p. 349, III, pp. 155–156, IV, p. 197.
51. John Ramsay, *Scotland and Scotsmen in the Eighteenth Century* (Edinburgh, 1888), I, p. 240.
52. George Hill, *Theological Institutes* (Edinburgh, 1803), p. 294.
53. The author was Harry Robertson D.D., minister at Kiltearn 1776–1815. John A. Lamb, 'Aids to Public Worship in Scotland 1800–1850', *Records of the Scottish Church History Society* 13 (1958), 171–185.
54. William Hanna, *Memoirs of the Life and Writings of Thomas Chalmers D.D., LL.D.* (Edinburgh and London, 1850), II, pp. 389–393.
55. *Cf.* C. G. McCrie, 'Revolution–Union–Decadence' in *op. cit.*, pp. 241–309.

BIBLIOGRAPHY

Don, A.C., *The Scottish Book of Common Prayer 1929* (London, 1949).
Dowden, J., *The Annotated Scottish Communion Office* (Edinburgh, 1884).
Graham, H. G., *The Social Life of Scotland in the Eighteenth Century* (London, 1906).
Lamb, J. A., 'Aids to Public Worship in Scotland 1800–1850', *Records of the Scottish Church History Society* 13 (1958), 171–185.
Leishman, T., 'The Ritual of the Church of Scotland', *The Church of Scotland Past and Present,* ed. R. H. Story (London, 1890), V, pp. 307–426.
McCrie, C. G., *The Public Worship of Presbyterian Scotland* (Edinburgh and London, 1892).
Schmidt, L. E., *Holy Fairs – Scottish Communions and American Revivals in the Early Modern Period* (Princeton, 1989).
Sefton, H. R., 'Thomas Chalmers and the Lord's Table', *Record of the Church Service Society* 28 (1995), 19–23.

Chapter Six

DISRUPTION TO UNION

Douglas Murray

During the second half of the nineteenth century the worship of the Presbyterian Churches in Scotland changed more than at any time since the seventeenth century. Major changes also took place in other areas of the life of the Church. The Disruption of 1843 resulted in a lessening of the hold of the Established Church over the nation and led to rivalry and bitterness in many communities. The relationship between the Church and the state was reconsidered and the move to disestablish the Church of Scotland, in which the Free Church joined the United Presbyterian Church, did not improve relations between the denominations. Yet it was not always a story of division. The union of the United Presbyterian and Free Churches took place in 1900, and negotiations were started before the First World War which led to the reunion of the two main Presbyterian Churches in 1929.

Significant changes also took place in the realm of theology. There was greater flexibility in theological thought and a growing unease about the position of the *Westminster Confession of Faith*. Earlier in the century John McLeod Campbell had been deposed from the ministry for teaching, in contradiction to the Confession, that Christ died for all people. Campbell linked the atonement to the incarnation and to the sonship of Christ and so gave rise to a dissatisfaction with the theology of the Confession. The place of the Confession was also challenged by developments in biblical criticism which were subject to action in the courts of the Church before their acceptance became general, seen particularly in the Free Church with the trial of Professor Robertson Smith of Aberdeen. The relation of ministers to the Confession of Faith was relaxed in different ways in each of the Presbyterian Churches in this period.

The Church also sought to respond to the changes in Scottish society brought about by increasing industrialization. The population declined in the Highlands and increased dramatically in the Lowlands, especially in the central belt of Scotland. Instead of living in close-knit rural parishes, most Scots people by the turn of the century were living in large urban areas. In response to such developments the pattern of church life was bound to change, and worship was no exception.

The services of worship of the Presbyterian Churches in the middle of the nineteenth century have been described as follows:

> The order of the first service was a psalm, a long prayer, the exposition of a considerable passage of Scripture, then, after a psalm and a shorter prayer, the sermon, a prayer ending with supplications for all conditions of men, a psalm or paraphrase, and benediction. When there was afternoon service it was the same, except that the sermon followed immediately on the first prayer. Standing at prayer and sitting at singing were the invariable attitudes.[1]

One advocate of reform described such worship as 'rudely chaotic',[2] while in the view of another even the published prayers of Scottish ministers were constructed on a wrong plan, or on no plan at all, and were 'often too fine, often too dogmatic, and often in bad taste'.[3] By the end of the period the worship of the reunited Church of Scotland had changed out of all recognition from what had taken place before the Disruption. Sermons were much shorter and were delivered from a script; prayers, too, were read rather than given extempore; organ music had been introduced to accompany congregational praise; hymns as well as psalms were sung; people stood to sing and sat to pray, instead of the other way round; Scripture was read without the lengthy addition of the 'lecture'; services were more structured; the main festivals of the Christian Year were observed in some parishes; Baptism was administered in church rather than in the home; Communion was celebrated more frequently; and service-books were being produced, not only by unofficial societies within the Church, but also by committees of the General Assembly.

Why did such changes take place? One reason was the Disruption itself and the ensuing rivalry between the denominations. The three main Presbyterian Churches were competing with each other and worship was one area which was examined with a view to attracting new members. Significant changes were seen first of all in the Established Church which was forced to regain the ground lost by the Disruption. With the departure of the more thoroughgoing evangelicals into the Free Church, changes in worship were also made somewhat easier. In addition, the move to disestablish the Church of Scotland led to an attempt to strengthen the national Church by making its worship appeal to a broader cross-section of the population.[4]

The improvement of the Church's services was also thought to be necessary because of an increasing secession of the upper classes to the Episcopal Church. The Duke of Argyll was one of the first to draw attention to the need to reform the Church's defective worship in order to stem the movement towards Episcopacy by members of his own class.[5] The secession took place, in his view, not because of any conversion to the principles of Episcopacy but because of the superior attractions of a more ritual worship. Young people of the upper classes were being educated at English public schools and were thus introduced to Anglican worship.[6] Others served in the armed forces where they came under the influence of a more liturgical form of service. For some the Presbyterian marriage services were so inadequate that they turned to the local Episcopal Church to meet that need.[7] Burial services at the grave were also uncommon in the Presbyterian Churches. The Anglican Church featured more prominently in the Scottish consciousness through the increasing contacts which were now possible through rail travel and with the growth of the national press.

Another weighty factor in the movement for reform in worship was the experience of those who lived and worked in the colonies. They were not only exposed to Anglican services but also felt the need for help in conducting worship when a minister was not available. The General Assembly of the Church of Scotland recognized this need by publishing *Prayers for Social and Family Worship* in 1863. One of the leading liturgical scholars and advocates of reform in worship in this period, Dr. George W. Sprott, was born and brought up in Nova Scotia, the son of a Scottish minister, and served in Canada and in Ceylon where he experienced the need for a more ordered worship. 'Our people abroad', he said, 'and the higher classes at home, are all familiar with the decency and good taste of the English liturgy, and they feel uncomfortable and are mortified if these qualities are wanting in the services of their own Church.'[8] Sprott's experience led him to study the history of worship and to become a leading exponent of liturgical change when he returned to Scotland in 1866. It is interesting to note that other Scottish ministers who had felt the need for a renewal in worship had also been ministering outside of Scotland and were thus exposed to other forms of liturgy. John Mason, minister of the Scots Presbyterian Church in New York, published *Letters on Frequent Communion* in 1798, and John Cumming, minister of Crown Court Church in London, brought out a new edition of *Knox's Liturgy* in 1840.[9] In the Preface to his edition, Cumming pointed out that the reformers had not been opposed to a liturgy and said that a recovery of the *Book of Common Order* would lead to great improvements in the worship of the Kirk.

In addition, there were two underlying reasons for the reform of worship, one historical and the other theological. The romantic revival of the nineteenth century, whose greatest exponent was Sir Walter Scott, led to an increased sentimental interest in the past. But there was also a renewal in the study of history and the Church shared in this development. As in the Church of England, with the Library of Anglo-Catholic Theology and the Parker Society, so in Scotland there was a return to the texts of the Church's history. The names principally associated with this study are those of George Sprott and Thomas Leishman. Leishman, the minister of Linton near Kelso, was the son of Dr. Matthew Leishman of Govan, the leader of the Middle Party, those evangelicals who did not 'go out' at the Disruption but stayed within the Established Church. Sprott's experience in the colonies led him, not to seek to imitate Episcopal practices, but to renew Presbyterian worship in harmony with its own traditions:

> When we are first become sensible of the defects in our own services, we are very apt to think the Church of England a model to imitate; but a further acquaintance with Christian antiquity, and with our own historical traditions and associations, has led me at least to think far otherwise. What we should look to as our model – in so far as we look to the models of later times at all – is the Reformed Church of which our own forms a part.[10]

Shortly after Sprott's return to Scotland, he and Leishman published a new edition of the *Book of Common Order* and of the *Westminster Directory for Public Worship* in 1868. Sprott also brought out an edition of other liturgies which had been contemplated in Scotland in the early seventeenth century.[11]

Sprott and Leishman concentrated upon the period immediately after the Reformation, before what they considered to be the 'baneful influence' of the English sectaries was felt in Scotland. They were able to show that such practices as the saying of the Apostles' Creed,[12] the use of the Lord's Prayer,[13] and the singing of the doxology after the psalms,[14] were features of reformed worship. They also showed that the *Book of Common Order* favoured the monthly celebration of Holy Communion and that the *Westminster Directory* had thought that Communion should be celebrated 'frequently'.[15] In particular they noted that the order of worship in the *Book of Common Order* was based upon the Lord's Supper as the norm even when it was not celebrated.[16] The prayers of intercession, for example, came after the sermon:

> It is in accordance with the usage of the first Christian ages, when the instruction rose out of the Scripture for the day, and the prayers for the body of the faithful, with the Creed and the Lord's Prayer, were part of the Communion Service with which the worship of every Lord's Day closed.

The ordinary service was thus kept in harmony with that of a Communion Sunday and was 'a testimony, as Calvin meant it to be, for the Lord's Supper as part of the complete service of the House of God'.[17]

The other underlying reason for the reform of worship was theological. Sprott and Leishman advocated the centrality of the Lord's Supper in worship, not just because the reformers based the usual Sunday service upon its celebration, but because of the theology of worship and the sacraments held by the reformers. The Scots reformers rejected the view that the sacraments are 'naked and bare signs', an outlook frequently but misleadingly associated with that of Zwingli, and affirmed the view of Calvin that they are means of grace. Yet it was commonly held that the true Presbyterian position was the former rather than the latter view. The popular conception of the sacraments was illustrated by the East Church Case in Aberdeen in 1882–83. A petition was brought against the minister, Dr. James Cooper, by eleven members of his kirk session who complained, among other things, about his 'novel and alien' preaching and practice in relation to the sacraments. Cooper was able to show that his doctrinal position was based upon the teaching of the *Scots Confession* and the *Westminster Confession*, and that it was the views of the elders, who held that the sacraments were nothing more than empty signs, which were at variance from the standards of the Church.[18] Even more important, in Sprott's view, was the consideration that the doctrine of the sacraments in the *Scots Confession* depended upon the doctrine of union with Christ by the Holy Spirit. In this view worship is a participation in the one offering of Christ to the Father. It was from this doctrinal position that Sprott and Leishman sought to reform the worship of the Kirk. They were 'high' churchmen, concerned with the place of doctrine in the life of the Church, and they reacted against what they considered to be a lack of concern for doctrinal principles by those who were called 'broad' churchmen.

The period in the Church of Scotland after the Disruption had been marked by moderation in doctrinal matters. A generation had grown up who were too young to have taken part in the Disruption but who had seen the bitter atmosphere which a stand on principle had engendered.[19] They came to suspect what they considered to be doctrine carried to extremes which had shattered Scottish church life as they knew it. They were tired of strife and wished to avoid controversy. Such 'broad' churchmen wished the national Church to tolerate a wide variety of opinions within its ranks, and were thus in favour of including different types of worship and of improving church services to appeal to a wider cross-section of the population. The pioneer of worship reform in Scotland, Dr. Robert Lee, the minister of Greyfriars in Edinburgh, approached the subject from the broad church position.

Lee was concerned that the Kirk was losing its character as a national Church, and was in danger of disestablishment. He was also exercised by the increasing number of secessions to the Episcopal Church because of the unsatisfactory nature of Presbyterian worship. But above all these considerations, Lee thought that the worship of the Church was in need of reform. Prayers tended to be too long, incoherent, repetitive, didactic and sermonizing in character. Worship, he said, should be distinguished by 'good taste, decency, propriety and solemnity, as well as by purity in doctrine and fervour of devotion'.[20] Worship for Lee had three elements, Word, Prayer and Praise, and a service was therefore to be constructed with these three elements in that order. A service should thus start with a scripture sentence, followed by a prayer and then by an item of praise. There then would follow another two sections, each starting with a scripture reading, and then the final section would start with the sermon, followed by prayer and praise. It will be seen from this order that Lee, in the words of his biographer,[21] 'lacked something of that tender reverence for Catholic usage' which characterizes the true liturgist. Nevertheless it was Lee, and not a liturgist of catholic tastes, who risked making the changes in worship which he considered to be necessary for the good of the Kirk. He went ahead with his innovations without consulting the presbytery, believing that some of the changes were sanctioned by the *Westminster Directory* while others were not forbidden by the law of the Church.

Lee took the opportunity of the reopening of Old Greyfriars in 1857 after a fire to make his changes. He invited the congregation to kneel for prayer and stand to sing and he read the prayers from a printed book which he had written. A later innovation was the use of a harmonium to accompany the praise in 1863. According to Leishman, the only change which could be described as an innovation was standing to sing. It was the one practice which he doubted had ever been prevalent in Scotland.[22]

The storm of controversy soon broke. Overtures against innovations in worship came before the General Assembly in 1858. The Assembly responded by enjoining presbyteries to secure uniformity and prevent divisions in the Church. In February 1859, Edinburgh Presbytery called Lee to task and condemned his order of service, apart from the postures for singing and for prayer. When Lee appealed to the Assembly, however, he was vindicated on all points except that of reading the prayers from a printed book. The opponents of liturgical change did not give up so easily. A committee of Assembly was set up in 1863 to consider innovations in worship and its report in the following year received a divided reaction from the Assembly, indicating a change in the thinking of the Kirk. A motion against the use of instrumental music and read prayers had to be withdrawn for lack of support, and a motion explicitly condemning Lee was defeated. The Assembly instead expressed a determination, when necessary, to enforce the law against innovations, and called on ministers to ensure that worship was conducted 'decently and in order'.[23]

In the following year, however, Dr. W. R. Pirie of Dyce, one of the principal opponents of Lee's practices who had been silenced at the previous Assembly because he occupied the Moderator's chair, succeeded in passing an Act which declared that the regulation of worship in parishes was to rest with the presbyteries of the Church.[24] Lee opposed the 'Pirie Act' maintaining that presbyteries could only decide on the basis of the law of the Church and that innovations should be left alone unless the peace of congregations was disturbed.[25] In effect the 'Pirie Act' was, in the words of Lee's biographer, 'a step considerably in advance of any that has been taken by preceding Assemblies in the way of facilitating the safe and orderly introduction of such changes in our usages of worship . . . provided that these changes be not inconsistent with any *express law* of the Church'.[26] Intended as an absolute check to progress in worship reform, the Act became instead an 'awkwardly worded charter of liberty beyond which the Church did not find it necessary to advance'.[27] Presbyteries did not always take action and they also varied in the judgements they pronounced.

Lee himself was to suffer further persecution in the courts of the Church since in December, 1865, he departed from custom and conducted a marriage service in church with read prayers, sung Amens, and a *Te Deum* to a Gregorian chant. The case, however, was indefinitely postponed in 1867 when Lee was paralysed as the result of a riding accident the day before he was due to defend himself at the bar of the Assembly. He died in the following year, no doubt imagining that the forces of reaction had prevailed. He was unable to see just how much the worship of Presbyterian Scotland would change during the remainder of the century.

An example of the way in which the attitude of the Kirk to worship was to change under the operation of the 'Pirie Act' is seen in the ministry of Dr. John Macleod at Duns and at Govan. After Macleod left Duns to take up his ministry at Govan in 1875, several of the practices which he had introduced were forbidden by the Presbytery of Duns as a result of a petition from over a hundred members of the congregation. The case came finally to the Assembly of 1876 which upheld the judgement of the lower court.[28] The congregation at Duns was forbidden to use certain symbols in the church building – the letters 'IHS' appeared on the cloth of the communion table and there was a cross on the cover of the baptismal font. They were also forbidden to hold 'any of the Roman Catholic or Episcopal Feast or Festival Days'. Macleod had held services on Christmas Day, Good Friday, Ascension Day and Pentecost. Macleod had also introduced the monthly celebration of Communion, whereas before it had been quarterly, and had abolished the twice yearly Fast Days which were held all over Scotland prior to Communion Sundays. The congregation were instructed that Communion should revert to the quarterly celebration and that Fast Days should be held. Finally, the congregation were told to stand for the benediction instead of kneeling as had become the practice during Macleod's ministry. On going to Govan, however, Macleod proceeded to introduce most of these practices and to change the services in other ways. None of his 'innovations' were forbidden by the Presbytery of Glasgow. A petition was presented in 1884 complaining of the irregular dispensation of Communion and the holding of special services during Easter Week, but it was dismissed by the presbytery. The judgement in the Duns Case thus did not represent the changing mood of the Kirk and was one of the last attempts by those opposed to liturgical change to stem the tide of reform. Writing about the case in 1904, James Cooper thought that, although it had been regarded at the time as a calamity by those in favour of reform, everyone now looked back on it as a 'mere absurdity'.[29]

There were, however, limits to what the Kirk would permit in terms of liturgical change. In 1903 the Assembly decided that Thomas Adamson, minister of St. Margaret's Church, Barnhill, Broughty Ferry, had exceeded what was permissible in the conduct of public worship. Adamson, a disciple of James Cooper, had gone much further in the area of ritual than his mentor, and Cooper and other high churchmen could not defend many of his practices on the floor of the Assembly. Adamson was thus not typical of the high church outlook or of the liturgical movement as a whole. The Assembly instructed Adamson to remove items such as a cross, candlesticks, and frontals, which gave the communion table the appearance of an 'altar', not to celebrate Communion with his back to the congregation but facing them from behind the table, and to discontinue using the *First Prayer Book of Edward VI* which included the 'Canon of the Mass'. The Assembly, however, made no judgement concerning Adamson's doctrine of Holy Communion and commended the more frequent celebration which he had introduced.[30]

One of the principal agencies for change in the Church of Scotland was the Church Service Society, founded in 1865 'to study the liturgies – ancient and modern – of the Christian Church, with a view to the preparation and publication of forms of Prayer for Public Worship, and services for the Administration of the Sacraments, the Celebration of Marriage, the Burial of the Dead, etc.' Although the formation of the Society owed much to the stimulus provided by Robert Lee, it was started by men whose interest lay in recovering the catholic tradition of the Church. Sprott had suggested the founding of such a society when still in exile in Ceylon, but it was left to three men to take the initiative: R. H. Story, then minister of Rosneath and later Professor of Ecclesiastical History and Principal of the University of Glasgow, J. Cameron Lees, minister of Paisley Abbey and later of St. Giles' Cathedral, and George Campbell, minister of Eastwood. Lee became a Vice-President of the Society after some hesitation.

The main way in which the Society carried out its work was by the publication of the service-book *Euchologion*, the first edition of which appeared in 1867. Seven editions were published in the following thirty years. The first edition consisted of two parts, the first of which contained orders for the administration of the sacraments, and the conduct of marriage and funeral services. The second part contained a lectionary and 'Material for the construction of a service for public worship on the Lord's Day', the material being arranged in fourteen sections ranging from scripture sentences and introductory prayers to collects, canticles and benedictions. The order for Communion followed the existing Scottish usage as far as possible but the language and some of its elements, such as the Apostles' Creed and the *Sanctus*, would be unfamiliar to most Presbyterian worshippers.

Material for *Euchologion* was gathered from a variety of sources, from the Kirk's own traditions, from Calvin and Knox, but also from

Eastern and Roman liturgies and from the *Liturgy and Divine Office* of the Catholic Apostolic Church. In the Preface the compilers denied that they wished to impose a liturgy upon the Church of Scotland. There were, they said, differences of opinion within the Society itself over whether a liturgy was desirable. If a liturgy were introduced into a Church which did not have a liturgical tradition it would have to be carried out slowly through the official channels of the church and not by an unofficial society. The Society had therefore set itself the task of preparing and collecting forms of prayer which could be fitted into the existing order of service. Members of the Society, it was said, enjoyed the privilege of free prayer, but 'free' prayer did not mean that the minister led devotions 'according to his own ideas or fancy, or as his spirit may be moved to pray'; he is at liberty to use whatever in the devotion of the whole Church is most suitable to his congregation's need. What many worship reformers favoured was a combination of free and liturgical prayer.

Not only were differing viewpoints over liturgy represented within the membership of the Society, there were different theological emphases as well. From the start, it was said, there were two parties struggling together in the 'womb' of the Society, the broad church party and the high church party. They differed over the place of doctrine in worship.[31] The broad church position was most fully stated in a 'Manifesto' submitted to the committee in 1888 by one hundred and forty-six members. These members thought that the services in *Euchologion* were 'too doctrinal in tone and expression'. The prayers of confession were 'statements of belief rather than of experience' while the prayers of intercession were too church centred and were not related sufficiently to the world and its needs. The world was treated as evil rather than as having potential for good. As a result of the 'Manifesto' a group of broad churchmen was given responsibility for preparing the morning and evening services for the fifth Sunday of the month in the sixth edition of *Euchologion* published in 1890.

The high churchmen took the opposite view as to the place of doctrine in worship. Dr. George Campbell, one of the founders of the Society, thought that their aims should be the 'preserving and presenting in a form of sound words the great doctrines and verities' of the faith. Unlike the 'Broad Church Manifesto' which minimized the difference between the Church and the world, Professor William Milligan of Aberdeen thought that the Church had a common life 'higher than the world's' and spoke of the Church as a 'distinct society'. The higher life of the Church is centred upon the continuing ministry of Christ in heaven as high priest, to whom the Church is united by the Holy Spirit.[32] Milligan did not wish to encourage sacerdotalism. The Church and its ministers were not priests in their own right but only by sharing in the one priesthood of Christ to the Father. It followed from Milligan's view that the sacrament of the Lord's Supper should have the central place in worship since it is there that the one offering of Christ is most fully set forth. In the Lord's Supper there is recalled, not just the death of Christ, but his continuing heavenly life. The sacrament should therefore be celebrated weekly as the main service of the Lord's Day.

Following from their view of the place of the Lord's Supper, high churchmen were to disagree with others in the Society over the order of service in *Euchologion*. The controversy arose, as did the doctrinal disagreement, over the revision for the sixth edition of the service-book. The order which had been used in the first five editions was based on the pattern for the celebration of the Lord's Supper, with the prayers of thanksgiving and intercession and the Lord's Prayer coming after the sermon. At a meeting of the Editorial Committee in 1888, however, it was decided that the Lord's Prayer should come after the first prayer and the prayers of thanksgiving and intercession before the sermon. Sprott dissented from this decision, his reason being 'besides the departure from Primitive and Reformed usage . . . that the order of the Communion which is the normal service of the Church should be followed as closely as possible at other times'. As W. D. Maxwell pointed out, this change in the order of service corresponded to the order of Anglican Matins where the sermon comes at the end of the service.[33] High churchmen were thus not among those who wished the services of the Kirk to be influenced by such Anglican patterns. James Cooper remarked that he had often been in disagreement with Dr. Donald MacLeod of the Park Church in Glasgow who had wanted to make the services in *Euchologion* more Anglican.[34]

After the disagreements over the place of doctrine in worship and over the place of Holy Communion, many of the high churchmen in the Society came to the conclusion that there was a need for another society in the Church of Scotland. They wished to emphasize the principles underlying worship, but such a task was beyond the scope of the Church Service Society. Dr. H. J. Wotherspoon of St. Oswald's in Edinburgh was concerned with the haphazard way in which many of the changes in worship had been introduced, without regard for doctrinal considerations.[35] William Milligan said that tasteful arrangements, music, flowers, pictures, embroidery and carved wood, and all that is included in an 'attractive service' may be good when they are expressions of great realities, but they could not occupy the place of the Gospel of God.[36] As a result a group of high churchmen founded the Scottish Church Society in 1892 'to defend and advance Catholic doctrine'. They continued to be members and office-bearers of the Church Service Society and were anxious to avoid any antagonism between the two societies. The Scottish Church Society had a different purpose from the other, more senior, society, for it was concerned primarily with doctrine, and while the doctrinal basis of worship was one of its main interests, it was also concerned with a wider range of church life and activity.

In spite of the disagreements which had arisen within its ranks, the Church Service Society could claim to have fulfilled a valuable function within the Kirk. By the turn of the century about a third of the clergy were members of the Society and over 10,000 copies of the various editions of *Euchologion* had been sold. The service-book had prepared the way for official publications to be produced by the General Assembly itself.

Societies similar to the Church Service Society were formed in the other two main Presbyterian Churches. The United Pesbyterian Devotional Service Association was founded in 1882 'to promote the edifying conduct of the Devotional Services of the Church' by the study of the history and literature of public worship and the practice of other denominations. Dr. Andrew Henderson of Paisley was the first President and Dr. William Dickie, then of Perth and later of Dowanhill, was elected the Secretary. Occasional Papers were published containing draft forms of various services and in 1891 these were collected and published as *Presbyterian Forms of Service*. The services in this book were offered as examples of the way in which worship might be conducted in the United Presbyterian Church. The first edition of four hundred copies was sold out quickly and further editions followed in 1892 and 1894.

The Free Church followed in 1891 with the formation of the Public Worship Association, the object of which was 'to promote the ends of edification, order and reverence in the public services of the Church in accordance with scriptural principles, and in the light especially of the experience and practice of the Reformed Churches holding the Presbyterian system'. The leaders of the Society included such prominent ministers as Dr. D. D. Bannerman of St. Leonard's, Perth, Professor A. B. Bruce of Glasgow and Professor W. G. Blaikie of Edinburgh. From the start the Society shaped its work with a view to the likely union of the Free Church with one or both of the other main Presbyterian Churches in Scotland. It was thought that a result of reunion would be a revision by the united Church of the *Book of Common Order* and the *Westminster Directory*. The Association aimed to prepare its members to take a useful part in the ultimate readjustment and improvement of Presbyterian worship. Papers were issued annually for private circulation among the members and in 1898 *A New Directory for the Public Worship of God* was published. Specimen forms were given for certain parts of the ordinary services, and fuller forms for special occasions, but the main part of the book was devoted to materials and suggestions 'which, while not repressing or hampering free prayer, should serve to guide or stimulate it'.

Contact between the United Presbyterian and Free Church Societies had taken place before the Union of 1900 and immediately afterwards the two bodies joined to form the Church Worship Association of the United Free Church. Various publications were produced including a book of *Services for Children* and an *Anthology of Prayers for Public Worship*. A service-book entitled *Directory and Forms for Public Worship* was published in 1909 as an attempt to combine the methods used by the previous books on both sides of the united Church. In 1923, when it was being discussed whether a new edition of the *Directory* should be produced, Dr. Millar Patrick, the authority on Scottish psalmody, persuaded the members of the Association to approach the General Assembly to authorize the preparation of an official *Book of Common Order*. Patrick presented the case to the Assembly and the project was approved. A committee was appointed and in due course the *Book of Common Order 1928* was authorized by the Assembly as the official manual of public worship. Apart from any merits or demerits of the book in Patrick's view, it accomplished two things.[37] It reconciled the United Free Church to the practice of having an authorized book for the Church's worship, and it prepared the way for having set up from the start in the united Church a standing committee of the Assembly charged with the oversight of 'Public Worship and Aids to Devotion'.

Another society with an interest in worship was the Aberdeen Ecclesiological Society, formed in 1886 mainly through the efforts of James Cooper. It was different from any of the other societies in that it was inter-denominational and was particularly concerned with church buildings. Monthly meetings were held, papers were read and discussed, and the annual *Transactions* of the Society were published. The Glasgow Ecclesiological Society was founded in 1893 and the two combined to form the Scottish Ecclesiological Society in 1903. Its objects were the study of the 'Principles of Christian Worship and of Church Architecture and its allied Arts, which are the handmaids of devotion', and the 'diffusion throughout Scotland of sound views, and a truer taste in such matters'. Cooper did not wish the Ecclesiological Society to be merely a gathering of antiquarians. Its object, he said, was to gain inspiration from the study of ancient buildings to help provide for the religious needs of the day.[38]

Much was achieved by the societies in providing published material to help ministers lead public worship, and in stimulating thought and action. Other changes in worship, however, became generally accepted by the Churches. Hymnals were published in all three of the main Presbyterian denominations. The need for a wider selection of praise than that offered by the Metrical Psalter had led to the publication of the Paraphrases as early as 1781. The Relief Church was the first to publish a hymn book in 1794, and after the union with the United Secession Church in 1847, the *United Presbyterian Hymn Book* was published in 1852. Needless to say, the compilers had to draw most of their material from sources outside of Scotland, and the book depended largely on English hymn writers such as Isaac Watts and John Wesley. Another book, *The Presbyterian Hymnal*, was published in 1876. After considering the matter for several years, the General Assembly of the Church of Scotland approved a hymn book. It was received with such little enthusiasm, however, that another improved version was published in 1870 entitled *The Scottish Hymnal*.

Most opposition to the introduction of hymns was found in the Free Church and was led by Dr. James Begg of Liberton who was closely associated with the founding of the Scottish Reformation Society and the Protestant Institute of Scotland. Begg fought against any tendency which seemed to lessen the hold of the Calvinism of the *Westminster Confession* upon the Free Church. He held firmly to the principles of the Disruption and regarded the demand for hymns as one of the most dangerous symptoms of the times. Certainly the increasing use of hymns showed that his own doctrinal standpoint was on the decline. The move away from Calvinist orthodoxy was seen particularly in the impact made by the American evangelists Moody and Sankey in 1874 and in the welcome given to *Sacred Songs and Solos*. Their campaign marked a change from the intellectual approach based upon the doctrinal orthodoxy of the Westminster standards to a more emotional approach based upon evangelical experience. The use of hymns showed the need of many Scottish worshippers to express their personal faith and to sing about such matters as the cross, the resurrection, and the Holy Spirit. Begg resisted the various moves to authorize the use of hymns but without success. A book containing hymns was eventually approved in 1873, and in 1882 a larger volume entitled *The Free Church Hymnbook* was published. All three main Presbyterian Churches had now approved the use of hymns, but it was not until 1898 that a joint hymnal was published. *The Church Hymnary* was the precursor of the *Revised Church Hymnary* of 1928, published just before the union of the Churches.

The introduction of organs to accompany praise took slightly longer. Early attempts to use organs at St. Andrew's Church in Glasgow and at Roxburgh Place Relief Church in Edinburgh were unsuccessful. Several organs were introduced in Evangelical Union and Congregational Churches in the early 1850s and, as has been seen, it was Robert Lee who led the way in the Established Church with the use of a harmonium at Greyfriars in 1863. The effect of the 'Pirie Act' of 1865 was to license the introduction of organs in Church of Scotland congregations, subject to the supervision of the presbytery concerned. By the following Assembly eighteen organs had been installed, and by the end of 1867 at least thirty-one organs were in use.[39] The ban on the use of organs in the United Presbyterian Church was removed in 1872. No doubt the playing of Sankey during the campaign of 1874 had helped to reconcile many Scots Presbyterians to the use of instrumental music in worship. The Free Church Assembly of 1882 received two petitions from congregations wishing to use organs, and seven overtures on the subject, five in favour and two against the change. A committee was set up which reported in 1883. Its findings were not unanimous, but a majority was in favour of giving liberty to congregations and after a lengthy debate this motion was carried by 390 votes to 259. From being absolutely prohibited, the organ soon became the most prominent feature of many Scottish Presbyterian Churches. Thomas Leishman considered the use of instrumental music to be an innovation but a welcome one.[40] On the other hand, H. J. Wotherspoon could speak of the organ as a piece of machinery set up 'like a Dagon in the sanctuary, that we may worship towards it'.[41] Clearly not all were in favour and it was not only the conservative Calvinists of the Free Church who had reservations.

Another development which took place gradually in this period was the observance of the main festivals of the Christian Year. Leishman considered that the evidence against their observance at the Reformation was not of a uniform character. He thought that Christmas and Easter were not to be kept in the post-Reformation Church because of the superstition which had become attached to worshipping at these time of year and that the main festivals could be observed when they were no longer connected with such superstition.[42] The Church, he said, should allow liberty for their observance without enforcing them. It could not, in any case, forbid ministers from mentioning the incarnation, resurrection and ascension of Christ on certain Sundays of the year. Four ministers in the Established Church held Christmas services in 1873: Dr. A Watson of St. Mary's in Dundee, Dr. A. K. H. Boyd in St. Andrews, Dr. Archibald Scott at Greenside and Dr. John McMurtrie at St. Bernard's in Edinburgh.[43] James Cooper was to follow a year later with a Christmas Day service at St. Stephen's, Broughty Ferry. In 1878 Cooper held Holy Week services at St. Stephen's, the first such services to be held in a Presbyterian church in Scotland in the nineteenth century. Indicative of the general acceptance of the practice, the General Assembly of the Church of Scotland received favourably an overture advocating the observance of the more important festivals of the Christian Year not long before the Union of 1929.[44]

The conduct of marriage and funeral services also changed quite considerably. By the middle of the nineteenth century it had become the custom that marriages would be solemnized at home or in the hotel where the reception was to be held. Services in church came to be more popular. Sprott pointed out that it was the practice in the period after the Reformation for weddings to be held in church, yet it was regarded as an unheard of innovation.[45] It was also important in his view that there should be a form of marriage service authorized by the Church so that members of the higher classes would cease going to the Episcopal Church for marriage rites. Sprott also wished there to be a proper funeral service to replace the usual Scottish funeral which was characterized by 'smoking and drinking'.[46] The customary ceremonies with whisky and biscuits to which Sprott objected were themselves an improvement on what had gone before when there was no service at all. They had developed from the practice of 'coffining' the body in a linen or woollen shroud for which an elder had to be present. In course of time the minister was invited and said grace before refreshments were served to the mourners. The grace developed into a prayer and the prayer into a short service with readings and an address. Thus the traditional service in the house before the burial developed. Funeral services in church, with hymns, readings and prayers, were still uncommon.

The use of service-books such as *Euchologion* led to a more orderly celebration of the sacraments. Baptism came to be administered in church rather than in the home, although it might still not be during the main service of public worship. Leishman considered that one effect of the practice of private Baptisms was that congregations no longer received teaching on the subject of this sacrament.[47] John Macleod, one of the leading critics of the practice of private Baptism, generally administered the sacrament at Govan in the church, but the Baptism took place after the morning service was over. James Cooper, as is evident from the diaries of his Aberdeen ministry, still administered a large number of Baptisms in private houses.

The celebration of Holy Communion changed in several important ways in this period. The practice of the congregation receiving the elements in the pews gradually replaced the old Scottish custom of going forward to take Communion seated round the table. The new practice had begun before the Disruption, the General Assembly failing to enforce the law of the Church and allowing several Glasgow congregations to receive Communion in the pews. It is interesting to note that high churchmen wished to see a return to the older method of different sittings round the table. James F. Leishman, who succeeded his father as minister of Linton, celebrated Communion in this way, a long table being set up in the restored chancel of the church.[48]

The traditional 'fencing' of the tables by the minister began to disappear in the 1860s and was modified, as in *Euchologion*, with a short exhortation before the Communion. Session disciplining became less severe and inquisitorial, and tokens were replaced by cards. The series of preparatory and thanksgiving services held over a weekend were being curtailed by the end of the century and Fast Days, which had degenerated into public holidays, began to disappear. R. H. Story moved the abolition of Fast Days at the Assembly in 1867. His congregation at Rosneath knew at first hand the undesirable effects of day trippers from Glasgow and Greenock spending the day in their parish. No final decision was taken by the Assembly but the practice gradually died out.

Two other innovations raised controversy, the use of unfermented wine and the use of individual cups. The growing temperance movement mobilized opinion within the Churches on the use of fermented wine at

Communion. The controversy first arose in the United Presbyterian Church and in 1876 several elders who had refused to partake of fermented wine or serve it to the people were deposed by the Synod. After a heated public debate the permissive use of unfermented wine came to be accepted in all three main Presbyterian Churches. Individual cups, too, came to have a permissive use. Research in bacteriology and public hygiene contributed to an uneasiness about the use of the common cup among a large body of opinion within the Churches, although the medical profession was divided on the question. In the Established Church, the Presbytery of Glasgow asked the Assembly for a ruling on the subject in 1907 and a committee was set up to study the issue. The majority of the committee wished to leave the use of individual cups to the discretion of ministers provided the harmony of their congregations was preserved. A minority report, however, argued that the innovation was against the law of the Church and that the danger to health had not been proved. The Assembly decided on a compromise between the two reports, that while they saw no sufficient reason for departing from the ancient and universal practice of the Church, they did not feel justified in forbidding the use of individual cups, although they regretted the introduction of a practice 'so novel and in many respects undesirable'.[49] The peace and harmony of congregations was not to be disturbed over the issue, and those who desired it were always to have provision for partaking 'in the manner heretofore in use'.

The frequency of Communion was increased, especially in urban areas where the twice yearly celebration gave way to a quarterly celebration. In rural areas and in the Highlands a twice or even once yearly celebration remained the norm. Even in the mid-twentieth century nearly half the congregations of the reunited Church of Scotland still celebrated Communion twice a year.[50] The first kirk session to institute a weekly Communion was not in one of the large city centre congregations but in Coatdyke Parish Church in Coatbridge in 1906 under the ministry of the formidable high churchman and temperance reformer, James Cromarty Smith. The celebration took place every Sunday at 8.30 a.m. and cards were not issued. Although Communion was celebrated weekly it did not become the main service of the Lord's Day, and the frequency of the main 'card' Communions remained at five times a year. A quite different pattern was followed by John Macleod who instituted a monthly Communion at Govan which was part of the main service.

By the time of the Union of 1929 the public worship of the Presbyterian Churches in Scotland had changed considerably from what had been customary at the time of the Disruption. But although the first meeting of the General Assembly of the reunited Church was marked by a celebration of Communion in St. Giles' on the day after the historic Act of Union, the Church of Scotland was still a long way from making the sacrament of the Lord's Supper the principal service of the Lord's Day.

NOTES

1. Thomas Leishman, 'The Ritual of the Church', in R. H. Story, ed., *The Church of Scotland, Past and Present* (London, 1890), V, p. 421.
2. R. H. Story, *The Life and Remains of Robert Lee* (London, 1870), I, p. 328.
3. G. W. Sprott, *The Worship, Rites, and Ceremonies of the Church of Scotland* (Edinburgh, 1863), p. 19.
4. Robert Lee, *The Reform of the Church of Scotland* (Edinburgh, 1866), pp. 36ff.
5. The Duke of Argyll, *Presbytery Examined* (London, 1848), pp. 302–303.
6. John Kerr, *The Renascence of Worship* (Edinburgh, 1909), pp. 143, 163.
7. *Ibid.*, p. 125.
8. Sprott, *Worship, Rites, and Ceremonies*, p. 19; *cf.* p. 49.
9. J. A. Lamb, 'Aids to Public Worship in Scotland, 1800–1850' *Records of the Scottish History Society* 13 (1957–59), 174–176. *Cf.* R. Buick Knox, 'Dr. John Cumming and Crown Court Church, London', *Records of the Scottish Church History Society* 22 (1986), 69–71.
10. Sprott, *Worship, Rites and Ceremonies*, p. 2.
11. G. W. Sprott, ed., *Scottish Liturgies of the Reign of James VI* (Edinburgh, 1871).
12. G. W. Sprott and Thomas Leishman, eds., *The Book of Common Order of the Church of Scotland, commonly known as John Knox's Liturgy, and The Directory for the Public Worship of God, agreed upon by the Assembly of Divines at Westminster* (Edinburgh, 1868), pp. xxxiii–xxxiv, 90. *Cf.* William McMillan, *The Worship of the Scottish Reformed Church, 1550–1638* (London, 1931), p. 114.
13. Sprott and Leishman, *op. cit.*, pp. xxxiii–xxxiv, 89. *Cf.* McMillan, *op. cit.*, p. 114.
14. Sprott and Leishman, *op. cit.*, p. xxxiii; G. W. Sprott, *The Worship and Offices of the Church of Scotland* (Edinburgh, 1882), p. 34. *Cf.* McMillan, *op. cit.*, p. 89.
15. Sprott and Leishman, *op. cit.*, pp. 121, 308.
16. Sprott, *Worship and Offices*, p. 15; Leishman, 'Ritual', p. 335.
17. Sprott, *Worship and Offices*, p. 15. *Cf.* McMillan, *op. cit.*, p. 117.
18. Douglas M. Murray, 'James Cooper and the East Church Case at Aberdeen, 1882–83: The High Church Movement Vindicated', *Records of the Scottish Church History Society* 19 (1977), 217–233.
19. H. J. Wotherspoon, *James Cooper: A Memoir* (London, 1926), p. 110.

20. Lee, *Reform of the Church of Scotland*, p. 45.
21. Story, *Life and Remains of Robert Lee*, I, p. 331.
22. Leishman, 'Ritual', p. 424.
23. *Acts of the General Assembly of the Church of Scotland*, 1864, pp. 52–53.
24. *Acts of the General Assembly of the Church of Scotland*, 1865, pp. 46, 48.
25. Story, *Life and Remains of Robert Lee*, II, pp. 160, 167.
26. *Ibid.*, II, p. 225.
27. J. R. Fleming, *A History of the Church in Scotland, 1843–1874* (Edinburgh, 1927), p. 204.
28. *Acts of the General Assembly of the Church of Scotland*, 1876, pp. 56–57.
29. James Cooper, *The Christian's Love for the House of God*, The Macleod Memorial Lecture, 1904 (Edinburgh, 1904), p. 35.
30. Douglas M. Murray, 'The Barnhill Case, 1901–1904: The Limits of Ritual in the Kirk', *Records of the Scottish History Society* 22 (1986), 259–276.
31. See Douglas M. Murray, 'Doctrine and Worship: Controversy in the Church Service Society in the Late Nineteenth Century', *Liturgical Review* 7:1 (May, 1977), 25–34.
32. *Cf.* William Milligan, *The Resurrection of our Lord* (London, 1884); William Milligan, *The Ascension and Heavenly Priesthood of our Lord* (London, 1892).
33. W. D. Maxwell, *The Book of Common Prayer and the Worship of the Non-Anglican Churches*, Friends of Dr. William's Library, Third Lecture (London, 1950), pp. 24–25; W. D. Maxwell, *A History of Worship in the Church of Scotland*, The Baird Lectures, 1953 (London, 1955), pp. 180–181.
34. Wotherspoon, *James Cooper*, p. 150.
35. H. J. Wotherspoon, 'The Present State of Church Music in Scotland', *Transactions of the Aberdeen Ecclesiological Society* 2:5 (1890–93), 38.
36. William Milligan, *The Scottish Church Society: Some Account of its Aims* (Edinburgh, 1893), p. 7.
37. Millar Patrick, 'The Church Worship Association of the United Free Church', *The Church Service Society Annual* 3 (1930–31), 82.
38. 'A Man Greatly Beloved', Tributes to James Cooper, *Transactions of The Scottish Ecclesiological Society* 7:2 (1922–24), 11.
39. James Inglis, 'The Scottish Churches and the Organ in the Nineteenth Century' (1987, Ph.D., Glasgow), pp. 171, 188.
40. Leishman, 'Ritual', pp. 423–424.
41. Wotherspoon, 'Present State of Church Music', 38.
42. Leishman, 'Ritual', pp. 353–359.
43. Wotherspoon, *James Cooper*, p. 97.
44. *Acts of the General Assembly of the Church of Scotland*, 1922, p. 64.

45. Sprott, *Worship and Offices*, p. 149; *cf.* McMillan, *op. cit.*, p. 269.
46. Sprott, *Worship and Offices*, pp. 167–168.
47. Thomas Leishman, *The Church of Scotland as she was and as she is*, The Macleod Memorial Lecture, 1903 (Edinburgh, 1903), p. 30.
48. J. F. Leishman, 'The Church of Linton in Teviotdale', *Transactions of the Scottish Ecclesiological Society* 4:3 (1913–15), 269.
49. *Acts of the General Assembly of the Church of Scotland*, 1909, p. 61.
50. G. B. Burnet, *The Holy Communion in the Reformed Church of Scotland, 1560–1960* (Edinburgh, 1960), p. 297.

BIBLIOGRAPHY

Barkley, J. M., 'The Renaissance of Public Worship in the Church of Scotland, 1865–1905' in Derek Baker, ed., *Renaissance and Renewal in Christian History*, Studies in Church History 14 (Oxford, 1977), pp. 339–350.

Cheyne, A. C., *The Transforming of the Kirk* (Edinburgh, 1983).

Drummond, Andrew L. and Bulloch, James, *The Church in Victorian Scotland 1843–1874* (Edinburgh, 1975).

Kerr, John, *The Renascence of Worship* (Edinburgh, 1909).

Leishman, James F., *Linton Leaves* (Edinburgh, 1937).

Leishman, Thomas, 'The Ritual of the Church', in R. H. Story, ed., *The Church of Scotland Past and Present* (London, 1890), V, pp. 307–426.

Ross, J. M., *Four Centuries of Scottish Worship* (Edinburgh, 1972).

Sprott, G. W., *The Worship and Offices of the Church of Scotland* (Edinburgh, 1882).

Sprott, G. W., ed., *Euchologion*, A Book of Common Order (Edinburgh, 1905).

Story, R. H., *The Life and Remains of Robert Lee*, I, II (London, 1870).

Wotherspoon, H. J., *James Cooper: A Memoir* (London, 1926).

Chapter Seven

EPISCOPAL WORSHIP IN THE NINETEENTH AND TWENTIETH CENTURIES

Allan Maclean

The nature of worship in the Episcopal Church in the period 1790 to 1930 was affected at least as much by the outside pressures of social, economic, political and literary change and stability as by the internal doctrinal stance of the Church. Though this may characterize other religious groups, the Episcopal Church has been more affected by outside pressures than many. This is not least because the Episcopal Church has depended on support from a laity, often articulate, who could wreck such a small ecclesiastical body if they withdrew their support, either to set up rival congregations (as did happen), or to join other religious groups (as also happened).

The principal factor in this history was the existence of two strains within Scottish Episcopacy. The one line descended from the non-juring Episcopalians, who had had a vigorous life, at times one of strength, but who had suffered from persecution and suppression after 1746, which led many to join the other Episcopalian body. This other group consisted of juring Episcopalians (or Qualified Congregations), who took the oaths to the Hanoverian kings and allied themselves closely to the Church of England and the Church of Ireland. Though Anglican in ritual, for it was the *The Book of Common Prayer (BCP)* which was their *raison d'être*, they had no ecclesiastical structure and were, in one sense, merely Anglicans-abroad.

The separation of the non-juring Episcopalians and juring Episcopalians was an anomaly that Parliament introduced. The non-jurors had the ecclesiastical structures, the jurors the stricter adherence to the *BCP*, but by the 1790s the political reasons for the separation had disappeared. The non-juring Scottish Episcopal Church was more and more seen as the sister church to the Church of England.

By the first decade of the nineteenth century, reunion between the two strains had been achieved and the Scottish Episcopal Church then consisted of the two distinct traditions: (*a*) the original non-juring descendants with an interest in the Fathers of the Church, primitive precedents and authority and a distinctive Scottish liturgy, witnessing to a history of liturgical independence and innovation, who were rapidly assimilating the *BCP* as a norm for worship; and (*b*) the former qualified congregations, whose adherence to the order of the *BCP* was now joined to ecclesiastical structures, with a new set of canons, rules and regulations passed in 1811.

The diversity was not destructive, though the liturgical rite was a point of contention, especially where a new congregation was founded, or there was a union between the two traditions. The Episcopal Church increased in committed membership dramatically, and its new adherents were largely people who had come into contact with the Anglican Church and admired its ordered services, and sometimes its doctrinal standards. Such contact was frequently through the armed services, schooling in England or intermarriage with Anglicans. There is evidence that socially the English connection appealed to some, especially in Edinburgh, where the Episcopal Church has been termed 'genteel and fashionable'. In the Episcopal Church they found a refuge from the controversies in contemporary Presbyterianism.

The Episcopal Church was not spared such controversies for long, for in the 1830s and 1840s in England a movement, contemporary with and similar in some respects to the Disruption, took the name of the Oxford Movement. It appealed to the historical continuity of the Church and its apostolic nature. It disapproved of Erastianism and sought freedom to re-assert the high theology of the Church, and its doctrines. In Scotland the movement found, in the old non-juring tradition, the survival of just such ideas, so that the adherents of the Scottish Liturgy were given a new vigour and vision. Though the results of this movement were gradually felt all over the Anglican Church, there was still a strong tradition of Anglican moderation, and it appealed to many in the Scottish Episcopal Church. The conflict between the two was strongly felt in Scotland, where the sides were more evenly balanced than in England – and it was expressed in the attitude to, and form of, worship.

Those who favoured Anglican moderation, and who in many respects were also Anglicizers of the Episcopal Church, won the day, largely through their majority in the high places. In 1864 Parliament lifted the final disabilities affecting the Scottish Episcopal Church and, hand-in-hand with this, in 1863 the canons were altered so that the *BCP* was enforced in all ordinary services and the English form of liturgy was given pre-eminence over the Scottish. Assimilation with the Church of England became the objective of the Church, and Bishop Wordsworth and others thought that this would make union with the Presbyterian Establishment easier. Those who upheld the Scottish Liturgy and traditional obedience to the Church were powerless. At the other end of the ecclesiastical scale, the Episcopalian Evangelicals had also found themselves restricted to the use of the *BCP* on all occasions – and, generally not having a high theological view of the Church, and suspicious of the high views of even the Anglicizers, some withdrew from the Episcopal Church, forming their own Evangelical Episcopal

Union. Sometimes called the 'Drummond Schism' after the Reverend
D. T. K. Drummond of St. Thomas', Edinburgh, they managed to
arrange a debate in the House of Lords in 1849, following a petition
from 'members of the United Church of England and Ireland, resident
in Scotland'.

In England, however, the *BCP* itself began to come under scrutiny
and reforms were introduced in the liturgical readings and, more
significantly, in the use of Prayer Book services. This change of mood
allowed the Anglicizers in the Scottish Episcopal Church to move along
the lines of liturgical and Prayer Book reform and even reconsider the
Scottish Liturgy. Draft revisions of the Scottish Liturgy, 1883–89, were
followed by an accepted text in 1911–12, which reinstated some of its
earlier authority.

After the First World War, further liturgical revision was undertaken
in Scotland and England. Though the new English Prayer Book was
rejected by Parliament in 1928, in Scotland there was no similar check.
In 1929 a new Scottish Prayer Book was published which included a
further revision of the *Scottish Liturgy*. The book was a sign of a new
mood in Anglicanism, with revisions to liturgies and some diversity of
practice accepted. For a time the Anglican and Scottish strains in the
Episcopal Church were able to work together, and soon virtually all
Episcopal churches were using the 1929 Prayer Book. Following the
1958 Lambeth Conference, in the 1960s and 1970s another round of
liturgical change was started, which included an ecumenical dimension.

Episcopalian forms of worship are tied to belief in the nature of the
Church and its task in the worship of God, by bible reading, praise and
prayer. This daily task is adapted during the year to the traditional feasts
and fasts of the Christian Calendar, by which Jesus Christ's life and the
life of the Church and its principal saints are recalled. It also upholds a
sacramental system of the assurance of God's presence in this world, by
the Church's particular action in certain circumstances and occasions.

Of the two traditions within the Episcopal Church, the non-juring
tradition used set forms of worship for most of its sacramental activities,
and at other occasional services, but regular Sunday worship was
usually of a freer and more extempore type. The Anglican tradition,
however, was accustomed to set forms of worship for all services,
including regular Sunday worship, and these set forms were all to be
found in the *BCP*.

Gradually, with the union of the two traditions at the beginning of the
nineteenth century, the Scottish Episcopal Church accepted more and
more of the forms in the *BCP*, to which they added their old services,
and in particular the Scottish Liturgy.

Underlying the form of the *BCP* services was the idea of the
continuous worship of God by the Church, day and night, every day of
the week. Although this was expected of parson and people in England,

the practice was largely non-existent among the people. Family prayers were sometimes said, but the parson was very lax in this as well (though in 1770 Dr. Abernethy Drummond wrote of the Scottish Episcopal clergy as 'clergymen who every day use the morning and evening service of the English Prayer Book').[1] Divine Service in England was usually said only on Sundays, in the morning and afternoon. The Morning Service was very long in its full form, consisting of Matins, Litany and ante-Communion (i.e. Holy Communion up to the end of the Church Prayer), though it was adapted and shortened. While this was familiar to the Anglicizing party, farther north the traditional Episcopalians were used to a version of the Morning Service nearer to the Presbyterian tradition, though the substance was the same, being composed of scripture readings and a selection of psalms.

In 1795 at Longside, Aberdeenshire, the Reverend John Skinner of Linshart (a poet much admired by Robert Burns, and known as *Tullochgorum*, the title of his best known work) started Morning Service with a psalm taken from the Assembly's Version, which he said was more intelligible to a country congregation than those of the popular English metrical version of Tate and Brady (produced in 1696). A precentor helped with the singing, but the service was largely Prayer Book. The congregation sang a hymn during the collection and the old man preached at the end of the service.[2]

At St. Andrew's, Aberdeen, his son's church, the English form of service was in use. The Prayer Book service had been introduced there in the 1730s. In the period 1795–1840 Morning and Evening Prayer were said every Sunday and there was a sermon at each. The Holy Communion was celebrated seven times in the year, Christmas Day, the first Sunday in Lent, Good Friday, Easter Day, Whit Sunday and twice in the Trinity season. Morning Prayer was also said on all the other Holy Days, on every Wednesday and Friday and on the Saturday before and the Monday after Communion, when that was on a Sunday.

The order for Sunday morning service started with singing verses from Tate and Brady's metrical psalms. Matins, as in the Prayer Book, followed, with its Confession, scripture readings, psalms, canticles, Apostles' Creed and prayers. The Litany was followed by a hymn, during which the minister went to the altar for the Lord's Prayer and the beginning of the Prayer Book Communion Service, with its Collects, Commandments (here, in Scottish fashion, a summary was used), scripture readings and Nicene Creed. During a hymn, the minister went to the pulpit to preach. After the sermon some more verses of Tate and Brady were sung and the prayer for the whole state of Christ's Church from the Scottish Communion Office was followed by more prayers and the blessing.

In the evening, Evensong also started with Tate and Brady verses, and then proceeded with a similar content to Matins. At the end there was a hymn, the sermon, psalm verses, prayer and blessing. After everything else came the anthem.[3] Psalms were invariably said in all churches at this period, but canticles were sung in many parishes.

The Canons of the first General Synod in 1811 aimed, among other things, at securing greater uniformity in the mode of conducting the public service of the Church. To that end, the clergy were ordered 'to adhere strictly to the words of the English Liturgy in the morning and evening service, unless where, for obvious reasons, resulting from the difference between a legal establishment and toleration, the Bishop shall authorize any deviations'.[4] This, however, did not mean that wholesale acceptance of the English precedent was contemplated, as their calendar was not enforced, but rather a simple requirement to attend the celebration of the Divine Service 'on the sacred solemnities' of Sunday, and 'such other holy days as have been usually observed by the Episcopal Church in this part of the United Kingdom'.[5]

A congregation like Fort William in 1836 had Divine Service performed twice every Sunday, in the forenoon in English, in the afternoon in Gaelic. At Kilmaveonaig Chapel, near Blair Atholl, Divine Service was performed twice every Sunday, Christmas Day, Good Friday and Ascension Day and at least six other days throughout the year.[6]

In the Canons of 1838, Canon XXVIII on the Uniformity to be Observed in Public Worship states: 'No Bishop, Presbyter or Deacon shall be at liberty to depart by his own alterations or insertions, lest such liberty should produce consequences destructive of "decency and order", it is hereby enacted that in the performance of Morning and Evening Service, the words and rubrical direction of the English Liturgy shall be strictly adhered to.' Furthermore, if any clergyman officiated or preached in any place publicly without using it, he was liable to suspension. This was particularly difficult for English Evangelical-style preachers, who did not stick to such restrictions. In 1822 the work of such preachers in Edinburgh had been the subject of discussion among the bishops.[7] Evangelical-minded clergy also found a new difficulty in the aftermath of the Oxford Movement, with its emphasis on order and tradition and its love of the Scottish Liturgy. It led them to withdraw from the Episcopal Church, with their congregations.

More and more frequently Morning Service took a similar form to Evening Service, with Matins alone, followed by a sermon and blessing. The Litany was not always used, or it was sometimes said separately in the afternoon. The Holy Communion was formed into a separate service, used on its own, though still after Morning Service. A new trend was for it to be said early in the morning, as a spiritual exercise with which to start the first day of the week, and this saw the end of the old custom of Communion tokens, which still survived in some traditional parishes (e.g. St. Paul's, Dundee).

By the 1870s there was quite a variety of practice, though St. Peter's, Peterhead, was not unusual in 1878 when, on Sunday, it had Holy

Communion at 8.00 a.m., except on the first Sunday of the month, when it was after Matins, which was always at 11.00 a.m., with sermon. Evensong with sermon was at 6.00 p.m. In the same year St. Thomas', Tillymorgan, had services at 11.00 a.m. and 5.00 p.m., 'A plain service of Matins, Litany and ante-Communion on Sunday mornings; Evensong in the afternoon', i.e. the old pattern survived, with Holy Communion occasionally.[8]

In more and more places, however, the psalms, canticles and litany were sung. In large city congregations a trained choir assisted in the Sunday services, at times almost to the exclusion of the congregation itself. In some cathedrals the choir sang the daily services, and at St. Mary's Cathedral, Edinburgh, consecrated in 1879, the full ritual of an English cathedral was established. In 1891 St. Mary's had seven resident clergy and Sunday services of Holy Communion at 8.00 a.m. and noon; Matins and Litany at 11.00 a.m., with Evensong at 3.30 p.m. and 7.00 p.m. Week-day services were Communion at 8.00 a.m., Matins at 11.00 a.m. and Evensong at 5.00 p.m.[9] The second Sunday Evensong at 7.00 p.m. followed the lines of the immensely popular English cathedral Evensongs, with a talented preacher and crowds of people. Other city churches introduced a similar service, largely as a background to a fine sermon.

The separation of the services, the changing pattern of early or sung Communions, as well as the personal practice of the clergy, suggested that some revision of services was needed. In 1871, in England, the lectionary of readings was revised and in 1872 shortened forms of services for week-days and additional services on Sundays were allowed. In England, too, the Athanasian Creed, which was most inappropriately said on certain festivals, was also under scrutiny. These various minor revisions allowed Scots, too, to look at the Prayer Book.

George Hay Forbes, the erudite liturgiologist and priest at St. Serf's, Burntisland, saw several defects in the Prayer Book, and made suggestions about the introduction to Matins and Evensong which were similar to, but fifty years ahead of, the revision of 1929. It is doubtful how widely read his views were, except among scholars. He also suggested changes in the Athanasian Creed to make its meaning clear,[10] but generally the Episcopal Church was still shy of any Prayer Book change. In 1872, the diocesan Synod of Moray unanimously passed a resolution in favour of the retention of the Athanasian Creed in all its integrity in the Prayer Book of the Church.

The attempts at revision in England, which encouraged a critical look at the *BCP*, coincided with Bishop Dowden's researches into the history and contents of the Scottish Liturgy. Several scholars began to re-discover its merits as a fuller and more appropriate service, though its reinstatement in Scotland took several decades, and this also held back general Prayer Book revision. In 1909 the committee appointed by the bishops to revise the Scottish Liturgy also took the opportunity to add to the Scottish Canons a schedule of 'permissible additions to and deviations from the Book of Common Prayer'. These acknowledged the changes that the clergy were already making, and were passed in 1912, published quite clearly with a line alongside them in *Common Prayer (Scotland)*. They included the alternative introductions to Matins and Evensong already sanctioned in England, and some thirty-six new prayers that could be used at the end of the service, largely composed by Bishop Dowden. New Tables of Psalms and Lessons were also sanctioned for experimental use in 1914.

After the 1914–18 War the old worshipping pattern and ritual began to be challenged at a deeper level than the authorization of accepted deviations. This was felt both in Scotland and England. Dean Perry, in *The Scottish Prayer Book*, says: 'After the great European War, the necessity for further revision of the Prayer Book was unduly felt. During that prolonged struggle of more than four years, the Church had played a great part in maintaining the spirit of her people. But when peace came, no institution in the country was so conscious of its failure or so keenly alive to its weaknesses as the Church.'[11]

In 1918 the Consultative Council on Church Legislation requested the bishops to nominate a Church Services Committee to consider the whole question of a thorough Prayer Book revision. Its liturgical sub-committee was chaired by Bishop A. J. Maclean of Moray, a first-rate liturgiologist, though not quite up to the standard of Bishop Dowden. It worked independently of, but parallel to, a similar scheme in England. The English New Prayer Book was rejected by Parliament, but in Scotland opposition was weak. In 1930 William Gillies, the Hon. Secretary of the Prayer Book Standards Defence Association, published *The Scottish Book of Common Prayer: Another Aspect*, in which he said that the new service-book 'in defiance of the Protestant standards of the Church, aims at and effects, to a considerable extent, the substitution of medieval accretions for the simplicity of primitive truth'. In March 1929, however, the Provincial Synod had confirmed its decision in favour of the *Scottish Book of Common Prayer*.

This Scottish Prayer Book was a complete revision and in some ways a fresh start. It not only legalized various customs that had developed, but it introduced new ideas and gave the Episcopal Church a spiritual treasure house. It drew inspiration from the English Book of Common Prayer (and its long history) and its Scottish additions; from the English rejected book of 1928; from the 1549 Prayer Book and the South African Prayer Book, and also from the ancient sources of medieval times and from the East. In morning and evening services the minor changes of 1912 were extended. A new canticle, the *Benedictus Es*, from the Book of Daniel, was introduced, and there was an opportunity to use a wide selection of extra prayers. A new inclusion in 1929 was the service of Compline, a late evening service which had its origin in early medieval times. It had been in use in theological colleges and supplied a late night service, which could also be used in Advent or Lent in parish churches.

The liturgical calendar in the 1929 book was extended beyond those saints included in 1912. More significantly, the 1914 lectionary of scripture readings was included, which was quite different from the revised English version. The Scottish Sunday lectionary was based on a three-year cycle, with a one-year cycle for daily readings. In the three-year cycle almost the whole of the New Testament and a considerable proportion of the Old Testament could be heard by the Sunday worshipper. The history of Judah was included in one year, the history of Israel in another, avoiding the previous confusion. The Psalter was arranged so that Sunday worshippers would use virtually every psalm at least once in a year, though this disrupted the ancient custom of the continuous cycle of psalms.

The Athanasian Creed was given a new translation, a new title, and made obligatory only on Trinity Sunday, when even then it might be used to replace the Apostles' Creed as an anthem.

Important changes were introduced in the Litany, the ancient form of penitential and intercessory prayer. Slight alterations to the Litany of 1662 were followed by an abbreviated version. A third very popular litany was introduced (the Second Shorter Litany), which drew largely from Eastern precedent, resembling one contained in the Liturgy of St. John Chrysostom, and concluded with a magnificent prayer from the Gelasian Sacramentary.

The principal treasure in the Scottish Prayer Book, both liturgically and theologically, is the Scottish Liturgy. Its history is both significant and romantic.

In his book *The Scottish Communion Office, 1764*, Bishop Dowden produced the theory, which is well accepted, that the 1764 Scottish Liturgy was the received text. From the turn of the nineteenth century this liturgy was the centre both of utter loyalty – from most of the traditional Scottish Episcopalians and the Tractarians – and of scorn, derision and fear, from the Anglicizers, the moderates, and those who wanted uniformity with the Church of England.

It was seen as a stumbling block at the time of the union between the two Episcopalian traditions, though this was smoothed over, with the acceptance of the 39 Articles. The General Synod of 1811 allowed liberty for any congregation which had previously used the English Office (i.e. the Communion Service in the *BCP*) to continue to do so, and then enacted that the Scottish Communion Office should be used in all consecrations of bishops; and that all bishops when consecrated must give their full assent to it as being sound in itself, and of primary authority in Scotland.

In 1863 the Canons were changed, partly for the ecclesiastical and political reasons of conformity with the Church of England. The

Scottish Communion Office was no longer declared to be of primary authority, and the English service was now to be used at Bishops' Consecrations and Synods. The Scottish Office could be discontinued in any church where the minister and a majority of the congregation wanted to change, but the opposite did not apply to the English Office. There were various restrictions on new congregations using the Scottish Office.

Though this action caused considerable unhappiness and George Hay Forbes took the Primus to court as far as the House of Lords (*Forbes v. Eden and others, 1865–67*) and lost, there is plenty of evidence of traditional congregations, like Kilmaveonaig at Blair Atholl, wanting to change to the English service at an earlier date. The controversy was bitter and prolonged. One Edinburgh cleric said, 'The Scottish Office, of obscure and schismatic origin, follows most servilely and literally the Roman form'.[12] He was totally mistaken, as the English Office is far nearer the Roman form of consecration prayer than the Scottish which contains an epiclesis, drawn from supposedly primitive and certainly Eastern precedent. Anti-Roman Catholic prejudice was used to support the Anglicizers in their assertion that the *BCP* rite was the only suitable one, not only for the Church of England, but for all the Anglican Communion of Churches.

By 1878, according to *The Directory of the Scottish Episcopal Church*, the Scottish Office was used, at least occasionally, by only forty-two congregations, half of which were in the united diocese of Aberdeen and Orkney. Brechin had six congregations using the Scottish Office, of which two in Dundee alternated it with the English Office. In Argyll diocese, after the influence of Bishop Ewing, only one congregation used the Scottish Office, Fort William at 8.00 a.m. Glasgow and Galloway diocese was uniformly for the English Office, except Jedburgh, with its particular Tractarian tradition.

By the 1880s circumstances had begun to change, with the new attitude to revision in England and a majority of the bishops in Scotland looking with more favour on the Scottish Office, which Bishop Dowden brought to their attention in his *The Scottish Communion Office, 1764* in 1883. They were anxious to remove the restrictions on the Scottish Office, but were also convinced that it needed revision first.

Since 1764 there had been various versions of the Scottish Office, more or less popular, of which the most significant were Bishop Abernethy Drummond's of 1796; Lord Medwyn's and his son William Forbes' version of Bishop Abernethy Drummond's, printed in 1844; the *Office for the Holy Communion* included in the Prayer Book of 1849, sanctioned by Bishop Torry, but which was condemned by the Episcopal Synod of 1850 as having no synodical or canonical authority and as 'not what it professes to be' (it was compiled by Alexander Lendrum, George Hay Forbes, another son of Lord Medwyn, and R. Campbell and was the Scottish Office with a few new rubrics);

and in 1862 George Hay Forbes' own *The Communion Office for the use of the Church of Scotland as far as concerneth the Ministration of that Holy Sacrament*. This last book was, so far as it is known, used only by Forbes' own congregation at Burntisland, but it is significant for its variations, since they come from the hand of 'the most learned liturgiologist in the Scottish Church since the death of [Bishop] Rattray'.[13]

The bishops believed that they should not re-establish the authority of a service for which there was no officially accepted standard text. At the same time they saw an opportunity to revise the 1764 text, so that it expressed acceptably the theological belief and practice of the Church. In particular, they were anxious about the Invocation of the Holy Spirit in the prayer of Consecration, which Bishop Dowden had criticized in his book, both in its wording and its bald statement.

After a great deal of study and consultation with experts in liturgical matters and with theologians, a revised text was issued (sometimes called *The Second Draft, 1889*)[14] along with a pastoral letter of explanation.[15] The principal change from 1764 was the re-wording of the Invocation that had been introduced in 1764, viz. 'may become' to 'may be'. '. . . We have aimed at coming as closely as a precatory form would admit, to the very words used by the Blessed Lord Himself. He did not say, "This *has become*" – but "This *is* – My Body". And similarly we pray not that the Bread and the Cup *may become* but that they *may be* His Body and His Blood'. 'Become unto us' and 'make' had been other suggestions which were rejected. Another change was a statement at the Invocation of the object of communion, 'that whosoever shall receive the same may be sanctified both in soul and body, and preserved unto everlasting life', drawn in part from the *American Communion Office*. Some eighteen other changes were proposed.

The subsequent discussions at the diocesan synods showed a great diversity of opinion, from the northern dioceses, who were alarmed by Bishop Dowden's criticism of the 1764 Invocation, which they believed had expressed and guarded the doctrine of the Real Presence, to those who opposed it because they saw it as part of a plan to give the Scottish Office an equal status with the English Office. It was evident that the peace over the eucharistic doctrine and practice, which the Church had begun to experience, could once again be shattered, so the General Synod in 1890 left both the Liturgy and its status untouched.

Bishop Dowden worked at a more suitable wording for the Invocation, with a nearer approach to the forms in the liturgies in use in the Orthodox Church of the East, which have a prayer that the Holy Spirit might be sent on the worshippers as well as on the sacramental elements. In a new edition of his book, almost completed, he had tentatively submitted a text when, in 1909, the bishops appointed the new Revision Committee for the Scottish Liturgy.

Bishop Dowden's suggestion was married to a suggestion of Dr. Bright (the eminent historian and liturgical scholar, and one time tutor at the Scottish Episcopalian Theological College, Trinity College, Glenalmond) in the *Church Quarterly Review*.[16] There he followed a dictum of St. Cyprian that in any alteration in the form of Invocation, the words employed should express no more and no less than that which Jesus Christ intended the sacrament to be. In other words, the prayer of Consecration was to leave the doctrine of the Real Presence where the Church had left it, undefined, revision proceeding on liturgical and not on doctrinal lines. The substance of the wording that thus resulted in 'humbly praying that it may be unto us according to his word' was derived from the words of Mary at the Annunciation.

Bishop Dowden was still influential in this version, along with Bishop Maclean of Moray. Some of the changes proposed in 1889 were incorporated. The offertory now included the offering of the bread and wine as well as the alms, which were all to be put on the altar before the familiar prayer, 'Blessed be thou ...'. Instead of the Ten Commandments, or the Summary, on week-days the Kyrie was allowed.

The collects for the sovereign and the reader's conclusion to the Gospel were omitted. The invitation to Communion was changed to the form in the English Office order. The prayer for further consecration was extended to include the oblation and invocation, so strangely omitted from the further consecration prayer in 1764. Seventeen post-communion prayers were introduced, some from the English Office, some from the 1889 draft, including one from the ancient Scottish *Book of Deer* and one a paraphrase of the *Altus of St. Columba*.

The deacon's role was more carefully stated. The old non-juring usage of a mixed Chalice of wine and water, and the reservation of the consecrated species 'for the sick and others who could not be present at the celebration in church', which were both practices of long standing among the traditional Scottish Episcopalians, were authorized in the rubrics. The name given to the revised Scottish Office was *The Scottish Liturgy*, and it was authorized by the Primus on behalf of the Scottish Bishops on 22 February 1912, and printed in *Common Prayer (Scotland)* alongside the text of the rest of the *BCP* with the permissible additions and deviations, including those to the English Office. At the same time, in the Code of Canons, the Scottish Liturgy was given a position of equality with the English Office, and reasonable liberty for its introduction into any congregation, thus reversing the trend that had resulted in the Canons of 1863. The permissible changes in the English Communion service allowed it to be celebrated in a form closer in some details to the Scottish Liturgy.

In 1921 Perry was able to say of the *Scottish Liturgy (1912)*, 'There is now not a cathedral in Scotland in which it is not in regular use, and in the majority of Scottish congregations it holds an honoured place and meets with increasing appreciation'.[17] The old edition of 1764 was also sanctioned for use in those congregations in which it had been employed prior to 1911, but the 1912 rite became immensely popular. So strong was this attachment that in 1929 no attempt was made at a complete revision, but several further changes were made, and existing practices acknowledged, all worked out by the adept hand of Bishop Maclean of Moray.

These further changes in the form of the Scottish Liturgy of 1929 and the permissible changes printed in 1929 for the English Office show that the Traditionalist element and the Anglicizers had come very close. The changes to the Scottish Liturgy were similar to those proposed in England in their new book, which was itself accepting many ideas tried out over the centuries in the various revisions and drafts of the Scottish Office.

Some of the changes incorporated in the 1929 version of the Scottish Liturgy, like the introduction of the *Benedictus*, had been suggested in the Scottish *Second Draft* of 1889, though it had not been included in the 1912 version. Other changes of 1929 were also incorporated in the new English (rejected) Prayer Book of 1928. The Ten Commandments could be shortened; the words of the Creed were altered to 'The Lord *the* giver of Life' and '*Holy* Catholic and Apostolic Church'. In the prayer for the Church the bishop is named, the Privy Council omitted and there is a direct petition for the departed. In both rites, too, there is a re-introduction of the *Pax*, or Kiss of Peace, signifying Brotherly Love, though in the Scottish Liturgy it is far more appropriately related to the breaking of the bread. Perry had suggested it in 1922, with the caution, 'No one with a sense of humour would think of suggesting the restoration of the literal Kiss, which even in the East has come to be represented only by a symbolical act'.[18]

Like the English draft, the *Scottish Liturgy, 1929*, divides up the service with titles, showing to the worshipper the various parts of the Liturgy. It also omits the first Lord's Prayer, gives fewer offertory sentences and adds more prefaces and post-communion prayers.

Significantly, it drops the 1912 introduction of Dr. Bright's suggestion in the Invocation 'humbly praying that it may be unto us according to his word'. Practice had shown that it was unnecessary and cumbersome. Its statement was obvious. The prayer of consecration, therefore, in the *Scottish Liturgy, 1929* follows the 1764 order of introduction and thanksgiving, the narrative of the institution, the oblation, the invocation, the prayers for acceptance of the action and a final thanksgiving. The 1764 wording is enriched by an added phrase after the Oblation, and at the Invocation, an introduction, a prayer for the Holy Spirit to bless the congregation, and a recital of the object of Communion (all as in the *Scottish Liturgy (1912)*). The *Agnus Dei*, 'O Lamb of God', familiar as a popular devotion in churches with a choral celebration, was now printed as an optional (but now authorized) extra.

This witnesses to the manner in which popular additions could be incorporated in liturgical revision.

The Scottish Episcopalian in 1929 was rather proud of his Liturgy, with its history and expression. Other Anglicans in general, whatever their church, looked with a certain envy at the Scottish Liturgy. Dr. Perry put it down to its richness of thought, its beauty of structure, its order of sequence and its dignity of expression. Its defect of two long consecutive prayers faded in the experience of worship.

The new Prayer Book also included revised rites for the Baptismal Service and the occasional offices. In Baptism there were various changes and modifications in the light of attitudes to original sin. With the old service there was a general feeling that it was difficult to understand, and the revised rite has headings to make the parts more distinct. The whole was enriched by a prayer for the blessing of the water and a later prayer for the blessing of the home.

Bishop Maclean, at the start of his Episcopate, told his clergy, 'We do not always use the means we have to meet the needs of our time with regard to public worship'. And later, when revision was under way, he commented that 'That which is plainly obsolete cannot tend to edification. We have to consider, not only ourselves, who have been brought up to certain things, and are thoroughly accustomed to them, but the next generation. Liturgical forms should not be considered sacrosanct simply because they are old'.[19]

For the traditional Episcopalians, a hundred years before, at the turn of the nineteenth century, the difficulty was in adapting themselves to these set forms and, in places, archaisms. Bishop Jolly and other Aberdeenshire clergy altered words quite often to make them more intelligible.[20] Bishop Maclean thoroughly disapproved of this, especially with the revised book, but Bishop Campbell of Glasgow had seen no harm in the practice.[21]

There had always been extra-Prayer Book services and prayers. In 1805 there were authorized services in Dunkeld diocese to remember Nelson's victory.[22] The rebuilding or consecration of new churches gave opportunities for extra rites, from the comparatively simple at Portnacrois Chapel, Appin, in 1815[23] and the fuller service at the consecration of St. Ninian's Cathedral, Perth, in 1850, to the elaborate celebrations at the consecration of the Cathedral of the Isles at Cumbrae in 1876, and at St. Mary's Cathedral, in Edinburgh, in 1879.

St. Mary's took upon itself the role of a sort of National Cathedral, until its aspirations were eclipsed by the restoration of St. Giles' for the Establishment. At St. Mary's there were many extra-liturgical services, including in 1902 a *Form of Service for the Coronation Day of their Majesties King Edward and Queen Alexandra*. This service was sanctioned by the Bishop of Edinburgh, but many clergy used extra-devotional services on all sorts of occasions, many of which were never sanctioned. In 1851 Cumbrae College at Millport produced a vernacular office book intended to enable its members to supplement the Prayer Book services with some from the Breviary. In 1871 T. I. Ball, later Provost at Cumbrae, produced a *Day Office of the Church*, which at the time was in advance of any other such Anglican production.

The Prayer Book and its changes are one aspect of worship in the Episcopal Church, but another is the manner in which worship was conducted and what was used to assist worship.

At the turn of the nineteenth century there were virtually no fine or adequate buildings, except St. Andrew's, Glasgow, and St. Paul's, Edinburgh, both of which were qualified chapels of the Anglican tradition. Rich congregations, mostly of the Anglicizing tradition, began to build adorned structures, such as new St. Paul's and St. John's, Edinburgh, together costing well over £30,000. Elsewhere, twenty congregations built or rebuilt between 1792 and 1810, twenty-seven between 1810 and 1830.[24] An adequate building was clearly conducive to worship, though there is evidence that many, of all ranks, were content to gather in an 'upper room' for the worship of God.[25]

Apart from the appeal of the Prayer Book language and rite, aesthetically, except in a few rich churches, there was little to aid worship. Even the clergy were loath to wear clerical vestments, for in 1811 the Canons enjoined the clergy to wear a surplice for the services, though this did not mean for preaching. Before this the clergy wore gowns and the bishops cassocks and gowns – but the surplice, being the Anglican custom, was fashionable.

Quite quickly the surplice became accepted, but at the same time some of the older Scottish customs of reverence during the services died out. Bowing the head in parts of the service was in very general use, and standing when certain passages in Scripture were read. The clergy during the Apostles' Creed turned to the altar.[26] It is strange that these were the very customs which people were criticized for re-introducing a generation later.

In the vanguard of the new discovery of worship by the Tractarians was the return to medieval precedent in church design, with its pleasure in the purity of the Early English style; the chancel as a distinctly separate part of the church, under a lower roof, for an ordered choir and clergy and as a sanctuary for an adorned altar; also the orientation of the building and the font near the door. St. John's, Jedburgh, and St. Columba's, Edinburgh, were early examples, with the architect John Henderson producing several structures in this taste in the 1840s and 1850s. Following him in the north, Alexander Ross of Inverness produced more elaborate designs, including St. Andrew's Cathedral, Inverness, opened in 1869. St. Mary's Cathedral, Edinburgh, showed this development to the full, where Sir George Gilbert Scott recreated a medieval cathedral, adapted to the needs of the Episcopal Church, but including Presbytery, Sanctuary, Transepts and Aisles, and drawing inspiration from the great medieval church buildings of Scotland and the north of England. Later, Sir Ninian Comper from Aberdeen recreated the complete medieval interior at St. Margaret's, Braemar (1899) and the Chapel of St. Margaret's Sisterhood.

The correct setting encouraged the clothing of the Prayer Book rite with more elaborate music and a fuller ceremonial, to complete the right atmosphere for worship.

The Episcopal Church had not shied away from music in church, and both traditions had installed organs and choirs where finance allowed. St. Andrew's, Glasgow, bought their organ in 1812, Keith theirs in 1815, and there are records of organs in the eighteenth century. Choirs to sing anthems, later the hymns and the canticles and, later still, the psalms, are also on record, as at St. Andrew's, Aberdeen, about 1800. St. Mary's, Dalkeith, the private chapel of the Duke of Buccleuch, opened in 1845, had a choir school and sung services. In 1880 the Choir School was founded at St. Mary's Cathedral, Edinburgh, as the continuation of the choir formed before the Cathedral was opened. The first choral services at St. Ninian's Cathedral, Perth, were in 1883.

The singing of hymns characterized Episcopalians in the early nineteenth century. As early as 1780 there is an Aberdeen edition of the Scottish Office with a hymn of fifteen verses 'to be sung during the time of, and after, the Communion'.[27] In 1781 there was printed *A Collection of hymns and anthems for the use of the Episcopal Church of Scotland*. In 1820 the Episcopal Chapel in Carrubbers Close, Edinburgh, and St. George's Chapel, Edinburgh, both produced collections of hymns and in 1830 the Bishop of Edinburgh sanctioned a selection of Psalms and Hymns which went into several editions.[28] With other Scottish Episcopal congregations producing their own collections, the Edinburgh diocesan synod instigated a Hymnal Committee to produce a hymnal, which was extended to all dioceses, after a petition to the College of Bishops. Dean Ramsay convened the committee, whose collection was approved in 1857, 'anxious to provide for divine services in the sanctuary, a consistent companion to the Book of Common Prayer, following the course of the church's year, and at the same time embodying the best specimens of earlier and modern hymns'.[29] Still other collections were made before the well-known English collections were generally accepted. The *Hymnal for Scotland* version of *The English Hymnal* introduced in 1950 became extremely popular.

Adding to the architectural and musical setting, the Prayer Book rites were enriched in the second half of the nineteenth century by a renewed interest in ceremonial, which the other factors encouraged. The restrained and very simple ceremonial of the traditional non-juring Episcopalians had been replaced by the formality of the Anglican tradition, along with the surplice. In many places it was not well performed by Scots unused to English ways,[30] but the renewed interest of the Tractarians led some clergy to question the long sermons in a prominent pulpit, a clerk as master of ceremonies, standing at one end of the altar to celebrate Communion, and making no special appreciation of the presence of Christ in the sacrament.

Bishop Wordsworth was an early advocate of facing east to celebrate, but he later changed back to the old way of standing at the north end of the altar, when he attempted conformity with the Church of England.[31] In the 1860s F. G. Lee, at St. John's, Aberdeen, introduced vestments, incense and a Sung Eucharist, and, like his successor, John Comper, had difficulties with the bishop over ceremonial.

As usual, as fashion changed in England, so the Bishops became more tolerant of the use of great ceremonial. In the early years of the twentieth century at St. Mary's in Glasgow, Bishop Campbell wore a chasuble (with a mitre) at early celebrations and at diocesan celebrations, though Provost Deane did not.[32] He did, however, hang a Sanctuary Light in front of the altar, and in more and more moderate congregations candles were introduced, though far into the twentieth century this was still opposed in some congregations. Some of these were descended from largely Irish congregations in the west of Scotland (e.g. St. John's, Greenock) and others were traditionally 'low church'.

In England, apart from those who adhered closely to Roman Catholic example (as some did in Scotland, too), a tradition of ceremonial and vesture developed, drawing inspiration directly from the medieval precedent, which fitted well with some of the Prayer Book rubrics, and the evidence of post-Reformation custom (usually called the 'Sarum' ceremonial). This tradition, aesthetically pleasing in a Gothic building, was generally accepted as the Anglican ceremonial. In Scotland there was a similar development. Provost Vernon Staley at Inverness was one of the adherents to the Sarum tradition, and wrote definitively on the subject. F. C. Eeles at Aberdeen rediscovered the eighteenth-century Scottish non-jurors' restrained ceremonial and recorded it in *Traditional Customs connected with the Scottish Liturgy*, in 1901.

The aesthetic appeal of some of the glories of ceremonial worship, an ancient, if revised, Liturgy, with its emphasis on thanksgiving, and the sacramental nature of the Church all tied in well with the medieval-style architecture of most Episcopal churches.

Bishop Maclean worked on three principles in 1929: (1) Great reverence for the forms of prayer of antiquity, (2) consideration of the varied needs of others, and (3) an attempt to do everything to the glory of God.[33] The resulting production of a book such as the 1929 *Scottish Prayer Book*, with its associated acclaim, inevitably led to a forty-five to fifty year period of settled use, though following the Second World War the College of Bishops saw the need for further enrichment. In 1948 *Services and Ceremonies for use on Ash Wednesday and Holy Week* were issued. These services were for use in addition to those provided in the Scottish Prayer Book. (A fully revised edition of the booklet was issued in 1967.) At the same period, some additions and permitted alternatives were sanctioned, which enriched the liturgical year by marking certain Saint's Days, including St. Mary Magdalene and the Lesser Feasts of the Blessed Virgin Mary.

Of far more lasting consequence were revisions made in the 1960s. Liturgical scholarship in both Anglican and ecumenical spheres had not ceased, and of particular influence was Dom Gregory Dix's *The Shape of the Liturgy*, published in 1945, which was both critical of the Anglican tradition and innovative in its conclusions about the liturgies of the Early Church. Its influence was clearly shown when the Lambeth Conference of 1958 received a Report about worship and the *BCP*, which urged Anglican provinces to revise their liturgies.[34] It listed 'suggested modifications or additions for the further recovery of other elements of the worship of the Primitive Church', and in Scotland these suggestions resulted in permission being given to certain alterations and deviations in the Communion rites. These included shorter forms of Confession and Absolution, the substitution of the Second Shorter Litany for the Intercessions, and clearer seasonal variations.

In 1966 these variations were incorporated in a booklet with grey covers called *The Liturgy*; and after a period of experiment it was re-issued, with additional alternatives and a further reordering of the rite, as *The Liturgy 1970*. This Liturgy, often termed 'The Grey Book', retained both the language of Cranmer and most of the familiar prayers of the Scottish Liturgy, but rearranged their order into a clear and distinct division between 'The Liturgy of the Word' and 'The Eucharistic Liturgy'. Within the latter, Dom Gregory Dix's now famous 'four-fold action' of Christ is explicitly shown, including a new separate heading of 'The Fraction'.

Professor Gordon Donaldson, an Episcopalian specialist of liturgical development and history, praised *The Liturgy 1970*, which he maintained successfully met the needs of worshippers in congregations, where the weekly Parish Communion had superseded Matins, a trend that was rapidly becoming the norm for most Episcopal congregations. This liturgy's distinct 'Liturgy of the Word' was, for him, in form something very like Matins. He noted that within the clear-cut general framework, there was scope for a great deal of variation as well as enrichment with an Old Testament Lesson, new versicles and responses, and various options for intercession. He commended the rite for restoring the Prayer for the Church to being a part of the Liturgy of the Word. In criticism, however, he did note that many of the cuts and omissions had in fact removed exactly those phrases and prayers that were part of the distinctive Scottish tradition, dating back to their introduction in 1637.[35]

The Liturgy 1970 has found a ready acceptance for over twenty years among those who prefer the traditional theology and the old language, but with the clearly defined and flexible nature of this distinctive rite. A parallel revision of the Baptismal rite was also produced.

Although the *The Liturgy 1970* was a departure from precedence, many people note a definite watershed in the distinctive liturgical tradition of the Scottish Episcopal Church dating back to 1774, and beyond to 1637, as liturgical revision after 1970 moved into new fields. This is seen in both the use of contemporary or new language and in the new theological concepts and emphases included in the liturgy and particularly in the Eucharistic Prayer. Certainly, the antecedents of the remarkable and much praised *Scottish Liturgy 1982* have more to do with ecumenical liturgical scholarship than any Scottish or even Anglican tradition. The same influence is also seen in the setting and ceremonial associated with new styles of worship. The Liturgy Committee of the General Synod has continued in a similar vein by producing a new Ordinal, and new Services including those for Daily Prayer, Baptism and Funerals, as well as extra Eucharistic Prayers, a new Calendar of Feasts, Fasts and Saints' Days, and the adoption of an ecumenical Lectionary, all of which are finding acceptance among Episcopal congregations.

NOTES

1. F. C. Eeles, *Traditional Ceremonial and Customs connected with the Scottish Liturgy,* Alcuin Club XVII (London, 1910), p. 105, footnote 2.
2. *Ibid.*, pp. 106–107, quoting MSS. of John Ramsay of Ochtertyre.
3. *Ibid.*, pp. 162–171.
4. *Code of Canons, 1811*, Canon xvi.
5. *Ibid.*, Canon xiv.
6. John Parker Lawson, *History of the Scottish Episcopal Church from the Revolution to the Present Time* (Edinburgh, 1843), pp. 497–498 and 493–494.
7. William Walker, *The Life of the Right Reverend Alexander Jolly, D.D., Bishop of Moray,* 2nd edn. (Edinburgh, 1878), pp. 106–108.
8. Charles T. Wakeham, ed., *Directory of the Scottish Episcopal Church, 1878* (Edinburgh, 1878), pp. 129 and 132.
9. Charles T. Wakeham, ed., *The Scottish Episcopal Church Directory for 1891* (Edinburgh), p. 133.
10. W. Perry, *George Hay Forbes* (London, 1927), p. 186.
11. W. Perry, *The Scottish Prayer Book, its Value and History* (Cambridge, 1929), p. 23.
12. W. Perry, *George Hay Forbes* (London, 1927), p. 37.
13. John Dowden, *The Scottish Communion Office, 1764*, new ed. (Oxford, 1922), p. 201.
14. *Ibid.*, pp. 235–249.
15. *Ibid.*, pp. 89–94.

16. 'Further Considerations on Proposed Changes in the Scottish Liturgy', *Church Quarterly Review* 29 (1890), 302–303.
17. W. Perry, *The Scottish Liturgy, its Value and History*, 2nd edn. (Edinburgh, 1922), p. 63.
18. *Ibid.*, p. 111.
19. W. G. Sinclair Snow, *Arthur John Maclean, Bishop of Moray, Primus* (Edinburgh, 1950), pp. 80 and 82.
20. William Walker, *op. cit.*, 2nd edn. (Edinburgh, 1878), p. 143. F. C. Eeles, *op. cit.*, pp. 152–158.
21. W. G. Sinclair Snow, *op. cit.*, p. 71, George T. S. Farquhar, ed., *The Right Reverend Archibald Ean Campbell D.D., late Bishop of Glasgow and Galloway* (Edinburgh, 1924), p. 125.
22. George T. S. Farquhar, *The Life of Jonathan Watson, Bishop of Dunkeld* (Selkirk, 1915), p. 106.
23. J. B. Craven, ed., *Records of the Dioceses of Argyll and the Isles 1560–1860* (Kirkwall, 1907), pp. 271–275.
24. Allan Maclean, *The Re-emergence of the Episcopal Church in Scotland* (Unpublished Edinburgh University thesis, 1972), p. 10.
25. W. H. Langhorne, *Reminiscences connected chiefly with Inveresk and Musselburgh* (Edinburgh, 1893), p. 54.
26. *Ergadiensis*, letter in *Scottish Guardian* (24 September 1888).
27. John Dowden, *op. cit.*, p. 198.
28. *A Selection of Psalms and Hymns adapted to the use of Protestant Episcopal Congregations*, 3rd edn. (Edinburgh, 1832).
29. *Hymnal for the Scottish Church (recommended by the Scottish Bishops), 1857.*
30. Robert Jameson Mackenzie, *Almond of Loretto* (London, 1905), p. 98.
31. W. Perry, *George Hay Forbes* (London, 1927), p. 87.
32. W. G. Sinclair Snow, *Frederick Llewellyn Deane, Bishop of Aberdeen and Orkney* (Edinburgh, 1952), p. 33.
33. W. G. Sinclair Snow, *Arthur John Maclean, Bishop of Moray, Primus* (Edinburgh, 1950), pp. 85–86.
34. *The Lambeth Conference 1958* (London, 1958), Part 2, p. 81.
35. Gordon Donaldson, 'Hopes Fulfilled: The "Grey Book"', *Liturgical Review* 5:2 (November, 1975), 21–8.

BIBLIOGRAPHY

Dowden, John, *The Scottish Communion Office, 1764*, new edn. (Oxford, 1922).

Eeles, F. C., *Traditional Ceremonial and Customs connected with the Scottish Liturgy*, Alcuin Club XVII (London, 1910).

Perry, W., *The Scottish Liturgy, its Value and History*, 2nd edn. (Edinburgh, 1922).

Perry, W., *The Scottish Prayer Book, its Value and History* (Cambridge, 1929).

Chapter Eight

ROMAN CATHOLIC WORSHIP

Mark Dilworth

The history of the worship of the post-Reformation Roman Catholic Church in Scotland is very largely the history of that Church's fluctuating fortunes. For most of the period under consideration, its worship was conditioned by the pressure exerted by its adversaries. The four centuries from the Reformation to the present day can be divided as follows:

From 1560 to *c*.1620, a period in which the old Church and its worship died out almost completely.

From *c*.1620 to 1697, a period of pioneer missionary effort, becoming gradually more organized.

From 1697 to 1829, a period of consolidation under its own bishops.

From 1829 on, a period of expansion in which the Scottish Catholic Church, free from external pressures save that of meeting the needs of its increasing numbers, was able to adopt or adapt to the changing trends. This is so vast a subject that only a brief outline can be given.

No study of post-Reformation Roman Catholic worship in Scotland has hitherto been published, and there is no single major source to draw upon. The present essay should, therefore, be looked on as a pioneering effort to sketch the main lines of the subject. It can most fittingly begin with an outline of Roman Catholic worship in its totality, as otherwise it is difficult to understand what lay behind the very diverse manifestations of Roman Catholic worship after the Reformation.

The central act of Roman Catholic worship is of course the Eucharist, usually called the Mass. It is always open to the congregation, at least in theory, to receive the consecrated bread (the host) in communion; in addition, the consecrated bread can be preserved and administered to those who for some reason, such as illness, cannot be present at Mass. In practice, then, the term Mass denotes the service, that is the communal act of worship, while the term Communion is used for the reception of the sacrament by the individual. At the heart of the Roman Catholic faith is the belief that Christ's sacrifice on Calvary is made present on the altar during Mass (though not repeated or added to in any way) and that the consecrated elements are no longer bread and wine but are the body and blood of Christ. By the late Middle Ages it had become customary to expose the consecrated host outside Mass for veneration. Of the seven sacraments, the Eucharist (Mass, Communion) holds the first place. Traditionally the sacrament of Penance (confession) has been used as spiritual preparation for Communion. Two sacraments are used as rites of initiation: Baptism, received in infancy, and Confirmation, administered at some point between infancy and the threshold of adult life. The sacrament of Anointing of the Sick, often termed Extreme Unction (an unfortunate latinized term for Last Anointing), is for those in some danger of death. Finally, there are two sacraments consecrating a person in his or her state of life: Matrimony and Holy Orders.

Consideration of Roman Catholic worship cannot be confined to congregational church services. Whether conducted in public or in private, all seven sacraments are part and parcel of Catholic worship and are necessary for its survival. In one sense, the sacrament of Holy Orders provides the key to the others. Only the bishop may ordain priests. Only the priest may say Mass (and thus provide Communion), hear confession or anoint the sick. Until recently only the bishop could administer Confirmation. Although the presence of a priest is not necessary for the remaining two sacraments, Baptism and Matrimony – since anyone may baptize and it is the husband and wife who minister the sacrament of marriage to each other – nevertheless the priest alone can provide the ceremonies on these two occasions.

The implications are clear. A supply of priests was necessary for the Mass and sacraments to continue. Another consequence of crucial importance followed from the nature of the sacraments, or at least from the discipline imposed by the Roman Church. The oil used for anointing the sick and for the ceremonies of Baptism could only be blessed by a bishop. If there was no bishop in Scotland, blest oil had to be brought in from abroad. The Latin formulae for administering the sacraments were strictly laid down, under pain of the sacrament being null and void; a service-book was thus essential. Stringent regulations also governed the vestments to be worn on such occasions, the nature of the bread and wine to be used at Mass (and this under pain of invalidity) and a great number of other related matters. Not only were priests necessary, but so were gear and material objects of various sorts.

Many other ceremonies and occasions have to be included under the head of worship. The most important was the Divine Office, recited each day in common in cathedrals and religious houses, or else in private from a breviary by the individual cleric.[1] Similarly there were great differences between the solemn ceremonies performed in major churches and monasteries and the simple rites carried out by a single priest in a small parish church or chapel. Funerals would be of frequent occurrence; so perhaps would be blessings of various kinds, whether of persons (e.g. women after childbirth) or things; exorcisms would be rarer. To these must be added various prayers and devotions, such as the rosary, performed in public or private.[2] Prayer for the dead would be made, and prayer through intercession of the saints. The doctrinal basis for these was belief in the Communion of Saints in heaven, in purgatory and on earth.

The background to all public worship was the Church's calendar, which provided great variety each year. Some feasts in this were fixed, e.g. Christmas, while the dates of the Easter cycle could vary by over a month. Daily observance varied from the most solemn of feasts to those of minor rank and to ferial (i.e. feast-less) days. The festal seasons of Christmas and Easter were preceded respectively by Advent and Lent, periods of fast and abstinence from meat. The greater festivals were preceded by a penitential vigil-day. Different points throughout the year were marked by litanies or processions or ceremonies of blessing. The three days before Easter Sunday had ceremonies not to be seen at any other time. The colour of vestments, altar coverings and so on varied according to season and day.

If the changing calendar provided variety in worship, other things contributed to its splendour – or at least, in smaller churches, to its visual impact. There could be crucifixes, statues and paintings; richness in the decoration of altar vessels, vestments and so on; perhaps such things as banners, flowers, bells, incense, extra candles. Gestures and actions (e.g. signs of the cross, genuflections) were prescribed for both clergy and congregation. Nevertheless the Church's liturgy was very much priest-centred. Lay people were obliged to attend Mass on Sundays and major feast-days and to receive Communion (the consecrated bread alone), usually preceded by Confession, once a year at Easter time. Their participation in the Latin liturgy was no doubt fairly passive. This could be compensated for, however, by religious confraternities and particular devotions, that is, prayer and meditation centred on, say, the passion of Christ.[3]

There was also a 'popular' side to worship, with medals, relics, agnus deis (pieces of blest wax stamped with a lamb) and similar objects being treasured as an aid to personal devotion. It was part of Roman Catholic ethos and tradition to 'incarnate' religion, that is, to integrate it into everyday life. Folk customs had grown up or perhaps had survived from pre-Christian times: recourse to holy wells and the like at certain times or in certain emergencies, pilgrimages to hallowed spots, bonfires or fairs on certain feasts. Christmas was associated with the winter solstice and evergreens such as holly, as was Easter with the spring and rebirth and so with eggs. No doubt the line separating religion from superstition was often overstepped in both private devotion and local custom, and some judicious pruning was badly needed. The purpose here is not to make any such judgement but simply to throw light on the worship and attitudes of Catholics in the post-Reformation period.

Period of decline – 1560–c. 1620

There are many uncertain areas with regard to the progress of Protestantism in the decades after 1560. The celebrated historian, Thomas Innes, for example, wrote that in 1580 'the Catholics, though not all publicly declared, were yet as numerous as the Protestants'.[4] It is beyond doubt, however, that Protestantism increased in strength, while Catholicism declined, so that eventually Scotland became over-whelmingly Protestant. Apart from the Jesuits, always few in number, who began to work in Scotland in the early 1580s, the Catholic clergy received practically no recruits. Their numbers steadily declined until, by the end of the century, pre-Reformation priests of Catholic sympathies must have been increasingly rare. The Protestant clergy, on the other hand, waxed correspondingly stronger as they tightened their grip on the parochial system. It is against this background that Catholic worship during these decades has to be seen.

The Reformation Parliament of August 1560 forbade the Mass under the severest penalties. For the next twenty years there were complaints about Mass being said in various places. Frequently the law pursued its course against the priests responsible, and in a few cases the death penalty was put into effect. In the years immediately following 1560, however, the campaign against Roman Catholic worship laboured under one great difficulty, namely the public knowledge that Queen Mary and her entourage (as well as a fair number of local people) regularly attended Mass in the chapel royal at Holyrood.[5] Mass was said also in various other places visited by the queen. At Christmas 1565 Darnley, the queen's husband, attended matins in Holyrood and heard Mass 'devoutly on his knees'. The marriage of Mary and Darnley and the baptism of their son James were carried out with Roman Catholic rites. On Mary's downfall in 1567, however, the chapel royal was purged of altars, statues and other Roman Catholic furnishings.

What appears to have been the only attempt to organize Roman Catholic worship on a significant scale took place in the west at Easter 1563. Archbishop John Hamilton, Prior Malcolm Fleming of Whithorn and over thirty priests were tried for 'attempting to restore Popery'. At one point 200 armed men gathered. Mass was said in various places, including four parish kirks and houses in and around Glasgow. In Paisley Abbey a dozen priests, secular and regular, supplied Mass and auricular confession.[6] According to Nicolas van Gouda, the papal envoy who visited Scotland in 1562, such boldness was not common. He reported that, apart from the queen's chapel, there was no publicly celebrated Mass or any Catholic sacrament; that the Bishop of Dunkeld had intended at Easter to provide Catholic preaching and sacraments but had been forbidden by the queen; that only in the houses of a few of the noble and wealthy was there Mass, and secretly at that.[7]

A slightly less gloomy picture is painted by the Jesuit Robert Abercromby in 1580. He speaks of religious priests, at Dunfermline in particular, reciting their daily office *privatim* (that is, presumably, in common but not in public) though with no other sacred rite. A few (he says) acted as teachers in households of the gentry, where they said office and Mass, while there was certainly Mass said secretly in Edinburgh. At Christmas 1581 Jesuits gave communion to 100 people in Edinburgh and preached and said Mass daily for Lord Seton's household.

The only places where Catholicism was practised openly for any length of time were in the south-west and the north-east. Lord Herries and the Maxwells gave their protection to Roman Catholic worship in Dumfries and New Abbey, where the long-lived Abbot Gilbert Brown regularly celebrated Mass. On 24, 25 and 26 December 1585 Lord Maxwell marched in procession from Dumfries to Lincluden (formerly a collegiate church), where Fr. John Durie, S.J., was officiating. On Christmas Day Durie sang the whole of the office and then celebrated the customary three solemn Masses. Guards had been posted on the bridge over the Nith to keep any worshippers away, but the people waded through waist-high water and attended Mass wet through.[8]

The protection of a powerful family and its head was needed for Roman Catholic worship to be practised with impunity. In the north-east this was provided by the Earls of Huntly and Errol, and there were frequent complaints about the persistence of Catholicism. On certain Sundays in 1579, 300 or more people were to be seen in the church at Turriff, clothed only in linen garments and imploring the aid of God and the saints, especially the Blessed Virgin. Some went on pilgrimage to the chapel of Our Lady of Grace (a few miles up the Spey from Fochabers), and rosaries were sold in Turriff market. In 1588 Jesuits freely celebrated Mass in Aberdeen, and it was complained that Catholics in the north had their house Mass at their pleasure and their public Mass in the laird of Leslie's chapel, with two 'idols' above the altar (presumably a crucifix and some statue or painting). Elgin, too, was marked by recusancy. One woman absented herself from the Protestant service to pray for 'hir friends departit' in the Chanonry kirk; another went there to pray on her bairn's grave. Two Elgin men helped Jesuits to say Mass in Lady Sutherland's house, and in 1595 a Jesuit was celebrating Mass in Elgin Cathedral. Before the Battle of Glenlivet in 1594, Jesuit priests administered confession and communion to the army of the northern earls and sprinkled their weapons with blest water.

References to Roman Catholic sacramental practice are not plentiful. When James VI's queen-consort, Anne of Denmark, was received in 1598 into the Roman Catholic Church, she heard Mass and was given Communion. Then, over the next two years, she received Communion nine times and would not set out for England (when James succeeded to the English throne) without receiving it once again. Lack of gear was an increasing difficulty. In 1569 four priests at Dunblane were first pilloried in their Mass vestments, then vestments, missals and chalices were burnt.[9] Lady Mar's chaplain had his service-books and vestments confiscated. An English Jesuit later reported on the scarcity and wretched state of Mass vestments in Scotland. It was said that English priests would be acceptable to Scots Catholics but could not help unless they were provided with altar vestments and travelling expenses.

A number of children were baptized in the chapel royal in the 1560s, and at the end of the century there were cases of children baptized by a monk of Pluscarden and by a stranger in a black plaid (presumably a priest) in a burn. A minister in Argyll, an ex-priest, was willing to baptize children according to either the old or the new rite; his memory was long respected! It must be supposed that what made the two rites so different was the Roman Catholic ceremonies: anointing with oil, the salt, the candle, the white robe, as well as the Latin language. No bishop was administering Confirmation, the other sacrament of initiation, but in 1585 it was reported that an Irish bishop had visited Scotland and confirmed at least 10,000 people in a short time – a figure that needs to be viewed with caution. Occasionally, too, there are references to weddings and funerals conducted with the old rites (no doubt, sprinkling of rings or coffin with blest water, and so on).

Anne of Denmark always carried with her a rosary and small cross, and Robert Abercromby wanted a supply of presents for women, such as rosaries, agnus deis and pictures, also girdles or ribbons which had touched the chair of St. Peter. It was, however, a man in Ancrum who had an 'idol' in his house. Those zealous for the reformed religion found much that disquieted them in the persistence of festivals and popular customs. Easter was celebrated in Edinburgh in 1562;[10] Christmas continued to be marked by the sale of 'great loaves', banqueting and papistical ceremonies. Fasting is always a less popular custom, but loyal priests observed the church fast-days – until, that is, they realized that such unsocial behaviour led quickly to their detection. There were constant complaints about people resorting to holy wells or shrines or observing festivals. Arrests were made at a pilgrimage one Beltane to the Cross Kirk in Peebles. Stirling in 1588 grieved the Kirk with 'superstitious ceremonies, pilgrimages and Christ's wells, fasting, bainfyres, girdls, carrells, and such lyke'.[11]

The year 1603 marked the end of an epoch, in theory at least, when the last of the Scottish Catholic bishops died in Paris. It made very little difference to the Scottish Catholics. About 1612, in addition to the handful of Jesuits, a few secular priests ordained abroad began to arrive.[12] Mass was being said in Dumfries openly and even with great solemnity; in 1609, however, the Roman Catholic equipment at New Abbey was confiscated and the aged Gilbert Brown retired to France.[13] If Catholicism was to survive in Scotland, something more was needed. The lack of leadership after 1560 is glaringly obvious; those in authority had aimed at success at the diplomatic level rather than among the people. When James VI achieved his ambition of becoming king of

England, likewise in 1603, the diplomatic efforts to restore Catholicism in Scotland had finally failed.

Pioneer missionary effort – c. *1620–97*
The pattern of Roman Catholic worship in the Lowlands and eastern Highlands did not change much during the seventeenth century. Only in the north-east was there a substantial Roman Catholic minority, protected by powerful families, chiefly the Gordons; elsewhere there were never more than small pockets of faithful Catholics. In noble households in the north-east there was often daily Roman Catholic worship, but elsewhere it was estimated that Mass was not usually celebrated more than three times a year, and with no advance warning. Priests not based in a noble house led an itinerant life, carrying around with them their Mass gear and the blest oils, as well as hosts consecrated at their last Mass, so that the sacraments could be administered even if there was no opportunity for Mass. It was their custom to pray for guidance as to how many hosts to consecrate, not knowing how many they would need before they could say Mass again. Catholics usually deprived of Mass valued it all the more, to judge from the report of a visiting priest that the Highlanders round Inverness assisted at Mass with such fervour that their sighs and ejaculations greatly distracted him.

Very different was the situation in a noble household. One elderly Jesuit said Mass daily and on Sundays and festivals delivered either a sermon to the people or an instruction to the household. Each evening he recited a litany in English with the household, followed by an examination of conscience and a point of meditation, after which he sprinkled them with blest water and gave his priestly blessing. Another Jesuit report describes persons of rank, relatives perhaps, travelling to a noble house to receive the sacraments at Easter. At these periods, he says, such houses resembled monasteries. There were morning prayers and Mass, then prayers and devotions each evening. This was in addition to each person's private devotions.

Catholics living near these houses could attend Mass on Sundays and feasts. Some priests, no doubt with the leave of their noble patron, exercised pastoral care for more distant Catholics. Gilbert Blakhal, chaplain to Lady Aboyne, said Mass almost every day; on Sundays and feast-days he preached to the household and Roman Catholic neighbours; during Lent he preached on Christ's Passion each Sunday, Tuesday and Friday. At intervals he set out for Aberdeen and Buchan, returning by Strathbogie; in each place where he stopped he spent one night in some house in order to 'say messe, confesse, communicat, and exhort the Catholicks be way of a short preaching'.

The Jesuits, naturally enough, encouraged the use of the Ignatian Spiritual Exercises. The rosary was in use as a private devotion; so were traditional prayers such as the *Te Deum* and various litanies. Fasting and almsgiving, at least among the gentry, were approved by their Jesuit chaplains. Jesuit reports often mention general confessions (that is, covering the penitent's whole life, not merely the period since his last confession) as a profitable spiritual exercise. One wonders, however, whether these pious practices (with the exception of the rosary) were widespread or confined to the privileged few.

Throughout the century priests had the same concern over necessary Mass gear, with hostile authorities or mobs seizing it when they could, and stressed their needs in reports to Rome. Priests continued to baptize children and bless marriages, but the absence of a bishop made confirmation impossible. It was, in fact, for this reason, usually omitted from Roman Catholic instruction. There was also difficulty at times over the blest oil needed for the anointing of the sick; in 1694 priests had received no new supply for five years.

Interesting details about Roman Catholic funerals have survived. There was a crucifix on the coffin, and in Aberdeen action was taken against men who painted crucifixes for funerals. Catholics were sometimes buried in abandoned pre-Reformation chapels. When William Ballentine, the prefect apostolic (that is, the superior of the secular priests, appointed by Rome in 1653), died in Lady Huntly's house in Elgin, Mass was said in the chapel, then the body was carried to the great hall, where it lay surrounded by torches. Three hours after sunset it was taken with great solemnity and over fifty torches to a grave in the Huntly aisle in Elgin Cathedral.[14] When another noble lady died, Gilbert Blakhal blessed earth to put on each side of her in the coffin and thus 'did bury her privatly in her chest, with Catholick ceremonayes' before the public funeral took place.[15]

Throughout the seventeenth century Catholics prayed in the ruins of Elgin Cathedral and visited the shrine and well of Our Lady of Grace near Fochabers.[16] There is a great deal in the Jesuit reports about practices like the sign of the cross, the use of blest water, visits to holy places, the wearing of pious objects like crosses, agnus deis or reliquaries, and a wealth of stories about their beneficial, not to say miraculous, effects on men and beasts and the forces of nature. In fact, this would seem to be the period of greatest polarization between Catholic and Protestant in Scotland. As the Kirk continued its efforts to extirpate sacred objects[17] (including, unfortunately, part of our cultural heritage) and customs connected with feasts or holy places, these did not diminish in importance in Catholic eyes. Alexander Leslie in 1681 wanted Rome to donate large numbers of pious objects (e.g. indulgenced medals) for the Scottish mission. Perhaps such polarization was only natural; perhaps the priests were influenced by their education in baroque Catholic Europe; perhaps the differences had to be stressed and these practices, inessential in themselves, were necessary for the survival of Roman Catholicism in a Protestant milieu.

No doubt the unprivileged Catholics observed the feasts and fasts of the Church's calendar as well as they could. In Aberdeen and Edinburgh the authorities kept watch at the sacred seasons, so that it was extremely difficult for a Catholic congregation to gather. St. Andrew's Day was kept and the veneration received new emphasis. Protestant Britain still adhered to the old Julian calendar and in consequence there were sometimes disputes and discrepancies over the dating of some Catholic feasts,[18] but the Scottish priests eventually took steps to ensure uniform practice.

The fortunes of the Catholics were naturally linked with the country's politics. At least one priest accompanied Montrose's mixed Scots and Irish army in his Highland campaigns of 1644–45, saying Mass and dispensing the sacraments in often primitive conditions. After James VII granted toleration for Catholics to worship in houses and chapels, an estimated 700 attended a chapel at Huntly and St. Ninian's chapel (in the Enzie) was being rebuilt. James' chief encouragement to the Catholics, however, was the setting up in Holyrood Palace of a Jesuit college, a printing press and a chapel royal. The king's chapel was opened on St. Andrew's Day 1686; then at Christmas there was a sung Mass and an evening service consisting of a hymn, a psalm and the litany of Our Lady. The choir comprised one salaried male singer and four Frenchwomen, who also sang a French Noel before Mass. During Low Masses the male singer had to sing a Latin antiphon or some verses of a hymn. These details come from a somewhat jaundiced critic, who considered both the ceremonial and the singing to be poor.[19] A year later Roman Catholic burials took place in the abbey church, but all was soon swept away by the Revolution at the end of 1688. The Roman Catholic chapels were looted, the priests forced to flee. At Holyrood and Traquair, to mention only two, rich furnishings were destroyed.[20]

The missionary work in the west Highlands and Islands deserves to be dealt with separately, not merely because of difference of language but because it was conducted quite independently and by Irish priests. Their success was astounding, for there was clearly a linguistic and cultural unity on both sides of the North Channel, and their mission field was apparently a religious vacuum apart from some residual Catholicism. The first concerted effort came in 1619 from Irish Franciscans, who over the next twenty years converted or baptized thousands of persons. The accounts of their hardships and dangers and successful evangelization make exciting reading. They preached daily whenever they could, sometimes, as in Barra, both before and after Mass. In Kintyre they worked at night, preaching and ministering, then saying Mass in two different places before dawn. In Eigg the priest explained the Mass and its different parts, the vestments and so on, then told the people to follow the Mass with silence and devotion; afterwards he preached on the Christian truths. One old woman asked why he had omitted the sign of peace, which she remembered from her distant youth. Often the priest could not say Mass: once, in Kintyre, there was no Mass for twelve days because the missal had been left in Islay; more often it was through lack of bread or wine. Even though they had their iron for baking the bread, wheaten flour was hard to get. They sent to Ireland or the Lowlands, or went themselves, to buy wine and flour. Once there was no wine, and thus no Mass, for two months, including Christmas Day; on another occasion, for six weeks there was Mass on feast-days only, through lack of bread.

The Franciscans heard confessions and gave Communion (when they had enough hosts), blessed marriages and baptized. In Islay they baptized on the beach, in South Uist in an open space. Like their brethren in the Lowlands they considered blest water and objects of piety important, and they petitioned Rome for supplies of these and the faculty to bless them and attach indulgences to their use. Even though their mission came to an end, other Irish priests followed them.[21] Perhaps even more important, the Franciscan friary at Bonamargy on the Antrim coast became a resort for Highlanders. About 1593 Highlanders had been making pilgrimages by sea to Croagh Patrick in Mayo. Now, in the 1630s, they crossed to Bonamargy: each year 500 went to be received into the Roman Catholic Church, accompanied by even more who were already Catholics. In one period of four months, 1,000 converts were received and afterwards confirmed by an Irish bishop.

So spectacular was the friars' success that the authorities in Rome were unwilling to believe their reports. It was a classic case of men undergoing dangers and hardships in the field, while the bureaucrats at home demanded impossibilities and skimped supplies. This was true also of the Lowlands, though to a lesser degree. There was no single superior of the various groups of priests, no co-ordination between them, no strategy. Both the priests in the field and the authorities in Rome took an excessively legalistic view of what could or could not be done by an 'underground' Church. The priests petitioned for permissions that would nowadays be taken for granted. The Irish Franciscans, like Robert Abercromby half a century earlier, asked for religious priests to be allowed to wear secular dress, Abercromby wanted priests to be able to say Mass in non-sacred places, the Franciscans wanted to say Mass using only part of a host and without candles. Sometimes Rome granted permission but with impossible conditions; when given leave to bless chapels and cemeteries, provided they used water blessed by a bishop, one Franciscan pointed out in a spirited reply that there was no bishop available to bless the water! On the other hand, Rome replied to the friars' petitions concerning fasting regulations that canon law already dispensed in cases of need. This legalism, together with the stress on relatively unimportant things, leads to the conclusion that, in the century after the Reformation, Roman Catholics had not yet worked out what was essential in their religious practices and what was not, what was necessary and what was dispensable.

Period of consolidation – 1697–1829
The secular clergy in Scotland had been growing in numbers and since 1653 had been organized under a superior, called the Prefect. Only a few years after the complete debacle of the Revolution, another step of far-reaching consequences was taken when a secular priest, Thomas Nicolson, was appointed bishop. Although his title was only Vicar Apostolic (signifying that his authority was derived from the Congregation of Propaganda Fide in Rome), he was the superior of the Roman Catholic Church in Scotland in its entirety. Both he and James Gordon, appointed his coadjutor and future successor in 1705, were capable and devoted men, who succeeded in unifying their Church and setting it on a steady course.[22]

A new epoch began when Bishop Nicolson arrived in Scotland in 1697. A Lowlander himself, he spent several months in 1700 visiting the Highlands and Western Isles, where he gave the sacrament of confirmation to 3,000 persons. Four years later he ordained a priest, Peter Fraser. In 1701 the Jesuits in Scotland made a formal submission to his authority. Bishop Gordon, likewise a Lowlander, went round the Highlands and Islands in 1707, confirming 2,242 persons and ordaining a priest in Knoydart. The next year he traversed the Lowlands, and in 1709 once more toured the Highlands, this time confirming 1,200.[23] In the space of a dozen years, Highlands and Lowlands had been united under the same bishop, and all priests in Scotland had accepted his authority. The sacraments of Confirmation and Holy Orders had returned to Scotland, and with two bishops in the country there was no longer any difficulty over supplies of blest oil for priests to use. A further step forward was taken in 1720 when John Wallace was ordained bishop in Edinburgh. In 1727 Lowlands and Highlands were each given a bishop of their own and four years later, again in Edinburgh, Hugh MacDonald was ordained bishop for the Highlands. In appointing bishops for Scotland, the Holy See usually gave leave for their ordination to be carried out by a single bishop and two priests instead of the usual three bishops.[24]

Politically, Scottish Catholicism made the disastrous mistake of aligning itself with the exiled Stuarts and Jacobitism. Naturally, it suffered for this during the 1690s, after the Jacobite rising of 1715 and especially after the failure of the '45. After Culloden the Catholic chapels (such as they were) were everywhere destroyed, the vestments and altar vessels burnt, the priests mostly imprisoned or banished. It should be said, however, that the rancour of the victors seemed to exhaust itself before many years passed, while the Catholics displayed considerable resilience in their power to reorganize themselves. Under the very canny guidance of George Hay, the greatest of the vicars apostolic (appointed coadjutor of the Lowland District 1768, succeeded to the full title 1778), the Scottish Catholics rehabilitated themselves as loyal citizens and began to play a part once more in the life of the country.

Guidelines were laid down for the Church in the Statutes agreed upon by the Scottish clergy in 1700 and approved by Rome in 1706.[25] Only those concerned with worship rather than discipline are relevant here, though it is difficult to separate the two aspects. Undoubtedly the Statutes aimed at producing a disciplined Church. Each priest was to be guided by the Roman Ritual and the instructions of St. Charles Borromeo (Archbishop of Milan and protagonist of the Counter-Reformation, who died in 1584); converts could not be present at Mass until they had made their profession of faith, nor sinners until they had amended; Easter duties (that is, communion preceded by confession) were to be fulfilled, but priests were not to give absolution unless the penitent had shown signs of amendment and was sufficiently instructed.

Other regulations governed the feasts and fasts. Besides Sundays, there were thirteen days on which the faithful were to attend Mass and were not to work; as for fasts, besides the forty days of Lent, they were to fast and abstain from eating meat on the ember days (another nine)[26] and the vigils of feasts (fourteen). The dates of the moveable feasts and fasts were to be announced early each year. This was undoubtedly a severe enough programme: sixty-five days of attendance at chapel and abstention from normal work, and sixty-three days of considerable discipline regarding the times of eating and the amount and kind of food.

Scottish Catholicism in the early eighteenth century was already heading for a most dangerous internal crisis. Priests who had studied at Paris were accused of Jansenism, a somewhat elastic term which, in the context of worship, implied being too rigid and demanding as regards the dispositions required for receiving the sacraments.[27] The accusers included the traditional opponents of Jansenism, the Jesuits. Certainly the Statutes seem rather strict in the conditions they laid down for confession and communion. Whereas seventeenth-century priests spoke of confession and communion being received monthly or weekly, and a Jesuit in 1632 was encouraging frequent communion, Robert Strachan declined to give absolution to some penitents at Holyrood in 1687.[28] There is no doubt of the tendency towards receiving the sacraments less frequently and only after longer preparation. In the end the crisis passed over, but English-speaking Catholics have been characterized by a residue of rigoristic Jansenism to the present day.

George Hay's lists in the 1760s would indicate that, if all his flock received communion at Easter, three-quarters did at Christmas, and a smaller number at the Assumption (15 August).[29] These were presumably the most popular times for communion. The Holy See granted seven annual plenary indulgences to Scottish Catholics in this same decade. One of the conditions for gaining a plenary indulgence was reception of confession and communion, and the indulgences may well have been offered as an incentive to receive the sacraments. There were also several Jubilee or Holy Years in the eighteenth century, and as early as 1733 Bishop Gordon published instructions of where in Scotland the special indulgences could be gained.

Small pieces of information here and there throw light on Roman Catholic worship: MacNeill of Barra in 1700 instructing his people on Sunday, in the absence of a priest; a woman in Braemar in 1706 keeping St. Ninian's fast, from noon of Maundy Thursday to noon on Easter Sunday. When Bishop Gordon toured the Western Isles in 1707, there was a sermon in Gaelic after the Gospel; then after Mass the bishop gave a short address, which was translated into Gaelic, and administered Confirmation. Times had changed for the better by the 1760s, for George Hay at Preshome wanted to reserve the Blessed Sacrament if he could acquire the necessary altar vessel, whereas the statutes of 1700 had forbidden it 'under existing circumstances'. The future bishop John Geddes, born in 1735, was baptized when one day old but had to wait until 1749 to receive communion and confirmation.[30] The well of Our Lady of Grace near Fochabers was still a place of pilgrimage, with cures being wrought there. The rosary continued to be a popular devotion.[31]

The fast from midnight until after Mass was carefully observed by the priests. All had to keep the days of fast and abstinence, and the bishops were unwilling to grant any general relaxation, though priests could give certain dispensations in particular cases. Curiously, Catholics in what had been the province of St. Andrews were allowed to eat eggs during part of Lent as had been the custom in the Middle Ages; others had to keep a stricter fast. They drank deeply after funerals, however, even though the prayers had been said in the house and the burial had been very quietly done. The Catholic Duke of Gordon, on the other hand, lay in state in St. Ninian's Chapel before being interred in Elgin Cathedral. Catholics continued to be married by the priest, in spite of legal difficulties they thereby sometimes encountered.[32]

The most notable change in Roman Catholic worship concerned the place where services were held. The Statutes had fixed limits of each priest's territory within which he was to operate, and by 1745 these mission stations in the north-east had their chapel, usually a converted room or barn. Almost all were burnt down in the reprisals after Culloden, but before long most were rebuilt. Indeed that at Preshome, opened in 1790, was recognizably a church building, the first Roman Catholic chapel of its kind. Chapels were built usually to replace buildings which had been destroyed but in some cases where no chapel had been before or where the existing chapel was now too small. Under Bishop George Hay, Scottish Catholicism entered on a period of consolidation: the feasts and fasts were slightly curtailed, the Statutes were modified, a *Rituale* for the use of Scottish priests was produced,[33] as well as some devotional works in Scottish Gaelic.[34] In the 1790s Roman Catholic editions of the Bible were published in Edinburgh.[35] It was now the custom to catechize the children at the altar rails on

Sundays.[36] In fact, the Catholic Relief Act of 1793 allowing public worship merely ratified the already existing situation.

For some time Catholic Highlanders had been enlisting in the army and Catholic Lowlanders had been praying at Sunday Mass for the Hanoverian dynasty. Then, in the 1790s, Britain and the Holy See became political allies, while French refugee priests were sympathetically received in Britain. Until then the Sunday service in Scotland had consisted of a sermon, long vernacular prayers and a Low Mass in Latin.[37] The time seemed right for introducing something a little more lively. The first moves seem to have come in 1789 from the priests at Aberdeen, Fochabers and the Highland chapel in Edinburgh. Indeed the latter introduced the carol *Adeste Fideles*, which soon had the apprentices whistling it in every street. Bishop Hay, cautious to the last, would not countenance any innovation which might attract unwelcome attention, and he continued to forbid singing of any sort.[38] A Benedictine priest in the south-west in particular met with his disapproval; this was Gallus Robertson, who not only wanted to have the sermon during Mass but had introduced what a conservative neighbour called 'singing and ranting Psalms of his own Translation'. In 1803, however, Hay retired and singing was permitted.

Roman Catholic worship blossomed in the first decades of the nineteenth century. The Comte d'Artois, brother of Louis XVI, lived with his entourage at Holyrood from 1796 to 1810. In 1802 the 'Holyrood silver' rescued in 1688 was returned there to allow exposition of the Blessed Sacrament. In 1803 a church recognizable as such was opened in Aberdeen and High Mass was sung at its dedication the following year. This was a step of some magnitude, for it required not only a priest but also two other clergymen to act as deacon and subdeacon, with vestments for all three, and a choir to render the compulsory Latin texts. With the resources of Aquhorties seminary (near Inverurie), these requirements were met. The Aquhorties press also printed a hymn book and a book of devotions.[39]

In 1814 a new Roman Catholic chapel with an imposing Gothic façade was opened in Edinburgh, and an even grander one in Glasgow three years later, the most magnificent and spacious in Britain. Meanwhile, in towns such as Paisley, the first chapels had been built to meet the needs of the Irish immigrants. These new chapels had their choirs; some of them even had their organs.[40] By 1820 High Mass was no longer a novelty and organs had been installed in many places. The older chapels had to make structural alterations to accommodate choir and organ. Ironically, this music was popular with Protestants, who were attracted by it to Catholic chapels and contributed generously to the collections, thereby helping the expansion to proceed. There was a need for trained organists, for hymn books and music, for more suitable vestments. These needs were gradually met. In 1816 Aberdeen again led the way by introducing Benediction of the Blessed Sacrament on special occasions; before long the practice became general and widespread. A most spectacular change in Roman Catholic worship had taken place in the forty years between 1789 and 1829.

Period of expansion and freedom – 1829–c. 1965
The year 1829 was a momentous one in the history of the Roman Catholic Church in Scotland. Highlands and Lowlands became much more integrated: not only did the Highland and Lowland seminaries amalgamate to form the new college at Blairs, but the three-fold division into Eastern, Western and Northern Districts (replacing the division into Highlands and Lowlands) began to take effect. Emancipation removed most of the legal disabilities of Roman Catholics. In 1829 too, for the first time Scottish Catholics had their complex liturgical calendar specially printed, and to this annual production a list of churches, priests and services came to be added. Today the *Catholic Directory for Scotland*, of all such annuals, has the longest unbroken run of issues, allowing one to trace the trends in worship year by year.[41] Two years later, in 1831, Rome was considering a petition from the Scottish bishops to have the obligation of certain feasts and fasts reduced, to conform with the practice in England.[42]

Over the next few decades the Church in the Lowlands, particularly the west, expanded enormously. As Irish immigrants continued to crowd into the industrialized regions, its centre of gravity moved from rural to urban areas, from the Highlands and the north-east to the central belt. There many churches were built where none had been before; they were bigger, too, intended to accommodate much larger congregations, while older churches were extended. The development was less striking in the east, but Edinburgh began to see spectacular Roman Catholic services. In 1831 the exiled cardinal-bishop of Rheims presided at Bishop Paterson's funeral. When John Menzies of Pitfodels died in 1843, Bishop Gillis stage-managed a most magnificent Requiem Mass and a funeral procession that had 50,000 people lining the streets to see it.

Sung Vespers on Sunday afternoons became quite common. An important feature of Roman Catholic life returned to Scotland when in 1834 the first nuns established a convent near Edinburgh. Other orders of nuns followed them, then orders of male religious, and from 1878, at Fort Augustus, the full office and Mass were sung or recited in public every day.[43] Meanwhile, in Scotland as in other countries, what has been termed the 'devotional revolution' took place as Catholics rediscovered the tradition of experiential religion. There was a proliferation of new devotions (or at least, new to Scotland): the Way of the Cross, the Sacred Heart, the Forty Hours exposition of the Blessed Sacrament. The focus was on parish life, with the priest at its centre. When parish missions began to be held, the confessionals were besieged, the altar rails crowded with communicants. At one parish mission in Glasgow about 1859, there were 3,947 confessions, 1,265 adults reclaimed, 165 first confessions, 35 Protestants receiving Catholic instruction. Many Irish immigrants were experiencing in urban Clydeside an organized devotional religion which they had not known in rural Ireland. Rosary and Benediction replaced the less obviously devotional Vespers as the standard evening service. 'May processions' in honour of Our Lady were introduced, and Corpus Christi processions of the Blessed Sacrament in late May or early June. Statuary was placed in churches to foster devotion: Stations of the Cross, statues of Christ and the saints, the Christmas crib with its various figures. Societies were founded to foster devotion and good works or to create solidarity in various groups in the parish, e.g. the mothers. It was a situation resembling the late Middle Ages in that a somewhat passive participation in the Latin liturgy was compensated for by non-liturgical devotions and fellowship. Roman Catholic life took on a very ultramontane, pro-papal ethos, with a fairly strong element of Mediterranean devotion and terminology.

By 1878 there were over 300,000 Catholics in Scotland, two-thirds of them in the west Lowlands. This expansion, not only in numbers but also in vitality and self-confidence, led Rome to conclude that Scotland was no longer a mission country. This was a conclusion given added force by the need to settle the open hostility between the Irish immigrants and the indigenous priests and bishops. Accordingly, in 1878, a hierarchy (that is, a national conference) of bishops was set up in Scotland: six diocesan bishops with *ex officio* authority in place of three vicars-apostolic with powers delegated by Rome.[44] As the new system came into operation, diocesan synods were held, with ceremonies not seen before. In each diocese one church was given the status of cathedral; somewhat unexpectedly, that of Oban became for some years the only one in the British Isles where the full celebration of the daily liturgical office was carried out. Aristocratic converts had contributed greatly to the advancement of Roman Catholic worship, by acting as catalysts or financing the building of churches. Perhaps the most important was the third Marquess of Bute, whose enthusiasm for the liturgy brought the Oban project into being.[45] Scotland also received a liturgical calendar that was more fully national, as the celebration of Scottish saints' feast-days was revived.[46] Pilgrimages too, were revived: at home to Iona, Whithorn and Dunfermline, abroad to Rome and Lourdes.

In the Lowlands this parish-based vitality could be, unkindly but with some justification, described as the Catholic ghetto.[47] In the Scots-speaking north-east, Catholic chapels were now in the towns rather than in the country. In the Gaelic-speaking Highlands and Islands, Catholicism remained mainly rural but places of worship were improved: a large slated building was termed *eaglais* (church), a smaller slated building was *caibeal* (chapel), while a 'black' or thatched building was *tigh-phobuill* (perhaps best translated as 'meeting-house'). The well-known Fr. Allan McDonald was, in Eriskay in the 1880s, introducing the 'devotional revolution' in Gaelic. He went further, with a Children's Mass in 1885 and his popular 'Gaelic Mass',[48] which anticipated the much later German *Betsingmesse* and the liturgical revolution of the later twentieth century.

Scottish Catholicism continued to grow in confidence. At Fort Augustus, the first national synod of bishops in 1886 and the centenary of Bishop Hay's death in 1911 were made into great liturgical occasions.[49] A centre of pilgrimage was set up at Carfin (Lanarkshire) and drew 30,000–40,000 worshippers one Sunday afternoon in 1928. In the 1930s a chronicler of Scottish Catholicism portrayed Scotland as a liturgical desert. In one sense this was justified, if 'liturgical' is taken in its stricter meaning of what concerns the official worship of the Church. Scotland was certainly deficient in public celebration of daily office and sung Mass. Universally, Dom Guéranger's *Liturgical Year* and his restoration of Gregorian chant were accepted as the ideal. Scotland did not match up to this; indeed the 'devotional revolution' of the previous century had led in a contrary direction. On the other hand, Pius X's encouragement in 1904 to receive Communion more frequently and at an earlier age was increasingly making headway, though less so in the conservative Highlands and north-east.

These were international influences, perhaps weaker in Scotland than in other European countries. In the mid-twentieth century the influences became stronger as well as more basic. A scriptural revival began to affect the Roman Catholic Church as it increasingly accepted the revolution in scripture studies. In liturgy, the rather academic and archaeological approach of Dom Guéranger gave way to emphasis on the doctrine of the Mystical Body, according to which the Church's liturgy is the worship of every baptized Christian.[50] Liturgical progress thus moved out from the monastery into the parish. Successive relaxations of discipline made fuller participation in the Church's worship easier. The fast before Communion was no longer from midnight but from three hours, then one hour, beforehand. The introduction of 'dialogue' Mass meant that not merely the 'server' but the whole congregation joined in the Latin responses. Allowing evening Mass, whereas hitherto it was permitted in the forenoon only, made attendance easier but had the side effect of ousting Sunday evening devotional services. There was also increased attendance at the reformed and simplified Holy Week ceremonies.

All this led to the immense changes effected by the Second Vatican Council. In the mid-twentieth century large congregations attended Sunday Mass in Scotland,[51] but in general they played a very passive role and congregational singing was impoverished. It is fair to say that the devotional revolution of the previous century had become stereotyped. Nevertheless, the latent vitality was there, and the number and proportion of Roman Catholics had increased steadily, from 325,000 (9 per cent of the population) in 1878 to 817,000 (15.7 per cent) in the 1960s,[52] although the influx of Irish priests and laity had diminished to almost nothing. Vatican II was to find in Scotland considerable potential for development, despite the numerical decline since the mid-1960s.

NOTES

1. For breviaries, see David McRoberts, 'Some Sixteenth-Century Scottish Breviaries', *Innes Review* 3 (1952), 33–48.
2. For the rosary from the fifteenth century on, see David McRoberts, 'The Rosary in Scotland', *Innes Review* 23 (1972), 81–86. Source references are intended to supplement the Bibliography.
3. See David McRoberts, 'The Fetternear Banner', *Innes Review* 7 (1956), 69–86.
4. William James Anderson, 'Thomas Innes on Catholicism in Scotland 1560–1653', *Innes Review* 7 (1956), 117. Copies of Innes' text are in the Scottish Catholic Archives, among Innes, Kyle and Clapperton papers.
5. For one episode, see R. Pitcairn, *Ancient Criminal Trials in Scotland* (Bannatyne Club 1833) I, p. *435.
6. *Ibid.*, I, pp. *427–430.
7. J. H. Pollen, *Papal Negotiations with Mary Queen of Scots*, pp. 123–126, 135–137. The translation given in Forbes-Leith, *Narratives*, is not reliable.
8. See also Odo Blundell, *Ancient Catholic Homes of Scotland* (London, 1907), p. 9; Mark Dilworth, 'Abbot Gilbert Brown: a Sketch of his Career', *Innes Review* 40 (1989), 153–155.
9. For a very similar case in 1607, see Pitcairn, *Ancient Criminal Trials* II, pp. 530–531. Missals and chalices in use are described in William James Anderson, 'Three Sixteenth-Century Scottish Missals', *Innes Review* 9 (1958), 204–209; David McRoberts, 'Some Post-Reformation Chalices', *Innes Review* 18 (1967), 144–146.
10. The resulting disturbances are described in Ninian Winzet's *Certain Tractates,* ed. J. K. Hewison (Scottish Text Society, 1888–90), I, pp. 123, 126. Winzet's *Four Scoir Thre Questions* also describe differences between Catholic and Protestant rites (*ibid.*, pp. 83–84).
11. *The Booke of the Universall Kirk of Scotland*, ed. Alexander Peterkin (1839), p. 331.
12. Anderson, 'Thomas Innes', 119; Donald Maclean, *The Counter-Reformation in Scotland 1560–1930* (London, 1931), pp. 93–94.
13. Blundell, *Ancient Catholic Homes*, pp. 155–157; Dilworth, 'Abbot Gilbert Brown', pp. 155–156; Maclean, *Counter-Reformation*, pp. 94, 97–99; Pitcairn, *Ancient Criminal Trials* III, pp. 252–254.

14. Gordon, *Catholic Church*, p. x (taken from the manuscript account in Scottish Catholic Archives, SM 2/29/6).

15. The practice is also described in *Memoirs of the Life of John Gordon, of Glencat* (London, 1734), p. 4.

16. See also William James Anderson, 'Prefect Ballentine's Report, circa 1660', *Innes Review* 8 (1957), 111, 125. Copies of Ballentine's text are in Scottish Catholic Archives, SM 2/3, 2/15/1.

17. For a case in the Highlands, see Maclean, *Counter-Reformation*, p. 300.

18. Richard Augustin Hay, *Genealogie of the Hayes of Tweeddale* (Edinburgh, 1835), p. 58. Rome upgraded St. Margaret's feast in the 1670s but we do not know how this affected Catholics in Scotland; see Mark Dilworth, 'Jesuits and Jacobites: The Cultus of St. Margaret', *Innes Review* (forthcoming).

19. Hay, *Genealogie*, pp. 55–56. The original of the passage cited in Anson, *Underground Catholicism*, pp. 83–84, is in the Scottish Catholic Archives BL 1/101/18. An insight into worship in the home at this time can be gained from William James Anderson, 'Catholic Family Worship on Deeside in 1691', *Innes Review* 18 (1967), pp. 151–156.

20. Hay, *Genealogie*, pp. 57, 60; Blundell, *Ancient Catholic Homes*, pp. 122–123. A contemporary valuation of the priests' gear lost is in Scottish Catholic Archives, SM 2/18/4.

21. For corporate Irish efforts, see Mary Purcell, *The Story of the Vincentians* (Dublin, 1973), chapter 3; Cathaldus Giblin, 'The Mission to the Highlands and the Isles c. 1670', *Franciscan College Annual* (Multyfarnham, 1954), 7–20; *idem,* 'St. Oliver Plunkett, Francis MacDonnell, O.F.M. and the Mission to the Hebrides', *Collectanea Hibernica* 17 (1974–75), 69–102.

22. Summary information on each bishop is given in James Darragh, *The Catholic Hierarchy of Scotland* (Glasgow, 1986).

23. Typescripts of the original reports of these episcopal visitations are in Scottish Catholic Archives, SM 3/1, 3/8.

24. The sets of papal bulls sent to each bishop can be reconstituted from the originals in Scottish Catholic Archives, SM 12.

25. A summary in translation is in Bellesheim, *History* IV, pp. 169–174. Contemporary copies of the full original text are in the Scottish Catholic Archives, SM 3/2.

26. This corrects the figure usually given. Three of the twelve ember days were in Lent and should not be counted twice.

27. A reappraisal of the significance and importance of Jansenism in Scotland is given by James McMillan, 'Scottish Catholics and the Jansenist Controversy: The Case Re-opened', *Innes Review* 32 (1981), 22–33 and subsequent articles: *ibid.*, 33 (1982), 23–30; 39 (1988), 12–45.

28. Hay, *Genealogie*, pp. 55–56; Anson, *Underground Catholicism*, p. 83.
29. Gordon, *Catholic Church*, p. 45, from original in Scottish Catholic Archives, IM 28/2.
30. For the impact made by Continental Roman Catholicism on John Geddes and a companion, see Gordon, *Catholic Church*, pp. 23–24.
31. See note 2. In 1697 leave was given by the Master General of the Dominicans to the Duchess of Gordon to have a confraternity of the rosary in her chapel (Scottish Catholic Archives, SM 3/10/5).
32. For this, at times misunderstood, subject see Anson, *Underground Catholicism*, pp. 340–341; Johnson, *Developments,* chapter 16.
33. Texts of the Statutes with amendments and additions in the hand of Hay and others are in Scottish Catholic Archives, SM 4/20. Printed booklets for the priests, *Instructiones* (1781) and *Rituale* (1783), are in SM 4/18, 4/19.
34. Donald Maclean, *Typographia Scoto-Gadelica*, pp. 1, 83–84. For later publications see *ibid.*, pp. 20, 87, 211–212, 305, 342–343.
35. William James Anderson, 'Father Gallus Robertson's edition of the New Testament, 1792', *Innes Review* 17 (1966), 48–59.
36. For an illustration see Anson, *Underground Catholicism*, p. 196; James Stark, *Priest Gordon of Aberdeen* (Aberdeen, 1909), opp. p. 56.
37. The lack of ceremonial and music can be readily explained by poverty of resources, the influence of Protestant neighbours and the desire to be unobtrusive. Having the sermon before Mass, whereas the traditional position was following the Gospel reading during Mass (see above, for instance: Bishop Gordon in the Western Isles in 1707), is less obviously explicable. Perhaps the priests wished to wear Mass vestments for the minimum length of time, when hostile interruption was always possible.
38. *A Collection of Spiritual Songs* (1791) sung to Scottish airs and a subsequent edition *A Collection of Spiritual Hymns and Songs* (1802), partly the work of Hay, are didactic rather than intended for worship. See Anthony Ross, 'A Collection of Spiritual Songs', *St. Peter's College Magazine* 19 (1949), 11–17.
39. Copies in Scottish Catholic Archives, CS 2/19, 2/26.
40. For music in the Aberdeen chapel, see Constance Davidson, *Priest Gordon* (London, Sands n.d.), pp. 50–54.
41. For this and other yearbooks and liturgical calendars, see David McRoberts, 'The Catholic Directory for Scotland, 1829–1975', *Innes Review* 26 (1975), 93–120.
42. Charles Burns, 'Additions to the *Fondo Missioni* Handlist', *Innes Review* 33 (1982), 35.

43. An outline from 1834 on is given in Mark Dilworth 'Religious
    Orders in Scotland, 1878–1978', *Innes Review* 29 (1979), 92–109.
    Reprinted with the same pagination in David McRoberts, ed.,
    Modern Scottish Catholicism 1878–1978 (Glasgow, 1979).
44. David McRoberts, 'The Restoration of the Scottish Catholic
    Hierarchy in 1878', *ibid.*, pp. 3–29.
45. Roderick Macdonald, 'The "Tin" Cathedral at Oban: 1886–1934',
    Innes Review 15 (1964), 47–55; David Hunter Blair, *John Patrick
    Third Marquess of Bute, K.T.* (London, 1921).
46. See, for instance, *Catholic Directory for Scotland*, 1899, pp. 74–76;
    Michael Barrett, *A Calendar of Scottish Saints* (2nd edn. Fort
    Augustus, 1919), *passim.*
47. An excellent general account is given in John Cooney, *Scotland
    and the Papacy* (Edinburgh, 1982).
48. Scottish Catholic Archives, Allan McDonald correspondence
    1884–91; John L. Campbell, *Fr. Allan McDonald of Eriskay, 1859–
    1905* (Edinburgh, 1954), pp. 15, 27; *idem*, 'The Sources of the
    Gaelic Hymnal, 1893', *Innes Review* 7 (1956), 101–111.
49. *Catholic Directory for Scotland*, 1887, pp. 216–218; 1912, pp. 249–
    251.
50. Two landmarks for Scripture and liturgy respectively are the papal
    encyclicals *Divino Afflante Spiritu* and *Mystici Corporis* (both
    1943).
51. See for instance John Highet, *The Scottish Churches* (London,
    1960), pp. 59–63; James Darragh, 'The Catholic Population of
    Scotland, 1878–1977', *Innes Review* 29 (1978) and McRoberts,
    Modern Scottish Catholicism, pp. 220–221.
52. James Darragh (*ibid.*, pp. 221–247) gives the most recent and
    sophisticated statistical analysis. A summary of statistics is given in
    Catholic Directory for Scotland, 1979, p. 501.

BIBLIOGRAPHY

Dilworth, Mark, 'The Counter-Reformation in Scotland: A Select
    Critical Bibliography' *Records of the Scottish Church Society* 22
    (1986), 85–100.
Bellesheim, Alphons, *History of the Catholic Church in Scotland*, trans.
    D. O. Hunter Blair (Edinburgh and London, 1887–90), III and IV.
Anson, Peter F., *The Catholic Church in Modern Scotland 1560–1937*
    (London, 1937).
Anson, Peter F., *Underground Catholicism in Scotland 1622–1878*
    (Montrose, 1970).
Forbes-Leith, William, ed., *Narratives of Scottish Catholics under Mary
    Stuart and James VI* (Edinburgh, 1885).
Forbes-Leith, William, ed., *Memoirs of Scottish Catholics during the
    XVIIth and XVIIIth Centuries*, 2 vols. (London, 1909).

Blundell, Odo, *The Catholic Highlands of Scotland*, 2 vols. (Edinburgh and London, 1909–17).

Gordon, J. F. S., *The Catholic Church in Scotland from the Suppression of the Hierarchy to the Present Time* (Aberdeen, 1874). The same work appears with other title-pages, e.g. *Journal and Appendix to the Scotichronicon and Monasticon* (Glasgow, 1867).

For more limited areas:

Sanderson, Margaret H. B., 'Catholic Recusancy in Scotland in the Sixteenth Century', *Innes Review* 21 (1970), 87–107.

Anderson, William James, ed., 'Report of Father Robert Abercrombie, S.J. in the Year 1580', *Innes Review* 7 (1956), 27–59.

Blakhal, Gilbert, *A Breiffe Narration of the Services Done to Three Noble Ladyes M.DC.XXXI–M.DC.XLIX* (Spalding Club, 1844).

Giblin, Cathaldus, ed., *Irish Franciscan Mission to Scotland 1619–1646* (Dublin, 1964).

Johnson, Christine, *Developments in the Roman Catholic Church in Scotland, 1789–1829* (Edinburgh, John Donald, 1983).

Catholic Directory for Scotland (1829–).

Aspinwall, Bernard, 'The Formation of the Catholic Community in the West of Scotland: Some Preliminary Outlines', *Innes Review* 33 (1982), 44–57.

The originals of Robert Abercrombie's Report and Blakhal, and many documents in Forbes-Leith, *Memoirs*, are in the Scottish Catholic Archives. The works by Gordon and Johnson rely heavily on the Blairs Letters in the Scottish Catholic Archives.

Chapter Nine

THE SCOTTISH TRADITION OF PREACHING

David Read

From the time of the Reformation the Scottish Church has been widely recognized as a begetter of preachers. To this day, whether we think that this reputation is justified or somewhat inflated, we have to live with it. Some may feel that there is more legend than fact behind this judgement today. Others may wish that the Church in Scotland could be celebrated rather for its saints, its devotional heritage, its liturgical contributions, its enviable solution of the Church-and-State controversy, or its enlistment of the laity in the government of the Church. The fact remains that in the estimate of the Christian world Scotland produces preachers: we are saddled with this tradition.

Nowhere is this reputation stronger than in the USA, where many are convinced that preachers rank second only to Scotland's leading export to that country. While immigrant preachers from other parts of the world struggle to acquire a standard American accent, the Scots maintain (and sometimes enhance) the lilt and cadences of their native tongue. To betray this origin is immediately to raise the expectation of powerful preaching, and even the weakest sermon can be greeted with acclamation if it is delivered with the throatiness of Harry Lauder or the rumble of Ramsay Macdonald. (Younger readers could ask parents to identify the above.) All this does not detract from the undoubted contribution of many distinguished Scottish preachers, whom many of us remember with immense gratitude, to the art and content of preaching in America, particularly among the Presbyterian Churches. The Churches of Europe and the Third World are not so apt to recognize this homiletic distinction, but the propensity of the Scot to travel to Europe or to what used to be called the 'mission field' served to propagate the Scottish style of preaching and its distinctive emphases.

But what are these emphases? What *is* the Scottish tradition of preaching?

Its origins are naturally in the turmoil of the Reformation. Scotland, like France, Holland, Hungary, and other European nations, was exposed to the power of the Word – the rediscovered impact of God speaking to the contemporary world through the content of Holy Scripture. From John Knox, fresh from Calvin's Geneva, through others who had drunk from the same source, the emerging Reformed Church in Scotland found the new centre of gravity in the pulpit. The exposition of the Word of God in the Reformed Churches created the new communions of Christian people, inspired them to battle for what they saw as a purified worship and a more scriptural and 'democratic' government of the Church, and was an instrument in the struggle for freedom from state control.

Thus from the beginning the Scottish tradition of preaching has been strongly biblical. The sermon was embedded in the act of public worship and never thought of as a kind of PS. in which remarks were made about suitable (or unsuitable) Christian behaviour or the need for financial support. There was in the Reformed tradition what could be called (but seldom was) a sacramental view of the sermon, and this has shaped Scottish preaching at its best. As in the celebration of Holy Communion ordinary elements of bread and wine become, through the operation of the Holy Spirit, the vehicles of the real presence of Christ, so in preaching the real, ordinary words of every day become, through the power of the same Spirit, the vehicle of the living Word of God. Hence there was a strong note of authority in the Scottish pulpit combined with a very concrete application of the scriptural text to contemporary life and manners.

This biblical foundation of preaching was modified and adulterated over the centuries after the Reformation, but it has remained a conspicuous element in the tradition. Congregations (at least until very recently) expected readings from both Old and New Testament in their Sunday worship, the announcement of a text, and its exposition. There was thus a healthy emphasis on the authority of Scripture which kept the practice of preaching from the blight of subjectivism and triviality which has infected certain areas of modern church life and worship. Just as a minister did not hesitate to preface a reading of Scripture with the words: 'Hear the Word of God', so there was an element of 'Thus saith the Lord' in the sermon. The biblical tradition also ensured that the sermon usually had theological backbone, and Scotland has enormously benefited from the firm alliance between the pulpit and the seminary, and the habit of drawing professors of theology from the ranks of practising preachers. (I think of the preaching skills of scholars eminent in their field, and of *obiter dicta*, like Professor H. R. Mackintosh remarking: 'What cannot be preached ought not to be believed.')

It has to be admitted that the passion for expounding the Word has not always kept within liturgical bounds. By the eighteenth century the sermon was not only extremely lengthy but was supplemented by a running commentary on Scripture when it was being read in the course of the service. Thus worship became more and more dominated by the sound of the preacher's voice and the congregation correspondingly passive. So one of the major principles of the Reformation – the participation of the people of God in the act of worship – was paradoxically undermined and the congregation which had been rescued from the position of mere spectators became mere auditors. It was not until the liturgical revival of some hundred years ago that the Scottish tradition began to be freed from the dominance of the spoken word, and the sermon to find its true place in the living worship of the churches. (The vestiges of this aberration can still be heard when attendance at divine worship is referred to as 'Going to hear Dr. So-and-So.') It has been difficult to persuade some church members that this isolation of the sermon and neglect of its proper place in the ordered expression of congregational worship was not in the true Scottish tradition, and that the use of collects, creeds and responses, for instance, in a balanced framework of worship links us with the reformers themselves. In the same way a restored emphasis on the sacraments of Baptism and Holy Communion is a return to the true tradition which was lost during the period when Baptism became 'private' and the Lord's Supper a very occasional feast.

There have been times, too, when the tradition of scriptural preaching was distorted by a lapse into a tedious rehearsal of the biblical material verse by verse, or by the excessive use of allegorical interpretation. Congregations were encouraged to believe they were listening to biblical preaching simply because the text was being re-worded or because some moral maxim was being illustrated from a tale from the Old or New Testament. (I once heard an Easter sermon on the text: 'They saw that the stone was rolled away' the point of which was simply that we often find that our difficulties have disappeared when we come to them!).

As in other Protestant Churches a crisis came for biblical preaching with the advent of critical scholarship and its impact on the proclamation of the Word of God. Towards the end of the nineteenth century the preacher faced the dilemma of whether to ignore the critical approach to the Scriptures that was gradually being accepted and taught in the halls of divinity and continue to preach as though he had never head of J, P, E and D or of any 'synoptic problem', or to risk startling his congregation with references to the human element in the composition of the Bible and the use of terms like 'myth' and 'legend'. If he adopted the former course, he was opening a chasm between his new understanding of the Bible through literary and historical criticism and the impression he was giving from the pulpit of accepting the pre-critical approach. If he chose the latter, he was exposed to charges of denying 'the truth of the Bible' and deeply offending some of the most devout and stalwart members of his flock.

The Scottish tradition of scholarship ensured that this crisis was faced at an earlier date than in many other countries and that it was fought through with a greater intensity. Although the older view of Scripture (later given the name of 'fundamentalist') persisted and is being constantly revived, the great majority of Scottish preachers learned to accept, often with thankfulness and relief, the new light that was being thrown on the nature and composition of the Bible, and to incorporate it in their proclamation of the Gospel. There was, however, in some quarters a weakening of the note of authority and a tendency to turn from exposition of the Scriptures to moralistic homilies, social commentary, or dramatization. Thus it was that in the thirties and forties of this century many Scottish preachers were ready to listen to the voice of Karl Barth and others who were speaking of the 'Word of God' with fresh power and instancy based on a theology that was in full revolt from a dominant 'liberalism' while accepting the critical approach to the Bible. For 'Neo-orthodoxy', in fact, the paradox of a Scripture that is *truly* human as well as *truly* divine was as necessary as the truly human and truly divine nature of Christ.

No one supposes that this particular emphasis has been the last word for the Scottish understanding of preaching, but it would be fair to say that some combination of a radiant belief that God speaks to us today through the biblical Word with an intelligent understanding of the nature of the book in its diversity of origin and literary genres stands within the tradition and continues to inspire what is most characteristic of the Scottish pulpit.

Some such historical appreciation will perhaps justify an attempt to summarize the contribution of this tradition to the Church Catholic.

(1) It is tempting to begin with a remark I once heard from a friend in the Church of England. 'What strikes me about the Scottish pulpit', he said, '*is the unique combination of scholarship and passion*'. It is probably true that in other traditions these qualities often seem to belong to quite different people. The scholar appears in the pulpit with his precise manuscript, his professional air, and delivers his sermon with the calm authority of one who knows. On the other hand the passionate preacher arouses the emotions, seeks to persuade and convert, and seems oblivious to any intellectual objections or cultural sensibilities in his congregation. It has been the strength of the Scottish pulpit that scholarship and passion have often been dynamically fused. (The long-running series of books entitled 'Scholar as Preacher' was a typically Scottish phenomenon.)

This tradition has its roots in the seminary where our professors not only had been, but still were preachers. I am thinking now of one of the greatest Old Testament scholars who had introduced us to the mysteries of the documentary sources of I Samuel. Breaking off one day to sketch the whole tragic life of Saul he ended the story of the rescue of his body by the men of Jabesh-Gilead with tears running from his eyes. Many will have similar recollections of immensely erudite scholars whose passions for the proclamation of the Gospel shone through the classroom lectures.

The Scottish Church has thus retained the conviction exemplified by Paul the Apostle that the powers of the mind can be harnessed to the burning desire to communicate the Gospel, and demonstrated by the unusual Dean of St. Paul's, John Donne, whose sermons were almost top-heavy with scholastic exposition but caught fire when the passionate poet broke through. It has never been considered in Scotland that the possession of academic qualifications should in any way inhibit a preacher from reaching the emotions or displaying the love of Christ that animates his soul. (It is simply for convenience that I am using the masculine pronoun when referring to the preacher. I am aware that, especially in this alliance of scholarship and passion, the tradition will open into new horizons as women increasingly occupy our pulpits.)

(2) Anyone trained for the ministry in Scotland has been exposed to the *discipline of sermon preparation*. In a day when ministers are apt to be suffocated by the sheer quantity of different tasks they are called on to perform, and are being tempted by slick 'How-to' techniques for the production of popular homilies, this element in the Scottish tradition sounds a needed warning. The voice of a long-dead professor sounds in the preacher's ear: 'Gentlemen, the curse of the ministry is laziness.' Or from another: 'The minister who is at his desk at 9 o'clock has one kind of ministry: the one who sits reading the *Scotsman* till 10 has another.' Today's laziness is not so much sheer idleness as letting almost any other pressing business encroach on the sermon preparation, and the reading of the *Scotsman* may now be the perusal of junk mail (which always seems extraordinarily attractive when the sermon beckons).

This tradition, I trust, will continue to haunt us. It means the acquiring of commentaries rather than little books of topical concern. It means honest work at exegesis. It means labouring to express theological insights in non-theological language. It means keeping the mind alive and avoiding the smooth little ruts in which our thoughts so painlessly move. It means considering the hours dedicated to the sermon as sacred as any other demands on one's time. It means keeping pace with congregations who are exposed, at least sometimes, to first-class minds in newspapers, magazines, radio and TV. It simply means taking the preaching task *seriously*. (I remember, as a probationer filled with the ideals of preaching to which I had been exposed, waiting one Sunday morning in the garden of the church where my laboriously prepared sermon would be delivered. Beside me sat an older preacher from another denomination who was on a similar assignment. He looked at his watch: 'Quarter to eleven! It's time I started thinking what I'm going to say.')

(3) Another note in the tradition is the *pastoral concern* of Scottish preaching at its best. This stems from the fact that preaching was never divorced from the care of a parish and sensitivity to the needs of its

people, whether church-goers or not. The discipline of scholarly research, careful exegesis, faithful exposition, and theological thinking, seldom came between the preacher and those to whom he was expounding the Gospel. While it was never in the Scottish tradition to lace a sermon with cheerful anecdotes about well-known characters, or indulge in pseudo-psychological therapeutics, there was normally a very human relationship between preacher and hearer based on a deep sensitivity to the joys and sorrows of their common experience. The sermon never dwelt in some intellectual or theological stratosphere but struck home to the needs of real men and women – most of whom the preacher knew in the intimacy of their homes. This tradition is endangered wherever churches become large, highly organized institutions, or where there is some kind of collegiate arrangement whereby one minister is the preacher, and another the pastor. Yet we can hope that no future experiments in adapting to changing circumstances will ever remove the preacher from the daily human contacts with those to whom he speaks on Sundays.

   (4) There is one controversial area of the preacher's calling on which the Scottish experience has light to shed. It could be called *the freedom of the pulpit to address social and national questions*. In recent years this has often been referred to as the 'prophetic note' in preaching, using the word 'prophecy' in its sense of 'speaking out', forth-telling rather than fore-telling. Unfortunately, the word has in some quarters come to be associated simply with being 'agin' the government or perhaps rather the establishment. So it is better to speak about the freedom of the pulpit to apply scriptural insights and convictions to specific questions of social and political controversy. In this thickly mined territory, the Church of Scotland has resolutely held to the belief that a preacher is not deviating from his Christian ministry when he speaks of his conscience in the name of God. The rightness of this conviction and the occasional wrongness of a preacher's judgement in particular cases is well illustrated from the example of John Knox. No one can deny that Knox believed it to be his sacred calling to use the pulpit as an instrument for carrying through a reformation that was sorely needed, and that his voice counted more than many political manoeuvres or movements of troops. He was not afraid of applying scriptural admonitions, or scriptural examples, to the current political uproar in Scotland. He believed that in those responsive congregations the 'people of God' had found a voice, and since this 'people of God' were the common folk who had been in the thrall of lords, temporal and ecclesiastic, his diatribes had strong political repercussions. From Knox's sermons, however, one can detect occasions when political zeal was more in evidence than strict adherence to the biblical text, and he could be accused of bending the Word to suit his purposes.

This is being evidenced in the Scottish tradition to this day. But the conviction that preaching ought never to remain solely in the realm of political and social concerns has prevented the Scottish pulpit from being an instrument of party propaganda. From time to time the bias of an Established Church towards the defence of the status quo has been reflected in the sermons of the parish pulpit but, on the whole, the unique nature of the Scottish establishment has preserved it from the taunt that it represents 'the Conservative party at prayer'. In the same way it is seldom that preachers whose sympathies are entirely with the political 'left' have abandoned a scriptural approach and become merely the mouthpiece of current party lines. The existence of a Church and Nation Committee of the General Assembly demonstrates the conviction that national and social issues are a proper concern of the Church and encourages the preacher to confront even the most controversial questions in the light of the Christian Gospel. And the politically varied composition of such a committee ensures that no preacher is likely to feel bound to defend or oppose any particular act of the civil powers from the standpoint of an accepted party line.

A word might be in order about the *mood* of traditional Scottish preaching. It is popularly recognized to be, on the whole, one of dignity and high seriousness. The preacher has not been expected to indulge in funny stories to, as Shakespeare put it, 'split the ears of the groundlings'. An exception to this has been the comparatively recent tradition of introducing a 'children's address' which, at its best, can be a helpful distillation of the main point of the sermon, but, at its worst, is little more than comic relief. Nor has the Scottish preacher been expected to indulge much in whimsical asides of a personal nature, or brush off serious questions with a quip. This is not to say that a typical Scottish sermon has always been lacking in humour but that the inherent dignity of divine worship and the high purpose of the sermon has ruled out a lapse into frivolity or bad taste.

Yet I confess that this mood of high seriousness has had an unfortunate result in the dehumanizing of the preaching of the Word at certain times in the Scottish pulpit, and I am not sorry to find a lighter note, an unashamed use of genuine humour, finding its way back in recent years. The old tradition of total and unrelieved seriousness often led to an artificial distinction between the man the congregation saw in the pulpit and the man they knew in their homes. This has led at times to a loss of the truly human side of the preaching paradox. The preacher became, not the *real* person through whom the real Word of God could be spoken, but a creature to be accepted for an hour or so on Sundays as a 'religious' being, speaking a 'religious' language. This element in the tradition has also had an unfortunate effect on the preacher. Just as at one period in the tradition congregations who violently objected to what they called 'ritual' in public worship found a release for their liturgical instincts in the ceremonies and rites of fraternal organizations, so preachers who assumed an invariable 'religious' pose in the pulpit found relief by being in great demand as witty speakers at Burns Suppers. It is all to the good that preachers today seem to be less afraid to be themselves in the pulpit, to let a humorous remark loose when it spontaneously occurs to them, and to find nothing incongruous in eliciting an occasional hearty laugh from the congregation. A sign that the truly human element in preaching is being recovered is the virtual disappearance of the 'minister's whine' that used to be heard so regularly and monotonously from the pulpit.

When considering the marks and the mood of the Scottish tradition of preaching, we have to confront the debatable question of whether the pulpit responded to certain facets of the Scottish character or was responsible for shaping them. Was the theological nature of the preacher the product of a national inclination towards metaphysics, or was the Scottish passion for asking the ultimate questions the result of hearing them endlessly rehearsed in the pulpit? To put it another way: Did the Scottish divines make the first question of the catechism: 'What is the chief end of man?' because that was a matter that deeply concerned the metaphysical Scot, or was it the constant repetition of this question with its answer that aroused a desire to philosophize in every Scottish breast?

I am inclined to the latter view. There is not too much evidence in the Middle Ages of a strong philosophical bent among the Scots. It is true that, after Chaucer, there was an outburst of poetry in Scotland which was not paralleled in the southern kingdom, and presumably his 'Boethius', with its wranglings about predestination and freewill, found an echo, but it would be hard to maintain that there was a natural inclination in the population at large for theological disputation. It was surely the arrival of the Reformation, and the peculiar shape and leadership it had in Scotland, that nourished the desire to wrestle with ultimate questions and the delight in theological argument that has been such a notable part of the Scottish tradition. (It throws a lot of light on national temperament to compare that first question in the catechism with that which our pragmatic neighbours to the south found most fitting: 'What is your name?')

The Scottish tradition of preaching has surely a lot to do with the eighteenth-century flowering of philosophy and metaphysics that had such repercussions in Europe and elsewhere. For the kind of preaching to which the entire nation was exposed was calculated to awaken the mind and kindle a passion for debate. It was in Scotland that the sermon penetrated most deeply into the minds as well as the souls of ordinary people. In the days before the modern distractions of press and television, the sermon was not only the unique spiritual stimulus of the week, but the mental pabulum as well. Its content would be discussed not only over the Sunday dinner, but throughout the week in the shops, the smithy, the bothy, and the tea-table. This lasted well through the nineteenth century, and, although the tradition may seem to have faded without trace by the late twentieth century, there is still a lively encounter between schools of philosophy and divinity, the Scottish contribution to modern philosophy is not totally divorced from its theological roots, and to this day a lively theological correspondence is more likely to break out in the columns of the *Scotsman* than of *The Times*.

It is not the purpose of this chapter to close on the note of 'Ichabod!' There is indeed much in the Scottish tradition of preaching that seems a mere memory, and there must be many of today's preachers who would gladly leave it there. No one wants to hear about the days when huge congregations lapped up sermons at 11 and 6.30 each Sunday, when the voice of the pulpit had repercussions at Town Hall (or even Westminster), when the parish minister rated high on the totem-pole, when almost every preacher issued his volume of sermons and apparently people bought them. The atomic age is here. The computer age is here. The secular society is here. Language, spoken or written, is undergoing strange convulsions. Yet the Word of God is not bound by any of these. And it may be that with the advent of an apocalyptic consciousness a new vitality will be unleashed as preachers wrestle with end-questions that are a neglected part of our scriptural heritage.

A sense of the tradition will keep us from resorting to the modern craze for 'techniques' instead of listening to the Scriptures and declaring with confidence a Word from God in the language of today. Whenever I am asked by an American lover of Scottish preaching: 'What was the homiletic secret you learned in seminary?' I am tempted to answer: 'There wasn't any. I never even heard the word "homiletics"'. An exaggeration; but I am thinking of the training by which one was exposed to the 'Scholar as Preacher' and the 'Preacher as Scholar' – each of them steeped in the high tradition of the proclamation of the Word.

Chapter Ten

THE SETTING OF WORSHIP

James Whyte

The traveller between Scotland and England is soon struck by one contrast between the two countries. In almost every English village one finds a medieval parish church, sometimes one of considerable magnificence. In Scotland pre-Reformation churches are few, and are sometimes only fragments incorporated into later building; and many are ruins. To what extent this reflects Scottish poverty, or the pillaging greed of the Scottish barons, or the neglect of fabric by the medieval Church, or the destructiveness of the Scottish reformers – or some combination of all four factors – is a question on which one does not find agreement.[1]

Of pre-Norman building only the merest fragments remain. The round towers at Abernethy and at Brechin are monuments of Celtic Christianity, but they are not buildings for worship. The tower and the ruined church of St. Rule at St. Andrews and the tower at Restenneth Priory near Forfar show signs of an Anglo-Saxon style of Romanesque.[2]

The 'Anglo-Norman penetration', as Douglas Simpson has called it, must have replaced many of the earlier buildings, probably not with the deliberate insolence of the conqueror to the conquered that marked the destruction of Saxon churches in England, but through a combination of the reforming zeal of Margaret and her son David, and the bland superiority of the new élite who were being attracted from England and France by gifts of land. The diocesan and parochial system was one fruit of this reforming movement; another was the foundation of many religious houses, and the introduction of new religious orders, from France and elsewhere.[3] These were later to work against one another, as the teinds from parishes were used for the endowment of the abbeys, and the needs of the parishes for spiritual care and church fabric were often neglected.

What the Anglo-Norman penetration did for church building was to encourage the free flow of European craftsmanship, as seen in the surviving nave of Dunfermline Abbey, with its reminiscence of Durham, or, by another route, in what is arguably the finest and best preserved of all our great churches, the Cathedral of St. Magnus in Kirkwall. The same craftsmen who built Dunfermline built the parish churches at Dalmeny and Leuchars, with the same exquisite workmanship and decoration. The parish churches that have survived from this period are all rural, and remarkably small. They are two-roomed buildings. The square chancel might sometimes have a little apse (as at Leuchars) but not always; the nave would be larger, and might be as much as twice as long, and in the arch dividing chancel from nave was the rood screen, usually of wood.[4]

To a later period, and the Gothic style, belong most of the burgh churches that remain. All have been considerably altered during the centuries. Some suffered more from nineteenth-century 'restorers' than they did from the iconoclasm of the reformers. The Cathedral of Glasgow is unique in retaining its original medieval rood screen – the only one in Scotland.

What was the state of church building at the time of the Reformation? There were about a thousand parish churches, some well-endowed, especially in the burghs, but many very poor. Over nine hundred had been given to religious houses or colleges, and were served by vicars.[5] Some of the rural churches were buildings of distinction, but many were simple, low, thatched buildings, and many, it seems, were in poor repair. The milking of the religious houses by the crown and the nobles through the appointment of 'lay commendators' meant the further impoverishment of the parishes.

Every parish church had a font, usually of stone with a lead lining, and a cover that could lock, to prevent the water from being used for the purposes of witchcraft. The font was at the door of the church which, normally, in a rural church was situated on the south wall at the west end. The church had also a pulpit, placed in the nave, on the wall or against a pillar. How much the pulpit was used, and how regularly, it is not easy to say, though there may have been more preaching, especially in the towns, than some Protestants have imagined.[6] The church also had an altar, or altars, in the smaller churches railed or screened off in the chancel area, in the larger churches in a chancel divided from the rest of the church by a rood screen. In addition to the 'high' altar the larger churches had many side altars, where Masses were said for the repose of the dead. In a church like Holy Trinity, St. Andrews, there were as many as thirty priests. Apart from a bench round the wall, and the stools which the people might bring with them, there was no seating. The church could be used for other things besides religious worship, and public proclamations were frequently made. Though they were often dark and ill-lit by candles, the churches would not be lacking in colour, with paintings on the plastered walls, and statues of the Virgin and saints adorning the altars.

The First Book of Discipline, 1560, has two things to say about ecclesiastical buildings. The second of these, towards the end of the book, is a section entitled 'For Reparation of the Kirkes'. 'Least that the word of God and ministration of the Sacraments by unseemlinesse of the place come in contempt, of necessity it is that the Kirk and place where the people ought publickly to convene be with expedition repaired with dores, windowes, thack, and with such preparation within as appertaineth as well to the Magestie of God, as unto the ease and commodity of the people.'[7]

McRoberts sees this as the need to repair the excess damage done by 'the rascal multitude', as Knox called them, in their cleansing of the kirks, but Professor Cameron, in his note on this passage, says 'The ruinous state of many churches prior to the Reformation is well attested'. It seems likely that there was damage caused by the mob in some places, but that what called forth this concern was the more general state of neglect into which the rural churches especially had fallen.

Behind this very practical concern certain principles can be seen. Just as the marks of the true kirk are the true preaching of the Word of God and the right administration of the sacraments, so the purpose of the church building is that the Word may be preached and the sacraments ministered in a seemly place and in a seemly manner. But the kirk is not in itself a holy place; it is the 'place where the people ought publickly to convene' for Word and Sacrament. So they have an eye both to 'the Magestie of God' and to 'the ease and commodity of the people'. 'Every Kirk must have dores, close windows of glasse, thack able to withhold raine, a bell to convocate the people together, a pulpet, a basen for baptizing and tables for ministration of the Lord's Supper. In greater Kirks and where the congregation is great in number, must reparation be made within the Kirk for the quiet and commodious receiving of the people.' Not till the next century were seats actually provided for the people, but here is expressed a concern that goes far beyond the basic necessity to have the kirks wind- and water-tight.

The other passage in the Book of Discipline which deals with church buildings begins in a very similar manner, but says something quite different. It is The Third Head, Touching the Abolishing of Idolatrie.[8] 'As we require Christ Jesus to be truely preached and his holy sacraments rightly ministered, so we cannot cease to require Idolatry, with all monuments and places of the same, as Abbeyes, Monkeries, Frieries, Nonries, Chappels, Chanteries, Cathedrall Churches, Chanonries, Colledges, others then presently are Parish Churches or Schooles, to be utterly suppressed in all bounds and places of this Realme (except onely Palaces, Mansions, and dwelling places adjacent thereto with Orchards and Yards of the same), as also that idolatrie may be removed from the presence of all persons of what estate or condition that ever they be within this Realme.' They added 'By idolatry we understand, the Masse, invocation of Saints, adoration of images and the keeping and retaining of the same. And finally, all honouring of God, not conteined in his holy Word.'

The negative consequence of the emphasis on the preaching of the Word and the ministration of the sacraments was a passionate rejection of idolatry. This is a passion which our more tolerant, or more slothful age finds difficult to understand. To us iconoclasm is the lamentable destruction of precious works of art and architecture; to them it was a mortal combat between faith and superstition.

The reformers saw the religion of the Middle Ages as full of holy relics, holy places, holy things. For them religion was a personal relationship between a gracious God and sinful men. Therefore for the reformers the veneration of relics and images was idolatry, a faithless attempt to manipulate God, in place of the faithful acceptance of His free grace. The Mass, where the veneration of the host rather than the receiving of communion had become the highpoint of the service, was the epitome of such idolatry. The cleansing, or 'casting down' of churches was an aspect of the attempt to replace superstition with faith, idolatry with the true worship of God. Where buildings were parish churches, or could be useful to the reformed faith as schools or colleges, the removal of altars and images was enough. Churches such as abbey or chantry churches for which there was no parochial or educational use were to be 'suppressed'. Their preservation would be a constant invitation to return to idolatry.[9]

Most of the cathedral and collegiate churches continued in use, at least in part, as parish churches. In Glasgow the cathedral was preserved entire, and partitioned so as to house three congregations – the Inner High Kirk in the choir, the Outer High in the nave, and the Laigh Kirk in the crypt. Similar use was made of the large burgh kirks in Aberdeen, Dundee and Edinburgh. In St. Andrews and in Elgin, on the other hand, there was an adequate parish church in the centre of the town, and the cathedral buildings were redundant. In places like Dunblane and Dunkeld the cathedral was larger than the parish required. Never, until the advent of Victorian romanticism, did anyone think of treating the large medieval church as a single space. The choir or chancel was separated off by the rood screen into a holy space, and no lay-person might enter it, unless he had the privileges of the monarch or a noble benefactor. The large church was a house with several rooms. Where all the rooms were not required, one (usually the choir, as in Dunblane) was taken and used as the parish church. Those parts of the building not in use did not then require to be maintained.

One aspect of reformed faith is the abolition of the division between the sacred and the secular which was central to the medieval world. It is impossible to understand the attitude of the Scottish reformers to church buildings and church furniture unless one understands that they repudiated as superstition all belief in holy places and holy things. The Negative Confession of 1580, later incorporated in the National Covenant of 1638, lists among the works of the 'Roman Antichrist' that are 'detested and refused' his 'worshipping of imagery, relicks and crosses; dedicating of kirks, altars, days', 'his holy water, baptizing of bells; conjuring of spirits, crossing, sayning, anointing, conjuring, hallowing of God's good creatures, with the superstitious opinion joined therewith . . .' The objection to holy places, days and things and to rites of consecration or dedication is rooted in the conviction that these already are God's good creatures, and need no mumbled incantations of men to make them so. That is also why churches were closed when not in use for the Sunday sermon or the daily prayers. To find God one did not have to repair to the holy building; in the homes of the people in family worship and in the hearts of the people in secret worship his presence is real and powerful.

A radical adaptation of church buildings was a natural outcome of the radical change in the understanding of the Church and its worship at the Reformation. The Church is not as much a hierarchically organized institution as a community of faith. The heart of worship is, as Luther said, that God Himself should speak to us through His most holy Word and we speak to Him in prayer and praise. So the church is not divided into a holy part (the chancel) for the clergy to enter, and a secular part (the nave) for the laity. Worship is not an event taking place on a distant altar to which the priests draw near, and from which the laity stand off, each one saying his own private prayers. The church must be ordered so that the Word may be preached in the midst of a believing people, and the people gather under the Word and round the tables of the sacrament. Reformed worship was intelligible, audible, corporate. The Gospel brought believers into new relationships, with God and with one another; and into new relationships to the Bible and to the sacraments. It would have been odd if this had not found expression in the spatial arrangement of their churches.

The preferred arrangement was simple and logical. In adapting existing churches they removed the altar and the font, as well as all images. In the smaller churches, which were mostly rectangular in shape, the pulpit was placed in the middle of the long south wall. The middle of the long wall was clearly the most convenient place for people to gather round to hear the preaching, and the south wall had windows which allowed the preacher to see, whereas the wall on the cold north side was frequently windowless. For Baptism, a basin was bracketed to the pulpit. When the Lord's Supper was to be celebrated, long tables were set up down the length of the church, so that the people might sit round them. At other times there was no table, and, at first, no seating save for the elders' seats around the pulpit. In the larger churches, the arrangement within whatever part of the church was in use was the same, save that there the pulpit might find its place (as it had formerly) against a pillar.

When extra accommodation was required, this might be found by introducing galleries or 'lofts' in the east and west ends, or, in the case of the smaller churches, by adding an aisle opposite the pulpit, giving the T-shape, which is the most characteristic Scottish church design. Despite the desire of the First Book of Discipline, seating for the people was slow to be introduced. Doubtless the laird and the craft guilds first introduced seating into their lofts, before it followed in the body of the kirk.

When new churches came to be built, they frequently followed existing models. Thus, the now ruined church of Kemback (1582) clearly had the pulpit between two windows (or doors?) on the south wall; the door for the people was at the west end of the south wall, as was common in medieval times; the belfry was on the west wall. What is not clear here is whether the aisle opposite the pulpit was (as some have thought) part of the original structure or whether it was a later addition. On a very different scale, Greyfriars, Edinburgh (1620) also followed a traditional model, that of the preaching kirk of the medieval friars – a wide hall-church, with pillars and arcades.

On the other hand, when the Town Council of Burntisland decided to abandon the medieval church at the Kirkton, and to build, in 1592, a new parish church on the hill above their prosperous harbour, they adopted also a new plan which appears to be entirely original. The church stands foursquare. Four great pillars take the weight of the tower, and arches go out to the buttressed corners. The walls have square-headed windows. The pulpit was against one of the pillars; against that opposite was placed, a little later, the canopied pew of Rossend Castle, which later became the magistrates' pew. The lofts on all four sides were for the craft-guilds of the town. In its completed form, with the signs of the guilds displayed on the panelling in front of their lofts, seats or pews below for the farms and estates, the magistrates' pew, and the space for the long tables in the centre of the church, it expressed beautifully the reformed ideal of a Christian community gathered, not simply as individuals, but in its secular structure, under the Word and round the tables of the Sacrament.

Burntisland is a magnificent structure, but it never served as a model. It may be good that there was no model, and that builders were free to experiment. Archbishop Spottiswoode intended the church at Dairsie (1621) to be a model. It is a simple rectangle in plan, with buttresses dividing the wall into bays that hold intricate three-light windows, in a survival-Gothic style. Despite its attractiveness it did not attract followers. The fact that it was designed to comply with James VI's Five Articles of Perth, and had a screened-off chancel area within, would not commend it to Presbyterians. For them, the T-shaped church served very well, especially in the rural areas, and it is the single most common design. It also, no doubt, commended itself to the heritors as simple and economical. (In many parishes the unwillingness of the heritors to go beyond their minimum obliga-tion in providing and maintaining the church building is well attested.) Some of these churches are plain, with rough workmanship; others, like Durisdeer (1699) or Monimail (1796) have elegance of style.

Rectangular churches continued to be built, some small, intimate and domestic, like Kilmany (1768) not out of scale with the cottages in the village below, and some, in the burghs, much larger and more commodious. In some of these latter, such as Cupar (1795) the curving front of a gallery, with its supporting pillars, softens and gives grace to what would otherwise be a severe building. Some of the smaller rectangular churches were enlarged later into T-churches. Cromarty was built as a simple rectangle in 1700. In 1740 it was enlarged by the addition of the north aisle, known as 'The Poors Aisle', because the Poor Fund was invested in the building, and the Fund repaid by the money from the seat-rents.

When Sir William Bruce was rebuilding Thirlestane Castle for the Earl of Lauderdale in 1673 he rebuilt also the parish church of Lauder, in the shape of a Greek cross, i.e. with arms of equal length. The effect internally is not unlike that of Burntisland. The pulpit stands against one of the internal corners. There is a steep gallery in each of the arms of the cross. The upper windows are fine examples of survival Gothic. The whole is surmounted by a little octagonal tower and spire. (It has been noted that some of the most interesting buildings of the seventeenth century were built during the episcopal periods. But it is also true that during the rest of the century conditions were not exactly favourable to church-building.)

One feature common in the earlier rural churches is the laird's loft, often with its retiring-room behind, where the laird could partake of a cold collation between the morning and afternoon services. If Presbyterians did not reserve a chancel for the clergy, they did reserve a loft for the laird, and exaggerated claims for the democratic or egalitarian character of the Church of Scotland receive a blow when we observe the fine woodwork, panelling, pillars and decoration of some of these lofts, expressing within a simple church the importance of the laird. But we can see another side to this if we compare the laird's loft to the magistrate's loft in the burgh kirks, or to the guild lofts. The whole community comes, in its secular order, to worship God. The laird at least was there, to be addressed by the Word, like anyone else. (Today many of the lofts are empty, either because there is no laird, but an anonymous company, or because he is an absentee, or an Episcopalian, as many of the landed gentry now are, or nothing at all.)

In their internal arrangement most, if not all, Presbyterian churches conformed to the norm of a central plan, with the pulpit centrally placed, usually in the middle of the long side, and the seating arranged so that the congregation gathered round; with provision for the long tables round which the congregation would sit for Communion, and a baptismal basin bracketed to the pulpit. These internal arrangements were not affected by changes in architectural style. Behind the pillared portico of a church built in the classical style would be an interior, more elegant perhaps in its detail, its panelling, its mouldings and its plaster ceiling, but still traditional in its layout. Some classical interiors, such as that of St. Mary's, Bellevue, Edinburgh (1824) are quite magnificent. Gothic revival architecture begins to appear before the end of the eighteenth century, and by the end of the next century even Free Presbyterian churches were being built with pointed windows. But this did not necessarily affect the internal arrangement of the building. The church of Glenorchy was built in 1811 in Gothic style. In plan it is an octagon, with buttresses at each corner, and a square tower. Inside the octagon the layout was quite traditional, with a horseshoe gallery, and a long table down the centre of the church opposite the pulpit.

A large amount of building in the eighteenth century was undertaken by the Secession Churches, and in the nineteenth century by the Free Church. The Scottish Episcopal Church also began to build with confidence, and in the west especially the Irish immigration meant a large increase in Roman Catholic churches.

Secession congregations tended to favour a broad rectangular plan, and a domestic style, with plain sash windows – the architecture of the meeting-house, which is the name they sometimes gave to their churches.[10] Few enough of these buildings are still in use, though some are still to be found behind the façade of the cinema which is now a bingo hall. The Free Church in 1843 faced an enormous task of building, and did so in a characteristically organized manner. The Provisional Committee had already, before the Disruption took place, set up a 'Building Section' or sub-committee to attend to this matter. They were concerned that 'the buildings should be erected with as little delay as possible, in order that those congregations who came out from the Establishment might be supplied with places of worship, and that they might be erected at as little expense as possible consistently with comfort.[11] Wealthy congregations were asked to make do with simple buildings and to assist their brethren until all should have 'decent places of worship'. Plans were provided of economical buildings and one had been erected on Lothian Road, using timber frame with brick curtain walls. The problem which vexed the Free Church was the refusal of certain landowners to make available sites on which to build. The early Assemblies are much exercised about this: already in 1843 the use of tents and of boats is suggested. There is no sign, however, that any theological thought was given by the Free Church to the design and internal arrangement of churches. They adhered to the tradition, save in one point. They did not generally make provision for the long tables. Thomas Chalmers himself had been the first to abandon the use of the long tables at St. John's in Glasgow, and to substitute the custom of serving the congregation in the pews. The Church of Scotland did not like this change, but could not stop it. The Free Church could welcome it more heartily.

There was, in the nineteenth century, a haemorrhaging of middle- and upper-class Presbyterians to the Scottish Episcopal Church. In part this was the result of the practice of sending their sons to English public-schools, of a general sense of the inferiority of things Scots to things English (the Scottish Episcopal Church was regarded, however inaccurately, as 'the English church'), and of a distaste for the barrenness and wordiness of Presbyterian worship. Indeed, G. W. Sprott, in his introduction to the 8th edition of *Euchologion* (1905), claimed that the influence of the Church Service Society on Presbyterian worship had helped to stem the loss of members to Episcopacy. However that may be, the Episcopal Church at this time produced some fine buildings, including their cathedral churches, whose Gothic revival architecture was suited to a worship deeply influenced by the Oxford Movement. The Roman Catholic church buildings of the nineteenth century were, on the whole, less distinguished, but some of their new building in the twentieth century has been striking in design. Oddly, their most distinguished architect, Jack Coia, showed no interest in the liturgical movement and some of his churches do not easily adapt to post-Vatican II practice.

Changes in the tradition of church building are the result not of changing architectural style, but of ecclesiastical choice. Sometimes such changes are the unintended consequences of other choices. Those who decided to abandon the use of the long tables probably did not foresee that the top table would then become 'The Communion Table', and even, to some, 'The Holy Table'. Those who struggled against ignorant prejudice for the introduction of an organ could not have foreseen the devastating effect their victory was to have on so many church interiors. Sometimes the changes are dictated by theological conviction, as in the Scoto-catholic movement, sometimes they are the almost unnoticed result of a change of emphasis, as with the evangelical pulpit. Sometimes a fashion seems to sweep the land, as in the outbreak of stone and marble fonts early this century. Such changes affect not only new churches as they come to be built, but the older churches as they are renovated, improved or restored. Before criticizing, as one must, the improvers and restorers of many of our churches, one must recognize that an antiquarian dislike of all change would condemn the church to being a museum or a mausoleum. A congregation which is alive will want to do more than simply preserve its building. Some of the most pleasing of our ancient buildings are those where each generation has left its mark, enriched its heritage, and one can read something of history and of present reality in the wood and stone. But this possibly happens only when there is a real respect and under-standing of what has gone before. But that is not always found, and what one generation recklessly abandons, another, later, may bitterly regret. But we cannot take away the right of those who come after us to disagree with us, and to undo what we have so painfully done.

The Scottish tradition in church-building was radically changed as a result of two quite different and apparently opposed forces – the evangelical movement, and the Scoto-catholic movement. The evangelical movement had an attitude to preaching, worship and church design significantly different from the earlier tradition, but the difference was so subtle as to make it appear only a development of what had gone before. Preaching still is central, but it tends to become the star performance. The pulpit becomes a platform, and now tends to be positioned on the end wall, perhaps because preachers prefer to have their audience in front of them, rather than stretching out to the sides.[12] The purpose of the prayer before the sermon is to heighten the emotional tension, and prepare the audience for the sermon: and many evangelists testified that they knew in the prayer whether their preaching would have effect that night. In a great preaching church such as Free St. George's in Edinburgh (1869) the pulpit became in effect a great box-stage, occupying one end of the building. Church has become theatre. To say this is not to dismiss as worthless this tradition; it is simply to recognize that it is different from the earlier tradition, and demanded a different setting.

Undoubtedly the greatest influence on church-building and the internal arrangements of existing buildings came from a movement which was never more than a small minority within the church – the Scoto-catholic movement. The movement's concern for 'worship and architecture' was expressed through the Aberdeen Ecclesiological Society (1886) and the Glasgow Ecclesiological Society (1893). Although the Ecclesiological Society (the name was reminiscent of the work begun by the Cambridge Camden Society, which the founders admired) was to include in its membership those of many denominations, and many whose interests were mainly antiquarian and aesthetic, according to the fashion of the time, the founders and continuing leaders of the Society, notably James Cooper and William Kelly, were motivated by theological assumptions and aims which are quite properly described as Scoto-catholic. The first President of the Aberdeen Society was the Rev. James Cooper, then minister of the East Church. An early (1886) minute states that 'the meeting was unanimous that the best results would be obtained by placing the pulpit at one side, the desk or font or both at the other, and the table in the centre further back, and the organ in the west gallery, with the choir (forming part of the congregation) in front of the organ'.[13]

Like the Anglo-catholic movement in England some fifty years earlier, and with astonishing parallels, the Scoto-catholic movement exercised an influence on the fabric of churches out of all proportion to its size.[14] Generations of ministers and architects came to accept standards of 'correctness' which represented a radical break with the Scottish Reformed tradition, and which went virtually unchallenged until the 1960s. The norms included the central position of the table, the side position of the pulpit (to be used only for preaching, and to be, if possible, outside of the 'chancel'), and the preference for the long-axis, vista building – that is, the assumption that a church has ends, at one of which you enter, and at the other of which things happen. Even the number and height of chancel steps could be judged by some afficionados 'correct' or 'incorrect'. Ancient and medieval symbolism was welcomed back into churches from which it had been banished since the Reformation. Crosses appeared in the apses and on the gable ends of churches.

The amount of activity was immense. The movement came at a time when the upper classes and the rising middle classes in Scotland were prospering and were becoming enamoured of things English, and ashamed of the barrenness of things Scots. Many were sending their sons to English public-schools. The gentry were marrying the daughters of English families. Since money was plentiful and labour was cheap, the reordering of churches on lines consonant with the theological principles of the movement and also congenial to those of genteel tastes was often possible. There must be very few of our ancient parish churches which did not receive some attention from the restorers. Many ancient buildings or parts of buildings which had been shut off or used as burial vaults were rebuilt and reopened for use: one such was the Norman church at Leuchars, long partitioned off from view. Of loving care for the past there was no lack – for the medieval past, that is. Of fine workmanship in stone and wood there was enough. And always the result was a church ordered within in accordance with Scoto-catholic principles. The process goes on strongly into the 1920s, as Fowlis Wester shows: indeed it goes on in small ways yet, though money and skills are now in short supply.

We owe a great deal to the restoration work which the movement inspired and encouraged, including the rebuilding of some of the larger churches which earlier generations had allowed to fall into ruins. Iona was rebuilt. The nave of Dunblane Cathedral was re-roofed, with the strange result that the congregation are now as far removed from their communion table as any medieval worshipper ever was from the altar. Some mistakes were made. It is possible that more constructive work and less destructive work was done by the restoration movement north of the border than had happened in the south, where Ruskin called restoration 'the most total destruction which a building can suffer'.[15]

In Scotland certainly there was less for the restorers to destroy than there was in the cathedrals and great parish churches of England. But many of our simple parish churches suffered at the hands of those who were without any respect for the earlier tradition of church-building. In 1906 D. Wishart Galloway had the task of restoring Careston Parish Church. Careston was a T-church, built in 1636, with a laird's loft in the north aisle. It had suffered from alterations in 1808, when the aisle was partitioned off to form a heating chamber and vestry, and other changes were made. Mr. Galloway determined to restore the aisle to its original use; but he 'restored' the church to what it had never been before. 'Two schemes occurred to me. Either the pulpit could be placed on the south wall, facing the aisle, as in the original arrangement; or the east portion of the church might be formed into a chancel and the pulpit placed therein. I chose the latter, as not only more in keeping with the general principles of ecclesiastical architecture, but as better fitted to express the ideas which underlie the worship of the Christian church.'[16] The architect might have restored the church; but he determined instead to improve it, according to what he believed were correct principles.

The process goes on, even at a time when these principles have been abandoned in Roman Catholic and Anglican thinking about church design, and central plans, expressive of a congregation gathered round Word and sacrament, abound. In 1962 the T-church of Garvald (1829) was 'restored' by having its galleries removed, a railed-off chancel created at the east end, all plaster taken off the walls (to reveal rubble) – an act of vandalism which did not even have the merit of the good workmanship which had marked some of the earlier 'restorations'.

The principles of the movement became those also on which new churches were built. When Alexander 'Greek' Thomson built his striking buildings for the Free Church in Glasgow in the mid-nineteenth century, he was free to follow his genius, remaining in general within the tradition of Free Church worship. Thus, St. Vincent Street (1859) with its rich interior decoration, Egyptian rather than Greek in effect, had a platform pulpit and horseshoe galleries. Thomas Pilkington's Barclay Church in Edinburgh (1862) is even more exotic, and has a double gallery, but is still clearly built for the Free Church preaching tradition. When P. MacGregor Chalmers was designing his churches early in this century he developed a distinctive style, but he was not following a tradition, he was seeking to create one. He was following a theory, put forward by Professor Cooper, that the Norman style and the apse were peculiarly suited to Presbyterian worship.[17]

The need to use cheaper building materials meant that most churches built between the wars lacked the grandeur and solidity of the MacGregor Chalmers churches, though Sir Robert Lorimer's St. Margaret's, Knightswood (1931) is a notable exception. In the post-war rush of church extension building financial restraints were more compelling, but at the same time new materials and new building techniques were providing exciting new possibilities for architects. Nevertheless, these churches all follow the same basic design, as though none other could be imagined. They are all long-axis buildings, with the focus on the 'east' end. This was not because of the detail of the church's brief to its architects, which seems to have been vague on anything other than the dimensions of a badminton court, but because the architects assumed that a church is a building uniquely without functional problems, where the architect is free to express religious feeling. The result is a series of buildings, some of which are pretty, but most of which are very weak. Wheeler and Sproson's church at St. Columba's, Glenrothes (1962) was the first where the architect gave independent thought to the requirements of reformed worship and the contemporary church. The church at Burntisland was the inspiration of this centrally planned church, though the lightness of its structure is as contrasting as could be to the solidity of Burntisland. Some time after this the Church produced a 'theological brief', and architects began to be more venturesome. Allan Rodger's St. Ninian's, Glenrothes (1970) is an attempt to solve the problem of 'ancillary buildings' by designing a many-roomed house for the family of God. This church, the most reformed of all in its conception, is at present being happily shared with the Roman Catholics. Some multi-purpose buildings have been designed[18] showing great imagination in the economical use of space, in contrast to the disastrous dual-purpose buildings of the post-war period, where you faced one way for secular activities and the other way for sacred ones.

The influence of the liturgical movement in other communions has at last encouraged some in the Church of Scotland to reconsider the ordering of their churches, and to rediscover within their own reformed tradition some emphases which the other Churches are only now beginning to discover. The reordering of St. John's Kirk, Perth, with the table in the crossing and the similar arrangement at St. Mary's, Haddington, and St. Giles', Edinburgh, are signs of a more thoughtful and theological approach to church arrangement. This needs to be neither a slavish imitation of the reformed past, nor a sentimental return to the supposed medieval, but an attempt, with due respect for the past, to express in the present the reality of the Church, its faith and its worship. The irony of history is that we seem set to do this at a time when there are no longer any churches waiting to be built.

Throughout this chapter reference has been made to pulpits and to tables. So much of the theology of the building is bound up with these that a word may be added about each.

It is interesting to compare the pulpits of Scottish churches with those of Lutheran and Catholic churches on the Continent. Continental pulpits are often elaborately, even flamboyantly, decorated and carved. Scottish pulpits lack all figurative decoration, save for the dove with the olive-branch sometimes to be found above a sounding-board. But they are beautifully panelled and proportioned. Such pulpits are found in St. Salvator's, St. Andrews; St. Columba's, Elgin (originally the pulpit of St. Giles', Elgin) and in Bo'ness. They are thrones for the Word of God, and in their dignity and restraint speak eloquently of the majesty of God. The two-decker pulpit allowed the reader, and later the precentor, to have his place. Dyke (1781) has a three-decker pulpit. Such pulpits were common at the same period in the Church of England, and were given a central position. In Scotland the position was almost always in the middle of the long south wall, and one can enter many Scottish churches and see the two large windows between which the pulpit was originally placed before it was moved by the 'restorers'. With the development of horseshoe galleries coming quite close to the pulpit there was a need for the pulpit to become higher (to the discomfort of those sitting below) but sometimes the opportunity was taken to make a striking feature of the pulpit stairs, as in Ardchattan (1836) and Logie Pert (1840).

In the late nineteenth century one finds the pulpit becoming sometimes a platform for the preacher, rather than a throne for the Word. One writer recalls the change with pride, 'When our church of 1847 was built there was a new pulpit erected, but it was after the old barrel-shaped style the like of which is seldom seen now ... In 1871 it was resolved to do away with the 1857 pulpit and substitute something more in conformity with modern ideas. The result was the present handsome platform pulpit which has been much admired ...'[19] In many churches, when the organ was introduced in the later nineteenth century, the only wall high enough to accommodate it was the wall behind the pulpit – the others being filled with galleries. It was this, rather than the desire to admire their new acquisition (some of them paid for by Andrew Carnegie) that led to the central position of the organ. This led not only to the pulpit appearing as an adjunct of the organ, but to its being pushed forward about six feet, which was enough to put the whole church out of joint. The Ecclesiologists were less successful in having the organ removed from its central position than they were in many of their other concerns. When the pulpit is returned to its original position, an awkward church can suddenly become graceful.[20]

The way we design a pulpit will say something about our attitude to preaching, and the way we position it will speak not only of its importance or unimportance, but also of the relationship between the preacher and the congregation. Some modern pulpits, themselves insignificant, and placed in a corner or in some indeterminate position, express uncertainty and an apologetic attitude towards preaching. In some small churches a pulpit might be strictly unnecessary. What matters is to make appropriate provision for the preaching of the Word.

The Scots insisted with an unshakeable determination that Communion was to be received sitting round a table. This was the practice John Knox had introduced in the congregation at Berwick, 1549–51. There is evidence for this practice in London at about the same time.[21] When the second Prayer Book of Edward VI was being prepared and it was proposed that Communion should be received kneeling, Knox and others wrote a memorial to the Privy Council. No document breathes more purely the spirit of the Reformation. Having objected on the negative ground that kneeling would encourage idolatry and superstition (an objection which led to the insertion of the 'Black Rubric' in the 1552 book), they conclude with a positive argument that kneeling is inappropriate because it obscures the joyful significance of the Supper.

Kneeling is the gesture of beggars or suppliants, who ask doubting whether they will receive or not. At the Lord's Supper our faith is that we are the sons and daughters of God, invited by our glorious King to His own table. Therefore at His table we sit 'as men placed in quietness and in full possession of our kingdom'. To do otherwise, they say, would be to betray our faith and to despise God's grace.

These views did not prevail; and Knox had to write to his old congregation at Berwick advising them to conform, for the sake of charity. But in Scotland, the Reformed Communion was always received sitting round a table. When churches were not filled with pews it was easy to set up, at the time of the Communion, a trestle table with benches, the table covered with a linen cloth. To this table the congregation came for the sacrament, minister, elders and people sitting together, each one serving his neighbour as the bread and wine were passed around the table. Since a large congregation could not be accommodated at one sitting, they came in relays till all were served. When churches were pewed, provision was made for the long table or tables, either in permanent form, a table running the length of the church (as at Ardchattan, Loch Broom, or Lochcarron) or by the adaptation of pews. Sometimes, as at Ceres and Durisdeer, box-pews were made, the dividing-boards of which could be removed so that a table could be set up from front to back of the church. In Durisdeer the aisle facing the pulpit was thus a communion aisle. Sometimes, as in Kilmany, Torphichen, Portmoak and many others, the backs of the front pews swivelled through an angle of 90 degrees to form a table-top. This arrangement is found in the church of Falkland, built as late as 1850. The churches of the Secession followed the same tradition. The plan for the new Burgher Kirk in Ceres in 1745 included 'cets [seats] which will be to be lifted at our sacrement'.[22]

The excessive amount of preaching that had become associated with the service of the long tables appears to be the reason for their abandonment by Dr. Chalmers in his city kirk of St. John's, Glasgow, in 1824. Why he did not dispense with the table addresses and keep the long tables is not so clear, unless it was that there was no churchyard for the communicants to go out into. The Assembly was extremely reluctant to allow the Zwinglian practice of serving the pews, but was unable to prevent it. The high church party in the Church of Scotland never approved of the change, interestingly enough. G. W. Sprott, writing in 1882, deplored the fact that 'the pew system has latterly become common'.[23] James Leishman of Linton rejoiced that the spacious restored chancel allowed him to minister Communion in the old manner, 'the worshippers receiving at a table extending the whole length of the chancel'.[24]

'It would appear to admit of no doubt that the Communion Table in the Church of Scotland is where the communicants – ministers, elders and people – sit together partaking of the Lord's Supper.'[25] Dr. Mair points out that this is the uniform law and practice of the Church since the Reformation, expressly provided for in the Act of 1645 for establishing and putting into execution the Directory of Public Worship. When the long tables have, recently, been omitted from churches, 'to cover the book-boards of pews with the linen tablecloth was regarded as equivalent. But the spreading of the tablecloth wherever the communicants are to partake still truly marks the communion table.' He goes on, 'From the use of pews the necessity has arisen of providing an adjunct to them on which to set the bread and wine. At the administration of the Supper this is only part of the communion table. At other times to call it the communion table may be convenient, but is evidently not quite correct, and tends to mislead on a subject of importance.' Mair wrote with the Barnhill case[26] in mind, and to stress that at the Supper the 'adjunct' must be so placed that it is seen to be only a part of that table at which all are sitting. Mair's words were soon forgotten. Although all Presbyterians seem content to retain the distinction between a table and an altar, the 'adjunct', separated from the rest of the table (i.e. the pews), begins to assume an importance of its own, whether or not the sacrament is being celebrated. It is referred to in the Book of Common Order as 'the Holy Table', and the design of many modern tables, with their solid fronts, suggests a hankering after the altar. When John Knox in his liturgy speaks of 'this Holy Table' he is not referring to the trestles and boards, set up for the occasion, but to the sacrament being celebrated.

The reformers had too vast and too personal a conception of the holy to tolerate its trivialization. That is why the reformed tradition in church-building is emphatically that of the meeting-house, not that of the temple. But the reformers might agree that we can make that distinction too sharply. The meeting-house, the house of the church, is a special place, for it is no ordinary meeting that takes place here, but the meeting of the Church with her Lord in Word and sacrament. In the minds of the worshippers something of God's holiness will be associated with this place. And even the first reformers wished the repair of kirks 'as appertaineth as well to the Magestie of God, as unto the ease and commodity of the people'.

NOTES

1. See George Hay, *The Architecture of Scottish Post-Reformation Churches* (Oxford, 1957), pp. 11–15; David McRoberts, 'Material Destruction Caused by the Scottish Reformation' in *Essays on the Scottish Reformation,* ed. D. McRoberts (Glasgow, 1962).
2. W. Douglas Simpson, *The Ancient Stones of Scotland*, 2nd edn. (London, 1968), p. 139.

3. During the years that the Cathedral of St. Andrews was being built, from 1160 to 1318, the bishops were French, as were the Augustinian Canons. Douglas Young, *St. Andrews* (London, 1969), p. 51.

4. There are examples at Birnie, Linton and Legerwood, but all much 'restored'.

5. See Denis MacKay, 'Parish Life in Scotland 1500–1560' in *Essays on the Scottish Reformation*, ed. D. McRoberts (Glasgow, 1962), p. 86; D. McRoberts, 'Material Destruction Caused by the Scottish Reformation', *ibid.*, p. 417.

6. Dom Gregory Dix, *The Shape of the Liturgy*, 2nd edn. (London, 1945), pp. 596–597.

7. J. K. Cameron, *The First Book of Discipline* (Edinburgh, 1972), p. 202.

8. *Ibid.*, p. 94.

9. Their destruction appears to have been fairly gradual, except in the ease of the Friars' Kirks, which disappeared almost completely.

10. The word is used in documents in the possession of Hope Park Church, St. Andrews, regarding the building of the Burgher Kirk. Later in the nineteenth century both the Free Church and the Established Church used iron churches as temporary and trans-portable structures in their church extension enterprise – an interesting use of contemporary technology.

11. *Proceedings of the General Assembly*, 1843, p. 39.

12. 'The end of the church that contains the pulpit and/or the Lord's table will, in accordance with common ecclesiastical parlance, be referred to as the east end of the church, while the end at which one usually enters will be described as the west end.' D. J. Bruggink and C. H. Droppers, *Christ and Architecture* (Grand Rapids, Michigan, 1965), pp. 21–22. Thus, a massive volume on Reformed Church Architecture begins with the quite gratuitous assumption that a church always has ends, at one of which you enter, and at the other of which things happen.

13. *Transactions of the Scottish Ecclesiological Society* 7:2. An illuminating account of the Scottish movement and its parallels with Anglo-catholicism is in an as yet unpublished thesis by Brian A. Rees, *James Cooper and the Scoto-Catholic Party: Tractarian Reform in the Church of Scotland, 1882–1918* (1980, Ph.D., St. Andrews).

14. See James F. White, *The Cambridge Movement* (Cambridge, 1962).

15. Quoted by S. Tschudi-Madsen, *Restoration and Anti-Restoration* (Oslo, 1976), p. 16.

16. *Transactions of the Scottish Ecclesiological Society* 2:1 (1907), 138. The architect who restored the church at Forgandenny, Mr. T. S. Robertson, writes without modesty of his own work, but hints

that it was not always appreciated. 'When cultivated people see an ugly and inconvenient place of worship, like what Forgandenny was, transformed into a beautiful and convenient place of worship, they feel in the presence of fine art, from which pleasure of the highest kind may be derived. There are not, however, many persons in Scotland who can fully appreciate art of this kind. Even of those most nearly interested, only a few know the value of the work that has been done for them. But, thanks to the Ecclesiological and Church Service Societies, this unfortunate state of affairs is being gradually mended.' *Transactions of the Scottish Ecclesiological Society* 1:2 (1905), 144–145.

17. Ian G. Lindsay, *The Scottish Parish Church* (Edinburgh, 1960), p. 82.
18. One such is St. Kentigern's, Kilmarnock.
19. David Webster, *History of the Kirkwall United Presbyterian Congregation* (Kirkwall, 1910), p. 134.
20. Cupar Old exemplifies this.
21. See Peter Lorimer, *John Knox and the Church of England* (London, 1875), pp. 30–38, 251–265, 267–289.
22. Document in possession of Hope Park Church, St. Andrews.
23. G. W. Sprott, *The Worship and Offices of the Church of Scotland* (Edinburgh, 1882), p. 132. Sprott also deplores the multiplication of table addresses.
24. James F. Leishman, 'The Church of Linton in Teviotdale', *Transactions of the Scottish Ecclesiological Society* 4:3 (1915), 269.
25. William Mair, *Digest of Church Laws*, 4th edn. (Edinburgh, 1912), pp. 92–96.
26. The Rev. Thomas Adamson, who had been assistant to the Rev. James Cooper in the East Church in Aberdeen, was appointed in 1884 as the first minister of the new charge at Barnhill, at the Broughty Ferry end of Monifieth. He was an enthusiastic ritualist, and proceeded, at first in the iron church provided, and later in the stone church which he had built according to his principles (and dedicated to St. Margaret, on St. Margaret's Day, 1895), to follow practices of worship and of church arrangement, including a dressed altar, candles, etc. which led to proceedings in the Presbytery of Dundee and in the General Assembly, and to the unwelcome attentions of the redoubtable Jacob Primmer. In dealing with the case in 1903 the General Assembly declared the law of the church that 'any other covering of it (the table) other than the customary white linen cloth is illegal, also the placing on it of cross, candlesticks, frontals and other appurtenances giving it the appearance of an altar.' (Mair, *op. cit.*, p. 95).

Chapter Eleven

WORSHIP SINCE 1929

Duncan Forrester

The Union of 1929 between the old Church of Scotland and the vast majority of the United Free Church engendered tremendous enthusiasm and many hopes for the future. For the first time in two centuries by far the largest part of Presbyterian Scotland was gathered within one denomination; Presbyterians who remained outside the union were, numerically at least, no more than sects. It seemed that the Church of Scotland was again in the true sense the national Church, the Church of the people, numerous, confident and committed to mission at home and abroad and also to further steps towards Christian unity. As far as worship was concerned, there had been some divergence between the Free and Auld Kirk traditions since the Disruption, but the differences were more matters of degree and general emphasis than clear-cut party divisions. The high church party had more influence in the Auld Kirk than in the Free Kirk, but there were high churchmen in both traditions, just as both sides had their low-church evangelicals. The worship of both Churches demonstrated abundantly the diversity which Professor Cheyne has shown to have characterized the worship of Presbyterian Scotland from the Reformation.[1] While some hoped for a greater degree of uniformity and central leadership, if not direction, in matters of worship in the united Church than had been practised in either of the component denominations, others, and probably a majority, were resolved to defend what had in practice become the unfettered freedom of ministers to conduct worship as they saw fit, allowing diversity and even idiosyncracy. The Act of Union said hardly anything about worship apart from drawing attention to the Westminster Directory as one of the standards of the Church, but it did set up a Committee on Public Worship and Aids to Devotion. In practice in neither of the uniting denominations had either Presbyteries or the General Assembly exercised much control or direct oversight in matters of worship since the controversies of the nineteenth century. But committees, societies and individuals could do something, if they felt so inclined, by way of persuasion, example and encouragement, and several groups were eager to influence the worship of the united Church.

The most prominent and significant of these 'pressure groups' was the Church Service Society, which now encompassed members of both Free and Auld Kirk backgrounds. The dominant tone of the Society had become by 1929 more high church, and it exerted very considerable influence in the Committee on Public Worship and Aids to Devotion, most of whose leaders were members of the Society. Two books illustrate well the nature and diversity of high church thinking on worship in the late 1920s and the 1930s: H. J. Wotherspoon's *Religious Values in the Sacraments* (Edinburgh, 1928) and D. H. Hislop's *Our Heritage in Public Worship* (Edinburgh, 1935). Both books are scholarly, devout and passionate appeals for the restoration of a catholic practice and understanding of worship in the Church of Scotland. Neither feels able to relate easily to what had become the mainstream tradition of worship in Presbyterian Scotland. Wotherspoon roots his thinking in reformed theology but blends with this a concept of a sacramental universe and other ideas borrowed from Anglicans such as Charles Gore and William Temple. The best that Hislop can say for reformed worship is this:

> What then did the Calvinistic service contribute to the idea of worship? What had it that could make amends for all that it had not, and its peers possessed? Lacking in stately ceremonial, without the glory of the mighty utterances which the spirit of worship had fashioned, divested of impressive ritual and without the dramatic movement of the soul's ascent, without the poetry of devotion – such it had not, and its limitations crowd thick upon our minds. It makes its appeal exclusively to the hearing ear, it forgets that human nature is more than a conscious mind, its temper is apt to be intellectual rather than devotional, its range is narrow, its language too often pedestrian and commonplace – these things it had. But one thing it was – the clearest illustration of the type of worship founded exclusively on the idea of Revelation. It drives home with concentrated energy the abiding truth of the Revelation of God. God has spoken and man, the creature and child of the Most High, can learn the Eternal Purpose. It has not the warmth and splendour of a picture with the glow and glory of colour, but it has the sharp distinctness of an etching with clear-cut line. Abstract in character it is without dramatic impressiveness, but it possesses the two qualities of abstract art, it has sincerity and dignity – a sincerity symbolized in its bareness, and a dignity which springs from the overwhelming sense of God on high and lifted beyond all moral striving.[2]

It is not surprising that those who were so disenchanted with much of their own tradition of worship should seek to transform it. Their intention was serious and they went about it with a will: it is a mistake to pay too much attention to what one might call the dotty side of Hislop's proposals.[3] Wotherspoon was a typical and leading high churchman; Hislop something of a maverick.

The most distinguished liturgical scholar from the group was W. D. Maxwell, whose magisterial edition and study of John Knox's Genevan Service Book, the immediate ancestor of the first Book of Common

Order, sometimes called 'Knox's Liturgy', set a new standard in the scholarly study of Scottish liturgical texts.[4] This was followed by *An Outline of Christian Worship: Its Development and Forms* (Oxford, 1936), a useful textbook on the history of worship which went through many printings, a collection of essays, *Concerning Worship* (Oxford, 1948), and *A History of Worship in the Church of Scotland* (Oxford, 1955). Maxwell never taught theology in Scotland, but went to be Professor of Theology at Rhodes University in South Africa – a reminder of the sad fact that there was remarkably little research or teaching on liturgical matters in the Scottish theological colleges so that students emerged and were ordained into a denomination which allowed them great freedom in the conduct of worship with only the sparsest acquaintance with the principles of worship and its history.

Maxwell was a considerable influence in the work of the Committee on Public Worship and Aids to Devotion, which produced a series of influential and much used books, the best known of which were the *Ordinal and Service Book for Use in the Courts of the Church* (First Edition, 1931, Second and Third Editions, with additional material, 1954 and 1962), *Prayers for the Christian Year* (First Edition, 1935, Second Edition, 1952) and *The Book of Common Order* (1940). The Ordinal contains a fine brief order for Holy Communion which was to reappear with some modifications and expansion in the 1940 *BCO*. The Ordination Service proper contains elements which are mandatory – the splendid Preamble concerning the Faith of the Church which was part of the Basis of Union, a series of questions to the ordinand, ordination by prayer in the course of which the Moderator and other ministers present lay on hands, the signing of the formula, and the declaration. *The Ordinal and Service Book*, however, has a full service, which in most presbyteries is followed very closely. This service, and in particular its prayer of ordination, has been influential far beyond the bounds of the Church of Scotland: both the Church of South India and the Church of North India found it a better model for their ordinals than the Anglican Prayer Book.[5] *Prayers for the Christian Year* was intended to encourage and facilitate the observance of the Christian Year by providing prayers and outlines of services for the major festivals and seasons. *The Book of Common Order* (1940) was built on the various editions of *Euchologion* and the two books which had been authorized by the uniting Churches shortly before the Union.* It was more than a 'directory' in that it gave the whole content of services and sets of rubrics, but less than a prayer book in that it was meant for ministers and not intended to be in the hands of the people, or to encourage a more responsive participation by the people in worship. Although it was authorized by the General Assembly, its use was in no way mandatory, even for the sacraments,

* The United Free *Book of Common Order* (1928) and the Church of Scotland's *Prayers for Divine Service* (1923 and 1928).

but it commended itself widely in the Church and played a significant role in enriching worship. It includes a range of material. A series of orders for morning and evening services follow roughly the pattern of offices such as Anglican matins and evensong rather than a *missa sicca*: prayers of invocation, adoration, confession and supplication, followed by scripture lessons, the Apostles' Creed, prayers of thanksgiving and intercession with the Lord's Prayer, the sermon, the offering and dedication, and the blessing, interspersed with psalms, paraphrases, hymns or canticles. The main order for the Lord's Supper (there is also a simpler and more informal 'Alternative Order' and two shorter rites) is one of the better fruits of the early liturgical movement, far superior to the Anglican 1929 eucharist and the like. In W. D. Maxwell's not entirely unprejudiced view it 'represents a long tradition brought to a high perfection, indigenously Scottish and Reformed and essentially Catholic. In its dignity of action, centrality of content, and felicity of expression, it provides a vehicle for worship entitling it to a place among the great rites of Christendon, and is rapidly being recognized as such.'[6] For a decade the *Book of Common Order*, and particularly its com-munion service, held a position of peculiar eminence among liturgical pundits, who saw it as expressing more fully the insights of the liturgical movement than most alternatives. But the publication of Dom Gregory Dix's *The Shape of the Liturgy* (London, Dacre, 1945) was something of a watershed, stimulating or provoking much radical rethinking on liturgical matters and influencing very deeply the next stage of liturgical revision, the first fruits of which was the Liturgy of the Church of South India (1950).

The *Book of Common Order* (1940) undoubtedly shaped for a generation the worship of the Church of Scotland, but it was used mainly as a model. Many ministers preferred to use the freedom in the conduct of worship which was given them by the Church, and not a few were uneasy at what they regarded as the Romanizing or Anglicanizing tendencies of the book. Besides, the general principle that the study of service-books and liturgical documents gives too uniform and simple an impression of change and diversity in the practice of worship applies with especial force to Presbyterian Scotland. If one speaks to older ministers and members of congregations about the changes which have taken place in worship in their lifetime one encounters developments of great importance which one could hardly discover mentioned in the service-books. In many parishes the decades after the Union saw a sustained effort to discourage Baptisms in the home and ensure that infants were baptized in face of the congregation at a Sunday service. That this was an innovation is evidenced by the fact that numerous churches provided themselves with fonts for the first time in the 1920s and 1930s. Similarly, there was a largely successful move to encourage marriage services taking place in the church rather than in a hotel or in the home. Many congregations were unaccustomed to saying the Lord's

Prayer together in worship, and older people can still remember controversies surrounding the re-introduction of this practice.

Sitting round the Table for Communion had disappeared everywhere by the late nineteenth century, but the 1930s was the peak of the introduction of that symbol that the neighbour was seen as a source of infection rather than fellowship, the individual communion cup. Arguments about hygiene, sedulously stimulated by the manufacturers as back-up to their energetic advertising campaigns, persuaded congregation after congregation to abandon the general use of the common cup in favour of the tiny glass phials, cumbrous trays, and little spring holders which between them disturbed the silence of the distribution with a distracting tinkling. A few churches arranged a compromise whereby at Communion the building was divided into four sections, in which fermented or unfermented wine was served in common or individual cups.

Except in the Highlands, the last vestiges of the old communion season disappeared in the 1960s. A Preparatory Service on the Friday before Communion had been almost universal, and the 1940 *BCO* assumes that it takes place, but by the 1970s few churches had either a Preparatory Service before Communion, or a Service of Thanksgiving after. Quarterly Communion became usual, although some congregations in the cities celebrated the Lord's Supper monthly and a tiny scattering had a celebration every Sunday. The collapse of the communion season marked the end of a specific sacramental tradition which at its best had nourished a rich and distinctive spirituality. It is hard to see as yet anything of real vitality which has arisen to take the place of what has decayed. Renewal of sacramental practice comes painfully slowly in the Church of Scotland.

The Victorian tradition of Scottish preaching hardly survived the Second World War. The membership of the Church of Scotland reached a peak in 1956, and has declined sharply ever since, but the crowds and the queues never really returned to the old 'preaching stations' after the War. There were, of course, diverse reasons for this. In part it had to do with the redistribution of population whereby people were decanted from the centres of the cities to the suburbs and the new housing estates. Middle-class suburban congregations flourished, but rarely attracted worshippers from a distance; numerous church extension congregations were launched in the post-war years with tremendous enthusiasm, but after fifteen years or so the going became much more difficult. But probably the most important factor was the development of the media, at the same time providing far more diversity of entertainment possibilities and conditioning people to expect incisive, predigested gobbets of information or stimulus to fill their much reduced attention span. Multitudes of people 'switched channels' from church to the television set at home. The cult of the popular preacher, once so significant a feature of the Scottish church scene, flourished up to the

War but declined sharply thereafter; no longer did crowds of 'hearers' (to use the term once a synonym for worshippers in Scotland) flock to hear notable preachers. A few still drew large congregations in the 1970s, but most of the people were ageing and nostalgic for an unrecoverable past. Secularization had made people suspicious of eloquence and advocacy in matters of religion, and there was a tendency to dismiss as bombastic what previous generations would have regarded as moving pulpit oratory. But suspicion of preaching has always been there in Scotland, as James Hogg's superb tale of the revivalistic preacher at Auchtermuchty who turns out to be the devil reminds us: 'and fra that day to this it is a hard matter to gar an Auchtermuchty man to listen to a sermon at a', an' a harder ane still to gar him applaud ane, for he thinks aye that he sees the cloven foot peeping out frae aneath ilka sentence.'[7] Modern Scottish preaching – apart from a few loquacious conservative evangelical ministers – is simpler, briefer, less elaborate than the older style; but it continues to be strongly biblical and theological and to emphasize the teaching role of the preacher. Indeed it is likely that the increasing use of the lectionary and the decline of the sermon as a *tour de force* have strengthened the sermon as an instrument of steady, carefully planned education of the congregation. And there is evidence to suggest that worship is now seldom considered merely as the preliminaries to the sermon, or the setting for the sermon. Rather, if the sermon is to play its proper role in the Church it must be integrated into the act of worship more adequately than was sometimes the case in the past.[8]

The desirability of observing the Christian Year had not stood particularly high in the Church Service Society's priorities – *Euchologion* simply contained a short section of 'Collects and Prayers for Natural and Sacred Sessions'. *Prayers for the Christian Year* has already been mentioned, and *The Book of Common Order* (1940) contained a two-year lectionary which followed a Calendar almost identical to that in the Anglican Prayer Book, save that saints' days, other than that of Scotland's patron, St. Andrew, were excluded. But Dr. Allan McArthur's scholarly study of the origins and rationale of the Christian Year, *The Evolution of the Christian Year* (London, S.C.M. Press, 1953), not only shed new light on the history and significance of the Calendar, but contained proposals for reform which were influential both within and far beyond the Church of Scotland, and have contributed substantially to the shaping of most recent Calendars and lectionaries.

The period from the end of the Second World War to the mid-1960s was in Scotland a time of large movements of population. Slums in the heart of the cities were 'cleared' and their inhabitants rehoused in corporation estates at the periphery. Huge new housing areas – Drumchapel and Easterhouse in Glasgow, Pilton and Niddrie in Edinburgh for example – sprang up, or expanded rapidly. New towns such as East Kilbride, Cumbernauld, Livingston and Glenrothes were established to take what was rather unpleasantly called 'the overspill' from the cities. Nor was it only slums that were demolished and handed over to the developers for conversion into shopping centres, offices, or industrial estates; middle-class housing in the city centres was also turned over to commercial use or torn down to make way for unsightly development, while the erstwhile inhabitants migrated to the suburbs. All this, of course, raised great problems for the Churches. Some city centre parishes lost the major part of their population within a decade and had to find a new role emphasizing week-day ministry to areas in which multitudes worked or played or moved about, but scarcely anyone lived, or close their doors and migrate in search of a congregation. A few 'preaching stations' managed to survive, drawing most of their congregation from a distance, but they were hard hit by the vast hiking of transport costs in the 1970s. In the suburbs and the housing estates the period from 1945–65 was the era of church extension, when new parishes were being established and new churches built at a rate which seemed almost to equal the prodigious scale of church-building in the aftermath of the Disruption. Flexibility and informality were the keynotes of the worship in the majority of the new churches, particularly in the heady early years in the housing estates. A more relaxed, participative and socially conscious worship seemed the order of the day, and the influence of the Iona Community was deeply felt in the many church extension charges with Community ministers.

The Iona Community from its inception in the 1930s as a response to the problems of the Depression had a special concern for relevant worship. The majority of its minister members were in industrial or church extension parishes and during the summer months large numbers of people visited Iona where the Community was rebuilding the Abbey, to share in the life and worship of the Community. The simplicity and grandeur of the Sunday morning celebration of the Lord's Supper impressed and moved several generations of young people, and the Community generated a new conviction that the eucharist was absolutely central to the life of the Church. The Iona celebrations were in all essentials simply 'standard Church of Scotland' (if one may use such a phrase), but the tone of informality, joy and relevance together with Communion every Sunday contrasted with the rather excessive solemnity which marked the quarterly Communions to which most Scots Presbyterians were – and are – accustomed. This, together with the daily morning and evening services, the Healing Services and the Thursday Act of Belief, in which people could make or renew their commitment to the Lord Jesus, gave a new vision of relevant, sustaining and challenging worship to many, and particularly to the young people who thronged the youth camps on the island. The setting of the Abbey, a magnificent ancient building on the site of one of the cradles of Christianity in Scotland, encouraged a sense of the numinous and was a constant reminder that our worship today is one link in a great chain of praise stretching back down the centuries. The Community used every opportunity to encourage reflection, teaching and discussion on worship and its relevance to the life of the world. Ministers and lay people alike found in Iona a new vision of worship and returned to the mainland to try to renew and revive worship in parishes up and down the land.

In the aftermath of the Second World War Scottish theologians gave more attention to worship than had been customary before. Donald Baillie's posthumously published *The Theology of the Sacraments* (London, Faber & Faber, 1957) lamented the neglect of the sacraments in his own Church. 'I must confess', he wrote 'it seems to me that in the tradition in which I have been brought up the sacraments mean very much less to the majority of good Church people than they did to their grandfathers.'[9] With characteristic clarity Baillie presents a sacramental doctrine which is both rooted in the Scottish Calvinist tradition and sympathetic to insights and challenges emerging from the ecumenical movement. Baillie believed in the centrality of the sacraments and the need for more frequent celebrations; and in this he is at one with almost all the Scottish theologians who have written on worship in modern times. T. F. Torrance made major contributions in an early essay on 'Eschatology and the Eucharist' prepared for the Faith and Order Conference at Lund in 1952,[10] which opened up a line of enquiry which has proved increasingly significant and rewarding. He also wrote extensively on Baptism and was the moving spirit in the Church of Scotland's Commission on Baptism which produced a series of weighty reports in the 1950s and an order for baptismal services which was used experimentally for a time but had to be thoroughly revised by the Committee on Public Worship because, in the words of *The Book of Common Order* (1979), 'It seemed to the Committee, in the light of experience, that the Church was perhaps unable to hear the word of God for the din of theological words'! Other theologians such as J. K. S. Reid, David Cairns and James Torrance also had substantial interests in the theology of worship and produced significant publications. The Torrance brothers' strong christological emphasis meant that they stressed that earthly worship is to be understood as participation in the ongoing worship of Jesus Christ as our High Priest.

But although there was important theological thought in the area of worship which had major and radical implications for the practice of worship it seemed to have rather little influence on what happened in most churches Sunday by Sunday. A gulf had opened between the theology and practice of worship and the kind of liturgical scholarship which had helped to bridge that gap in the past was markedly lacking. Since Maxwell, and Allan McArthur's book discussed above, there have been no really major liturgical publications in Scotland and no liturgiologist in the Church of Scotland of the stature of Maxwell or the 'Fathers' of the Church Service Society. This lack of serious and forward-looking liturgical studies backing up a coherent policy for the renewal of worship has been reflected in the declining influence of the Church Service Society since the War. But the Society continued for a time to be the dominant influence on the Committee on Public Worship and Aids to Devotion, which has been responsible for several recent publications to which we now turn.

A good indication of the nature and variety of worship in the Church of Scotland in the late 1960s is to be found in a volume entitled *Worship Now* (Edinburgh, St. Andrew Press, 1972) compiled by a group of leading churchmen and including services, prayers and meditations composed by a considerable number of ministers. 'We were convinced', wrote the compilers, 'that it would be a great help and encouragement if recent experience were shared, both in relation to "middle of the road services", and in relation to more original types of prayer and service'. The material is diverse and indeed uneven, and the book shows that abundant use is being made of the freedom allowed to ministers in the conduct of worship, that this is throwing up some material of lasting value as well as a good deal that deserves to be forgotten, and that there appears to be no particular line of development, no movement towards a goal, perceptible in contemporary worship in the Church of Scotland.

After a long period of gestation the Committee on Public Worship and Aids to Devotion produced a new *Book of Common Order* in 1979. There was no doubt that the 1940 *BCO* needed replacement, or at least radical revision. It had been in advance of its time, but it had long been overtaken by liturgical developments elsewhere and appeared stodgy, old-fashioned and even pompous when compared with the new services of the Anglican and Roman Catholic Churches, and indeed when set alongside the new productions of many other Presbyterian Churches as well. The 1979 book affirms very strongly the centrality of the Lord's Supper – whereas the 1940 book, as we have seen, started with several orders for morning and evening service, the new book offers three full orders for Holy Communion and only a bare *missa sicca* outline for a Sunday service when the Lord's Supper is not celebrated. This, presumably, is because the Committee hopes that the Church of Scotland will move rapidly to having weekly Communion. But meanwhile the Committee provided material for non-sacramental services in both a contemporary and a traditional vein in *Prayers for Contemporary Worship* (Edinburgh, St. Andrew Press, 1977), in a companion volume to *BCO 1979, Prayers for Sunday Services* (Edinburgh, St. Andrew Press, 1980), and in *New Ways to Worship* (Edinburgh, St. Andrew Press, 1980).

The orders for Holy Communion in *BCO 1979* use different idioms, said to correspond roughly to the language of the Authorized Version, the Revised Standard Version, and the New English Bible. This suggests an inadequate recognition that there is a distinction between the language of worship and the language of biblical translation. It also means that *BCO 1979* makes no serious attempt to present a model of contemporary liturgical English which is resonant, allusive, theologically rich, rhythmical, dignified, balanced, flowing and clear. Instead we are presented with a variety of possibilities, but it has to be said that none of them is particularly striking or attractive. No modern form of the Lord's Prayer is included in the book, and none of the new material can hold a candle to such recent compositions as the splendid post-Communion prayer in the Anglican *Alternative Service Book*, 'Father of all, we give you thanks and praise . . .' The rest of the book is composed of sound, but on the whole unexciting, orders for Baptism, Confirmation, marriage, funerals and the ordination of elders, together with the lectionary, collects, and proper prefaces.

The Book of Common Order 1979 was not greeted with great enthusiasm, either by the reviewers or by many in the Church of Scotland. It is on the whole canny and sometimes pedestrian, perhaps because it is the fruit of so many compromises. Whether it will do much to encourage that most desirable of reforms in worship – 'the Lord's Supper every Sunday' – depends on its ability to commend itself to ministers and congregations. It quickly evoked a counterblast: the *Reformed Book of Common Order* published by the National Church Association. This quaint and conservative production, produced by the Presbyterian equivalents of the followers of Archbishop Lefebvre, sees the *Book of Common Order 1979* as part of a Scoto-catholic conspiracy to detach the worship of the Church of Scotland from its roots and standards in Knox's *Book of Common Order* and the *Westminster Directory*. But it can be shown that the *Reformed Book* itself substantially tones down the sacramental teaching of these standards in producing a book which is archaic in language and turgid and insular in contents.[11]

A new hymn book, *The Church Hymnary, Third Edition* (London, Oxford University Press, 1973) was produced by the Church of Scotland in association with several other Presbyterian Churches, replacing the *Revised Church Hymnary* of 1928. The new hymn book removed a good many sentimental Victorian hymns and saccharine tunes, included a section of Scottish metrical psalms, some prose psalms, some Gelineau psalms, and some newly written psalms and paraphrases, together with a fairly small and unadventurous selection of modern hymns. The music included a number of specially composed modern pieces by leading composers such as Kenneth Leighton, and the general mode of the music could be described as classical and pure, the most favoured composers being Orlando Gibbons and Ralph Vaughan Williams. A number of 'old favourites' had disappeared, and some of the music was far beyond the range and resources of most congregations. The book was structured to correspond to the ideas on the shape of the service being advocated by the Public Worship Committee, with three main sections (Approach to God, The Word of God: His Mighty Acts, and Response to the Word of God), a greater range of Communion hymns, and settings for the Kyrie,

Sanctus, Benedictus qui venit, Agnus Dei, and Gloria – these last all sadly in traditional language only, and with music rather complicated for the average congregation. The book was criticized for undue conservatism, for attempting to displace the complete Scottish Psalter by incorporating the best-known metrical psalms, and for largely disregarding recent hymnody; but a new hymn book could not possibly please everyone, and *The Church Hymnary, Third Edition* is undoubtedly enriching the worship of the Church of Scotland and the other churches which use it.

The Church Hymnary, Third Edition and the 1979 *Book of Common Order* proved to be the last of a long line of 'top-down' publications, intended to influence and shape the worship of the Church of Scotland. They were received by many as expressing a party line – theological, aesthetic and liturgical – which commanded the allegiance of a declining proportion of the Church. In more ways than one they were the end of a road.[12] A number of important developments, some of which started as early as the 1960s, did not find expression in either book.

In the area of hymnody, Ian Fraser as Warden made Scottish Churches House, Dunblane, a nest of singing birds in the 1960s. Hymn writers and musicians from all over Britain gathered there and produced a steady succession of hymns of great freshness and variety. Some proved to be ephemeral; others have been widely used around the world, and bid fair to become part of the world Church's heritage of praise. But the Dunblane initiative left no mark on *CH III*.[13] Meanwhile a new spring of worship and hymnody emerged in Iona, associated with names such as Kathy Galloway, Graham Maule, Douglas Galbraith and, above all, John Bell. John Bell and Graham Maule in particular were prolific in the production of hymns of remarkable quality, initially published in little pamphlets and 'Wee Worship Books', and quickly finding their way into standard collections around the world. The Iona Community established the Wild Goose Worship Group[14] which propagated these hymns and other Iona forms of worship throughout Britain, and overseas as well. Hymn writing was supported by the production of prayers and forms of worship of great sensitivity and freshness, often quarrying into what was, or what was believed to be, the Celtic tradition of spirituality, and using popular folk tunes to great effect. Work on experimental worship also went on in other centres, like Carberry Tower, where Jock and Margaret Stein were the Wardens, and at the Church of Scotland's art and drama centre, the Netherbow in Edinburgh. The new material was accessible particularly to young people, in whose eyes the fact that none of it had the official imprimatur of the Church of Scotland was a positive asset.

The direct impact of Iona on the worship of the Church of Scotland became even more marked when Iona people became the major influence in what was now called the Panel on Worship, John Bell in due course becoming its convener. He was the moving spirit in the production of the immensely successful supplement to *CH III*, *Songs of God's People* (1988). This was a 'catholic' compilation in a new sense. There were a few old favourites which had been omitted from *CH III*; there were evangelical choruses; there were chants from Taizé; there were contemporary hymns from Africa and Asia; and there was a substantial offering of excellent modern hymns from Scotland, not all of them by John Bell and Graham Maule. In some circles *Songs of God's People* seemed virtually to displace *CH III* – unfortunate, since on its own it offers a somewhat unbalanced diet. As I write, steps are under way to produce an ecumenical supplement to *CH III*, and the major task of producing a new edition of the *Church Hymnary* has started.

Just eight years after the production of *BCO 1979*, the General Assembly of 1987 instructed the Panel on Worship to 'proceed without delay with the production of a new *Book of Common Order*'. This move reflected widespread dissatisfaction with the 1979 book, and a desire on the part of some to return to the tradition expressed in *BCO 1940*. The compilers were aware that they were working at a time of flux and experiment, when inherited forms and understandings of worship were being reviewed and often rejected, and when the impetus of the Church Service Society seemed largely spent. The *Book of Common Order of the Church of Scotland*, 1994, does not reflect or impose a liturgical orthodoxy. It makes no claim to being mandatory or prescriptive. John Bell introduces it thus:

> This is a **common** book, it belongs to all the people of God. In the reformed understanding, worship is not the right or the rite of an ordained caste, but is the duty, joy and prerogative of all believers . . . The book also reflects the common heritage of prayer and devotion of the whole Church, drawing from the orthodox wellsprings of liturgy and from the lay heritage of Celtic spirituality originating in these shores.
>
> It is also a book of **order**. In worship we engage as the Body of Christ in an encounter with almighty God. This engagement should never become a rambling incoherence of well-meaning phrases and gestures. It should exhibit that deliberate and historical patterning of sentiment and expression which befits the meeting of the sons and daughters of earth with the King of Kings. Further, in public worship as distinct from personal devotions, it is important that the whole congregation sense a purpose and direction in their representation before God. They should never be placed in the position of being spectators at a performance which is entirely dependent on the aesthetic, emotional and spiritual whims of its leaders.[15]

Accordingly the book is a substantial resource for worship that is likely to be more widely used than its predecessors because of the variety of material that it offers. It is at pains to use inclusive language, and unlike its predecessors, it promotes the agreed modern language versions of the Lord's Prayer and the common liturgical responsive elements. Like *1979*, the new *Common Order* assumes the centrality of the Lord's Supper in Christian worship, but unlike *1979* the new book does not attempt to put everything into a eucharistic straitjacket. There are five orders for Holy Communion, the first including three alternative Action Prayers, the most interesting of which is adapted from John Knox's Genevan Service Book of 1556.[16] The other two prayers represent the modern eucharistic norm of the Church of Scotland and a eucharistic prayer of ecumenical provenance. The Second Order is Celtic in ethos, and the others are for special occasions. There is a splendid simple order for use with children. The Order for the Baptism of a Child is indebted to the liturgy of the French Reformed Church. The baptism comes before the promises, and includes a fine Declaration:

> N . . . ,
> for you Jesus Christ came into the world:
> for you he lived and showed God's love;
> for you he suffered the darkness of Calvary
> and cried at last, 'It is accomplished';
> for you he triumphed over death
> and rose in newness of life;
> for you he ascended to reign at God's right hand.
> All this he did for you, N . . . ,
> though you do not know it yet.
> And so the word of Scripture is fulfilled:
> 'We love because God loved us first.'

There are five varied and imaginative orders for morning and evening services, a variety of structures and resources for weddings and funerals, numerous services for special occasions, the Revised Common Lectionary, and a very considerable treasury of prayers and meditation.

Common Order 1994 has been warmly welcomed, and it seems likely that it will be very widely used within the Church of Scotland and beyond. It must count as probably the major contribution to the renewal and refreshment of worship to emanate from the Church of Scotland in the second half of the twentieth century.

The Scottish Episcopal Church responded to a post-war crisis of declining numbers and radically reduced resources with great imagination and vigour. A Church which had, not undeservedly, for long been regarded as 'spiky' and defensive, high church in a rather old-fashioned way and resistant to change, found a new role for itself in Scotland, in many places setting the pace in ecumenical developments, pioneering new patterns of ministry, and treating the problems facing the denomination as opportunities rather than threats. The new vitality of this small denomination would not allow it to rest content with the *Scottish Prayer Book* of 1929. In 1970 a cautiously revised eucharistic order was published in what was known as 'The Grey Bookie', more correctly *The Liturgy*, and authorized for optional use. This was superseded by a remarkable communion rite issued first as *The*

Experimental Liturgy 1977 and then, after revision in the light of experience of its use, as the *Scottish Liturgy 1982*. This glorious, flexible and theologically rich rite has a clear, classical structure and sets a new standard in fine modern liturgical English, without the baldness of some recent Anglican productions or the archaism of much Presbyterian liturgical language. The liturgical and theological erudition of Dr. Gianfranco Tellini, formerly of Coates Hall and presently Rector of Dunblane, and the poetic gifts of Bishop Michael Hare-Duke helped to shape this fresh and rich liturgy, which is regarded by some knowledgeable people as the finest modern rite in English. In the mid-1980s the Episcopalians produced a new Ordinal, which has been widely praised. At present the major, and very difficult, liturgical work is the revision of the rites of initiation.

The Roman Catholic Church in Scotland in recent times has had the reputation of being rather conservative and slow to throw itself into the mainstream of national life. Its leaders were canny rather than charismatic and loyally led the Church through the turmoils of trans-formation engendered by the Second Vatican Council. Cardinal Gray for a number of years headed the Vatican's Commission on English in the Liturgy. The renewal of worship enjoined by Vatican II was carried through gradually and with great pastoral sensitivity, so that in Scotland only very small numbers of people associated themselves with Archbishop Lefebvre's dissident movement of traditionalists. The changes carried through were indeed far-reaching. Most important, perhaps, was the change from Latin to the vernacular. Rome had the advantage of proceeding straight from the use of a dead language to contemporary English in worship without passing through Elizabethan English, and this has saved the language of the new rite from the half-understood archaisms and sheer mumbo jumbo (e.g. 'world without end') which disfigure the worship of other traditions with a longer heritage of insisting that the language of worship should be understood by the people. The old solid high altars built against the east wall were replaced everywhere by freestanding altars or 'Tables of the Lord', the priest celebrating Mass facing the people, who often now gathered around the altar. Minor altars are to be few in number. In these and other ways the symbolism suggests powerfully that the Mass is a banquet in which the whole People of God participate actively, rather than something done by a priest while the people watch or busy themselves with their own private devotions. Ceremonial has been pruned and the ritual simplified so that the structure of the Mass is now far clearer, all sorts of devotional accretions having been removed. For many Roman Catholics there has been an exciting rediscovery of the Bible in the aftermath of Vatican II, and in the Mass the new lectionaries ensure that there is extensive and well-integrated scripture reading, while biblical homilies are obligatory except when there are very few people present.

Congregational singing has become the norm, and Roman Catholics in all but the most traditionalist parishes are happy to use hymns like 'Amazing Grace', Scottish metrical psalms, and evangelical choruses alongside more usual Catholic items. Charismatic Renewal has been increasingly influential in the worship of many parishes, and this has encouraged a great deal of participation by the laity, in reading the lessons, offering prayers, and acting as 'eucharistic ministers' who share in the distribution of Communion and take the hosts to those who are house-bound. Communion in both kinds has become increasingly common, although many of the older and more conservative are still reluctant to receive the chalice.

It is no exaggeration to say that the worship of the Roman Catholic Church in Scotland, as elsewhere, has been *reformed* by the Second Vatican Council. This is not to deny that there are still substantial differences in the theology and practice of worship between the Roman and the Reformed traditions, but Rome has assessed and renewed its worship in the light of very similar criteria to those which the Protestant Churches recognize – the Bible and the practice of the early Church on the one hand, and the need to nourish and sustain the witness of God's people in the modern world on the other. Protestants who encounter Roman Catholic worship in Scotland for the first time are often much surprised because it differs so much from the stereotype of 'the idolatry of the Mass' which they have inherited. Paradoxically it is less sacerdotalist and more participative, expressive of the corporate priesthood of all believers, than much Protestant worship and it is simple, biblical and relaxed as well. It is to be hoped that in such a situation the varying traditions will realize that they have much to learn from one another, and that more sharing in worship is now possible and desirable than has been conceivable since the Reformation.

The visit of Pope John Paul II in May 1982 marked a turning point in more ways than one. A conservative Pope found a Scottish Roman Catholic Church in many ways more conservative than himself. The Pope strongly encouraged Scottish Roman Catholics to assert their Scottishness, to give up timidity and to enter the mainstream of Scottish life, where they certainly have much to give. The impact of the Pope's warm personality and transparent goodness had an extraordinary impact on a Scotland with a not undeserved reputation of being dour, Presbyterian and increasingly secular. The Mass in Bellahouston Park and other events in the course of the visit led most Scots, sometimes reluctantly, to recognize the living spirituality and worship of the Roman Church in Scotland. The Pope's call for Christians of various confessions to 'walk hand in hand' towards the goal of greater obedience to the common Lord, a fuller unity, and a truer sharing in worship seems likelier of fulfilment now than anyone could have conceived possible before the Papal visit.

As an earnest, a foretaste of what it to come, consider this fine Communion hymn, one of several by the Edinburgh Jesuit theologian, Father James Quinn, which have been included in the *Church Hymnary* (No. 568), and are now widely used in the Church of Scotland:

> Father most loving, listen to thy children
> Who as thy family joyfully forgather,
> Singing the praises of the Son, our Brother,
> Jesus beloved!
>
> We stand attentive, listening to God's Gospel,
> Welcoming Jesus as he speaks among us
> Mind and hearts open, ready to receive him,
> Lips to proclaim him!
>
> Father in heaven, bless the gifts we offer,
> Signs of our true love, hearts in homage given!
> Make them the one gift that is wholly worthy,
> Christ, spotless victim!
>
> Father, we thank thee for thy Son's dear presence,
> Coming to feed us as the bread of heaven,
> Making us one with him in sweet communion,
> One with each other!
>
> Praised be our Father, lovingly inviting,
> Guests to this banquet, praised the Son who feeds us,
> Praised too the Spirit, sent by Son and Father,
> Making us Christ-like!

And what of the future? In matters such as worship we should expect the wind of the Spirit to blow where it wills, and no meteorologist can predict this wind with accuracy. But some possibilities and some problems deserve to be mentioned. As far as the Roman Catholic Church is concerned the changes in worship over the last twenty years have been remarkable both for their scope and their significance, amounting in Scotland as elsewhere probably to the most thoroughgoing and theologically based renewal that Christian worship has seen since the Reformation. That so much that has happened in Roman Catholic worship is congenial to a reformed understanding of worship and even to reformed practice suggests a major movement of convergence pregnant with constructive possibilities. The renewal of Roman Catholic worship is an irreversible change, and even if there is now a pause for consolidation it is likely that there will be more growth and development in a tradition of worship which has shown more resilience, adaptability and spiritual vitality than most observers had thought possible prior to Vatican II. The Scottish Episcopal Church has imaginative and scholarly leadership as its new eucharistic liturgy gradually gains acceptance in most congregations, and is pressing ahead with liturgical revision.

The smaller Presbyterian Churches, and particularly the Free Church and the Free Presbyterians, have allowed their worship to ossify and have been almost totally unaffected by the liturgical movement, new insights into the theology of worship, or ecumenism. In their own eyes their worship is preserving evangelical purity; to others, and to many of their own young people, it is tedious, didactic and sombre. The worship of the Church of Scotland is almost impossible to assess because of its extraordinary diversity, and the absence of any coherent and effective movement for renewal of worship makes prediction difficult. Almost every form of Christian worship can be found somewhere in the Church of Scotland, and if there is such a thing as 'the normal Church of Scotland service', it has changed, but not dramatically, since 1929, and at present there is neither an agreed direction nor any great enthusiasm for substantial renewal or reform. There is not a little complacency about the state of worship in the Church of Scotland, yet a disturbing number of people find that services are often dreary and shapeless ministerial monologues, and even a Moderator of the General Assembly spoke of the worship of the Church as having 'gone stale'.

There are, of course, congregations where the worship has an encouraging vitality and a sense of joyful participation, and situations where well-considered steps towards a renewal of worship are being taken with real pastoral sensitivity. But the impact of Iona on the worship of the Church of Scotland might now be compared with that of movements such as Parish and People which transformed the worship of the Church of England in a few decades. Nevertheless, neither presbyteries nor the General Assembly exercise much effective oversight in matters of worship, nor do they give as much leadership as they sometimes did in the past. The amount of time spent in discussion of matters of worship in courts higher than the kirk session is negligible, and the kirk session, according to the law of the Church, has no responsibility for the conduct of worship apart from regulating the times of service. Legally the minister conducts worship as the agent of the presbytery, and is responsible to the presbytery for the worship of the parish. In practice the minister is almost entirely free from effective presbyterial oversight of his conduct of worship. In many congregations there is an enervating inertia in matters of worship, or a few members of the congregation seem to exercise an effective veto on any kind of liturgical renewal.

But, for all that, change in worship is inevitable in the Church of Scotland. The important questions for the future are about the kind of change, and the pace of change, and the handling of change. For change in a matter as important as worship is always disturbing and must be introduced with great sensitivity, with much explanation and education, and with a very clear distinction between what is important and what is trivial or peripheral. The kind of changes the writer hopes to see include a rediscovery of the dynamic complementarity of Word and sacrament, a restoration of the centrality of the Lord's Supper by making its celebration the principal act of worship Sunday by Sunday, a far greater sense that in worship the whole people of God participate in an action, rather than listening to a ministerial monologue, more flexibility, informality and spontaneity within a simple, orderly structure, more dove-tailing of worship and the life of the world, and far more ecumenical learning and sharing in matters of worship. For worship must be constantly reformed, thoroughly evangelical, and truly catholic and ecumenical if it is manifestly to be, in Karl Barth's words, 'the most momentous, the most urgent, the most glorious action that can take place in human life'.

NOTES

1. A. C. Cheyne, 'Worship in the Kirk: Knox, Westminster and the 1940 Book' in Duncan Shaw, ed., *Reformation and Revolution* (Edinburgh, 1967), pp. 70–81.
2. D. H. Hislop, *Our Heritage in Public Worship* (Edinburgh, 1935), pp. 182–183.
3. Hislop, for instance, advocates reservation and reverencing of the sacramental bread (p. 255) and communion in one kind as a way of avoiding controversies about fermented and unfermented wine (p. 252).
4. William D. Maxwell, *The Liturgical Portions of the Genevan Service Book* (Edinburgh, 1931), re-issued by the Faith Press (London, 1965).
5. T. S. Garrett, *Worship in the Church of South India* (Ecumenical Studies in Worship No. 2, London, 1958), pp. 53–54, 60.
6. W. D. Maxwell, *A History of Worship in the Church of Scotland* (London, 1955), p. 183.
7. James Hogg, *The Private Memoirs and Confessions of a Justified Sinner* (London, 1947), p. 184.
8. This emphasis is shown particularly well in two outstanding volumes of Warrack Lectures on Preaching: Oswald B. Milligan, *The Ministry of Worship* (London 1941), and Thomas H. Keir, *The Word in Worship* (London, 1962).
9. Donald Baillie, *The Theology of the Sacraments* (London, 1957), p. 40.
10. Published in Donald Baillie and John March, eds., *Intercommunion* (London, 1952), pp. 303–350; reprinted in T. F. Torrance, *Conflict and Agreement in the Church* (London, 1960), II, pp. 154–202.
11. Duncan Forrester, 'Recent Liturgical Work in Scotland', *The Expository Times* 91:2 (November, 1979), 39–44. *Cf.* A. Stewart Todd, 'The Ordering of Liturgical Worship', *Liturgical Review* 7:2 (November, 1977), 11–19.

12. One should also note the publication of *Hymns for a Day* (Edinburgh, 1982) by the Committee on Public Worship and Aids to Devotion. This was intended to be a supplement to *CH III* and consisted of hymns by modern writers, a few of whom were Scots. It followed the Christian Year according to the lectionary in *BCO 1979*.

13. See *Dunblane Praises No. 1*, 1965, *Dunblane Praises No. 2*, 1967, *Dunblane Praises for Schools*, 1970, *New Songs for the Church Book 1: Psalms, Children's Songs, Ballads, Hymns*, and *New Songs for the Church Book 2: Canticles*, 1969. Ian Fraser wrote an account of the Dunblane workshops in 'Beginnings at Dunblane' in the Festschrift for Erik Routley, *Duty and Delight* (Norwich, U.S.A., 1985).

14. So called because of the suggestion that the Celtic Church used the wild goose as an image of the Holy Spirit.

15. *Book of Common Order of the Church of Scotland* (Edinburgh, 1994), p. x.

16. *Cf.* William D. Maxwell, ed., *The Liturgical Portions of the Genevan Service Book* (London), 1931, pp. 125–127, and *Common Order*, 1994, pp. 134–136.

INDEX

197